DANGEROUS
RELIGIOUS
IDEAS

DANGEROUS

THE DEEP ROOTS OF SELF-CRITICAL FAITH

RELIGIOUS

IN JUDAISM, CHRISTIANITY, AND ISLAM

IDEAS

RACHEL S. MIKVA

BEACON PRESS
BOSTON

BEACON PRESS
Boston, Massachusetts
www.beacon.org

Beacon Press books
are published under the auspices of
the Unitarian Universalist Association of Congregations.

23 22 21 20   8 7 6 5 4 3 2 1

This book is printed on acid-free paper that meets the uncoated paper
ANSI/NISO specifications for permanence as revised in 1992.

Text design and compostion by Kim Arney

Library of Congress Cataloging-in-Publication Data

Names: Mikva, Rachel, author.
Title: Dangerous religious ideas : the deep roots of self-critical faith in
    Judaism, Christianity, and Islam / Rachel S. Mikva.
Description: Boston : Beacon Press, 2020. | Includes bibliographical
    references and index.
Identifiers: LCCN 2020013318 (print) | LCCN 2020013319 (ebook) |
    ISBN 9780807051870 (hardcover) | ISBN 9780807051887 (ebook)
Subjects: LCSH: Abrahamic religions. | Christianity—Doctrines. |
    Islam—Doctrines. | Judaism—Doctrines.
Classification: LCC BL425 .M55 2020 (print) | LCC BL425 (ebook) |
    DDC 202—dc23
LC record available at https://lccn.loc.gov/2020013318
LC ebook record available at https://lccn.loc.gov/2020013319

*This book is dedicated to my father,
Abner Joseph Mikva (z"l),
who spent his life trying to make
profoundly good but still
imperfect systems . . . better.*

CONTENTS

PART I

DANGEROUS RELIGIOUS IDEAS

INTRODUCTION

The most intense love that humanity has ever known has come from religion, and the most diabolical hatred that humanity has known has also come from religion. . . . No other human motive has deluged the world with blood so much as religion; at the same time, nothing has brought into existence so many hospitals and asylums for the poor; no other human influence has taken such care, not only of humanity, but also of the lowest of animals, as religion has done. Nothing makes us so cruel as religion, and nothing makes us so tender as religion. This has been so in the past, and will also, in all probability, be so in the future.[1]

No one asked the Hindu monk Swami Vivekananda to prove these assertions during his 1896 lecture in New York, and some are surely exaggerations. His pronouncement rang true because it articulated the consternation felt by so many about the role of religion in human history. People value their faith for its capacity to inspire goodness, fashion meaning, connect communities, and open gateways to the sacred. At the same time, they have long recognized and struggled with the ways in which religion is wielded as a weapon to oppress people, to deepen division and justify violence.

The recent flurry of publications about the destructive power of religion should not suggest it is a recent discovery; historical events simply pushed it more to the center of our attention at the beginning of this twenty-first century. Most of these discussions, however, focus on holy war, fundamentalism, and other limited aspects of religious experience. When I begin my course on "Dangerous Religious Ideas," I first ask my class what they would put on the syllabus. Primarily faithful Christians studying for a master of divinity degree, the students hesitate briefly. They frequently start with someone else's ideas; reflecting the current climate of anti-Muslim bias that infects even progressive and pluralist spaces, jihad is almost always mentioned first. Then we get to extremists of all flavors. As students start to think more critically about their own traditions, however, they quickly realize that just about any religious idea could make the list: God, scripture, Messiah, sin. The board quickly fills with all the essentials of faith, each at some time having played an integral role in devastating harm.

ALL RELIGIOUS IDEAS ARE DANGEROUS

All religious ideas are dangerous, including those embraced by moderates and progressives. Take God, for instance. Faith in a divine being has at times inspired murderous intolerance for those who do not share it. This is undoubtedly an extreme example, but even today atheists find it difficult to get elected to public office in the United States. Indeed, over 40 percent of Americans assert that one must believe in God in order to be an ethical person.[2] Theists in opposing camps on reproductive justice, gun safety, tax policy, and a host of other divisive issues frequently presume that God is on their side, while heaping moral condemnation on their adversaries. God becomes an idol carved in our own image, a "yes-man" who endorses our politics and prejudices.

Scripture has been used to uphold slavery and condemn LGBTQ+ individuals, to inflict harsh punishment and legislate discrimination. Presumptions of its divine source and perfect quality have led to heresy trials, burning of books, resistance to scientific learning, and aggressive suppression of countervailing ideas. Even those who try to read scripture critically sometimes find themselves internalizing negative impressions about religious others or defending rotten ideas. My students, for example, are surprised when they realize how much of the New Testament's anti-Pharisaic polemic they have absorbed and how it has shaped their understanding of Judaism. Even though they know better, they catch themselves denigrating "the law" as contrary to the spirit and suggesting that ancient Judaism was too parochial—prompting Paul to invent universalism (like Al Gore invented the internet).

Some people claim that destructive and hateful expressions are not real religion: the great religions of the world are, in essence, religions of peace, love, and goodness. Such essentialism identifies manifestations of religion that stray from these values as deviant or heretical. Ironically, this attitude is not all that different from that of fundamentalists who believe their interpretation of religious tradition to be the only authentic one. It also fails to recognize that even this idealized vision carries dangerous power. "Peace" can be (and has been) the value that perpetuates injustice, "love" the emotional catalyst for oppressive interference, and "goodness" a culturally constructed perspective imposed on others. We may believe that certain embodiments of religion are not what God wants or that they are not worthy expressions of our tradition. We can definitely argue that oppressive teachings claiming to rely on literal interpretation of scripture are still filtered by human hands, but we cannot declare that such things are not religious. Given the textual and historical record, it is fair to conclude that religion can be expressed violently and nonviolently, with grace or cruelty, as Swami Vivekananda said. After all, religion consists of humanly constructed responses to what a community understands as divine revelation or sacred path. The range of responses reflects the full spectrum of human personality, culture, and imagination.

We also hear the excuse that "dangerous" religion is merely the prop of those who wish to gain political or economic advantage, to defend or advance their power. Violent struggle, enduring discrimination, and brutal judgment may be justified in sacred texts and tradition, but according to this line of reasoning they derive primarily from the political, social, and psychological needs of the central group. People distort religion, taking advantage of its ability to motivate and mobilize. These claims have merit, but religion is not an innocent bystander. It is an integral part of human nature and a powerful influence in society, playing important roles in the unfolding of history. Even as a force used by others in harmful ways, the power of religion requires critical attention. This is not to claim that religion is more prone to violence than secular ideologies, a myth that William Cavanaugh rightly challenged for the ways it ignores or justifies the violence of the nation-state.[3] This book is simply trying to grapple with religion's role.

I am not persuaded by scholars, like those in the new atheist camp, whose overreaching accusations identify religion as the cause of all destructive human behavior. Pointing to sacred text and history, they associate all forms of religion with obscurantism, superstition, violence, and oppression.[4] Nor do I embrace the conclusions of social scientists who, in trying to understand the religious impulse, explain it away entirely. Marx reduced it to the temporarily necessary illusion resulting from an oppressive class structure, and Freud to a "universal obsessional neurosis" that humanity should outgrow.[5] Religious belief is surely affected by class and power structures, and it meets certain psychological needs, but such catalysts can tell only part of the story. These dismissive analyses share the assumptions that religion is somehow detachable from human experience and that the world would be better off if we simply eliminated it completely. Even if one embraced the goal, religion is deeply inscribed within human experience, making its erasure highly unlikely.

SELF-CRITICAL FAITH

By insisting that dangerous religious ideas are not limited to extremists, I attempt to reckon with the harm committed in God's name and to refine religion in a crucible of critical inquiry. There have been many efforts to shed the dangerous dross while preserving the transformative power of religious concepts; this book explores, celebrates, and expands upon them. Yet in some elemental way, the productive and destructive materials of religious thought are bound together. To take the analogy one step further, the purest states of metals and ideas are not found in nature; they are always blended with other substances that are integral parts of how they come to be. What makes religion a powerful force for good is to a large extent the same as what makes it potentially dangerous.

Keith Ward offers a comparison with liberal democracy. Most people in the West see democracy as a virtuous system for communal governance. But at the same time, some of democracy's core values can easily inflict suffering: majority rule has oppressed minorities, empowered electorates have opted for racist leaders and policies, democratic governments have waged unnecessary wars to "protect their freedoms," and wickedness has more than once won out in the marketplace of ideas.[6] Ward's primary inference is that all powers can be corrupted, including religion. Mine is different; I believe the flaws are built in. All religious ideas are dangerous, and self-critical faith is essential. It is my contention that most religions of the world have known it all along. This book is not simply a reading of scripture and tradition that tries to call out the threats and resist them. It is a reading of scripture and tradition that sees the seeds for this work planted deep in the soil of religious thought, designed for us to cultivate.

Aware of religion's tremendous power both to harm and to heal, with no way to permanently separate these potentialities, the traditions transmit their sacred stories alongside tools for penetrating self-examination and ongoing self-improvement. This does not mean that all adherents embrace self-critical faith or that religious institutions readily undertake reform. Nor does it suggest that all changes are for the better. But a careful tilling of the soil with these seeds serves as the natural defense against religion's most perilous inclinations and yields a bountiful crop of understandings that might not otherwise grow.

The purposes of this study are diverse: It challenges assumptions about which religious ideas are considered dangerous by extending the analysis beyond "extremisms." It demonstrates how the constructive capacity of religion is bound up with its power to divide, discriminate, and destroy—qualities all deeply embedded in the human psyche and society. Illuminating the shared struggle of the Abrahamic faiths to address this tension, the book excavates their rich interpretative traditions. Long before the advent of historical-critical analysis, the fluidity of interpretation could help to check religion's absolutist tendencies by showing how scriptural texts are always mediated humanly. Central religious doctrines and practices were contested, not unanimous. Most importantly, the book makes the case that Judaism, Christianity, and Islam all constructed mechanisms for self-critique and correction that are integral to their teachings.

This inheritance of self-critical faith challenges religious leaders to be more thoughtful in teaching and preaching within their communities, and more cognizant of the potential damage religious concepts—even those that lie at the heart of faith—can do. It challenges skeptics to see the tools of self-critical faith as vital resources for contemporary discourse, both secular and religious. It asks adherents, wherever they identify on the progressive–traditional spectrum, to recognize the dangers of spiritual complacency. A mature engagement with religion, one capable of nurturing its full potential for bringing blessing into the world, must face forthrightly the shadow side and claim it as its own. It cannot be that "the dark side of religion is all in the mind, heart, and company of 'the other,' those people who have the wrong God, the wrong books, the wrong nation in which to live"[7]—or the wrong interpretation.

This project also speaks to interreligious engagement. While interfaith work often focuses on shared values and inspirational teachings, we require tools for building relationships across differences and for addressing problematic material as well. A group of Jewish, Christian, and Muslim scholars working together on a Just Peace paradigm, for instance, struggled to articulate the need for the project. After all, their religions were traditions of peace! Then they agreed to bring each other their "worst text"—one that revealed the violence embedded in each of their scriptural traditions—and suddenly a path opened before them:

> It made us each less defensive and more open. Muslims and Jews did not have to say, "You Christians have used the New Testament to justify killing many of us"—the Christians had already said that. Christians did not have to accuse the others of justifying persecutions or attacks based on their holiest texts—Muslims and Jews had already said that. . . . We each developed a hermeneutic—a method of interpreting scriptures—that showed respect for those problem passages but did not use them to cause harm.[8]

The shared struggle of self-critical faith is the essential glue of a diverse society. Social power intervenes here; it is easier for privileged religious voices to admit the ugly stuff. But no tradition can remain vital—and they certainly can not thrive together—without continuing to cultivate these capacities.

Self-critical faith does not require that we discard tradition as hopelessly misogynistic, homophobic, authoritarian, and parochial (even though it can be all those things). Instead, it recovers the diversity of voices that inculcate, substantiate, and perpetuate problematic elements—as well as those that stand in counterpoint. It reveals how religions remain developing, dynamic organisms so that we may wield our truths more gently. It insists on continuous reflection and repair in religious thought. It also illuminates fresh teachings for our time, providing the social critique that has always been a vital part of religion's role in human history.

Dangerous religious ideas do not remain contained within theological writings and houses of worship; they continually travel into the public square. Focusing primarily on the United States, this book addresses their ongoing impact on society and culture, interrogating the role of religion in the public sphere and seeking to shape the voice of public theology—how we talk about and embody religious values in our collective public life.

METHODOLOGY AND STRUCTURE

Beginning with scriptural sources and collecting diverse voices in the history of interpretation, I explore ramifications of core religious themes that can be considered dangerous in Judaism, Christianity, and Islam. I also excavate resources within the history of these religions that have served or can serve to address these hazards. Counter to the tendency to select only those texts that portray religion in the best light, or only those that prove it to be a destructive force, I wrestle with the tension between them to highlight religion's substantial self-critical capacities.

The traditions of Abraham, Sarah, and Hagar constitute the "family" of religious thought and practice with which I am most familiar. For brevity, I reluctantly refer to them by the patronym *Abrahamic*, although this minimizes the significance of the matriarchs and also runs the risk of effacing differences between Judaism, Christianity, and Islam.[9] I use the term *religion* to discuss a quality common to these three traditions, even if it does not apply universally. This shorthand should not suggest that the broad variety of spiritual expression has been forgotten.

Scriptural sources and their interpretations serve as the foundation of this study for several reasons. They are seen by "Peoples of the Book" as the basis for much of religious life, providing an extensive and explicit record of how particular aspects of faith and practice were to be understood, embraced, and embodied. A review of scriptural exegesis also reveals broader possibilities of meaning that have been obscured through the sifting of history and processes of normalization. No teaching has always meant what we now think it means. The interpretive arguments demonstrate how Abrahamic traditions have long recognized our limited capacity to fashion institutions that fully embody God's vision for humanity. Similarly, the mechanisms for self-critique and correction I identify are not modern inventions of reform traditions, but integral to religion itself. Lastly, as Georgia Warnke wrote, the history of interpretation shapes our present: "The way in which we have understood the past and the way in which our ancestors have projected the future determines our own range of possibilities."[10] Admittedly, lived religion has never been identical to the written record, which tends to privilege the experience or perception of intellectual elites (primarily literate men who studied and taught these texts). Nevertheless, the sources represent crucial aspects of Judaism, Christianity, and Islam.

This approach is natural to me as a student of exegesis, but some caveats are in order. First, the traditions cannot be reduced to their scriptural dimensions. Although I begin my discussion of Judaism with Tanakh, for example, this must not obscure the fact that Judaism as we know it today is much more a rabbinic project. Secondly, discussion of the diverse scriptures is not an invitation to qualitatively compare them, since they were composed centuries apart from each other under very different circumstances. Instead, this overly ambitious glimpse into multiple traditions is designed to examine how they collectively wrestle with the implications of their teachings—teachings that trace back to scriptural foundations. Lastly, my review of exegetical history within Judaism, Christianity, and Islam is necessarily sporadic and impressionistic. My overarching interest is the range of voices, read together, in the way that religious traditions historically understood them, as concurrent aspects of a complex heritage.

The first task of this book is to unpack the meaning of dangerous religious ideas (chapter 1). What makes a religious idea *dangerous*—and is that always a bad thing? What makes it a *religious* idea, and how do concepts that may not be religious in origin acquire additional weight when affirmed by religious teachings? How do religious *ideas* come to shape the course of human history? For these inquiries, I incorporate scholarship on religion and culture gleaned from the disciplines of sociology, psychology, anthropology, evolutionary biology, and neuroscience. These lenses collectively reveal how religion is woven through every facet of human development and experience, contributing to its amazing staying power and making it impossible for the dangers to be permanently excised.

Parts II and III each begin with a core religious idea and the dangers it entails. We need to understand why these ideas are attractive, often both *in spite of* and *because of* their power to harm. Subsequent discussion examines readings of the tradition—historical and contemporary—that manifest or resist the hazards, amplifying the voices of those who demonstrated a capacity for self-critique. Each section concludes by reflecting on how the problems and possibilities manifest in our world today.

In part II, the theme is scripture, frequently granted supreme authority, presumed to define the good and to override other ethical perspectives— even though its meaning is determined by human beings (chapter 2). Yet the tools for interpretation in Judaism, Christianity, and Islam, explored in chapters 3 through 5, have historically functioned as a check on the ultimacy of scripture. They emphasize the multivocal nature of sacred texts and interpretation, recognizing how change and conflict establish pluralist canons of religious history. They also reveal a surprising humility, making room for doubt, accommodation of human limitations, and the sometimes slippery nature of truth. Nonetheless, scripture continues to be wielded as a weapon. Chapter 6 discusses the ways that contemporary readers try to navigate this challenging terrain, including a focused reflection on scripture and politics in the United States that reveals the ongoing potential for benefit and harm.

In part III, chapter 7 introduces a matrix of interrelated ideas—chosenness, election, supersession, and salvation—where conquest and the evaluation of difference emerge as two of the most prominent dangers. Chapters 8 to 10 explore diverse Jewish, Christian, and Muslim interpretations, from scriptural references to early modern expressions. For much of history, competing religious claims played out in art, literature, and governance but the traditions again show themselves to be aware of the dangers rooted within. They transmit teachings that warn against abuse and emphasize beneficial dimensions of the concept. We see some of the same driving forces—the will to meaning and pleasure, the cultivation of community, and the preservation of cultural values—embedded in both fruitful and harmful expressions. Yet the former try to distill aspects of chosenness that can fuel human spirituality without exploding into darkness. Unfortunately, election always carries with it the burden of associated dangerous expressions, and even careful articulations often convey faint echoes of bias. Chapter 11 presents modern examples, including discussion of nationalism as a secular version of the idea. In this time of tremendous social diversity and global connectivity, the moral ambiguity of election looms large.

As religious ideas continue to thread through our social fabric, the final chapters of the book address religion in the public square. Chapter 12 debates the proper place of religious discourse in our collective conversation and public policy. Protected but not privileged speech, religious convictions should never be allowed to stifle debate or operate as a trump card. At the same time, religion's capacity to challenge norms can have social value. The chapter takes up the theme of reward and punishment as a test case. Justice in the United States is largely focused on punitive measures. A quick review of religious sources, however, reveals much broader conceptions of justice—mixing restorative, retributive, distributive, and procedural elements that can transform our thinking.

Religion has too much to contribute to be ignored, and it is too thickly woven through human existence to disappear. But its ongoing role in public life in the United States makes cultivating the deep roots of self-critical faith more urgent. Ultimately, we have to learn how to do this work together, subjecting other people's religious ideas to rigorous scrutiny as well, without prejudice. Religious ideas cannot receive a pass without impairing the nation's democratic culture. Given the transformative encounter with science, technology, and global culture, religious thought requires collective critical engagement in order to speak intelligently in the postmodern age. There are many ways to do this badly, but critique is distinct from criticism, with a more holistic approach and healing objective.[11]

The themes of the book were selected because they are found in all three traditions, though distinct in their articulation, and because they typify the existential bundle of danger and possibility. Is scripture a sacred call to advance justice and mercy amidst God's creation, or a selectively read authorization to marginalize people with whom we disagree? Is chosenness an aspirational covenant to become worthy of God's blessing and an extension of it in this world? Is it a foundational narrative with communal and transcendent purpose, or a claim of superiority and exclusivity? Is salvation a divine promise that we can be "right with God" despite our failings, that God acts in history to alleviate suffering, that existence culminates in fulfillment of the divine vision for creation—or a catalyst to divide the world into the saved and the damned, to impose faith in an attempt to "rescue souls," and to privilege a single path? Does the concept of reward and punishment serve to enact some measure of justice in the world and to discern meaning in suffering—or to encourage retribution and blame victims for their plight? In short, yes. Scripture, chosenness, salvation, and reward and punishment have meant all these things at some point in the history of interpretation—and their assigned meanings have had consequences.

WHO AM I?

My own context and orientation surely influence this book, so I offer a few relevant details. I am a committed progressive Jew. As a religious person, I am pained by the devastation wrought in God's name and hopeful that the religious project can do better. I have a personal stake in this work. As a political and religious progressive, I must acknowledge that my own perception of the traditions—what the texts mean and how I read them, what I define as dangerous that needs undoing—is not universal. Each of the traditions has a rich diversity, one that frequently makes *intra*religious engagement more challenging than the interreligious sort. At the same time, I believe that the critical difference for engaging this work is not whether one identifies as progressive or traditional, but whether or not one recognizes the long history and obligatory nature of self-critical faith.

My Jewish background and training in Jewish studies certainly mean that I am most familiar with that tradition; the risks of writing about other religions that are neither my own nor my primary field of expertise are considerable. While I study Christianity and Islam as well, the place of any bit of information I absorb takes on meaning amidst a much larger landscape of understanding that I have not thoroughly traversed. Claiming to identify what another person's tradition teaches or should teach takes a lot of nerve; it also requires appreciative knowledge, collegial support, and clear conviction that the challenge is a shared one. We learn about our own traditions in studying each other's.

Judaism also shapes my religious imagination. Abraham's dispute with God about Sodom and Gomorrah, as recorded in the Hebrew Bible, challenges the God of justice to do justly—and Abraham bargains with the Almighty until God agrees to spare the cities entirely if ten righteous individuals can be found (Gen. 18). It is one of countless narratives in Jewish tradition that radically affirm the moral stature of human beings. We acknowledge that we are not always right, but we must explore the ethical implications of all our actions and defend our conclusions. Jewish texts show Job confronting the tidy theologies of his friends, the sages radically reinterpreting Torah, and Abraham defending his vision of justice even over against God. So I believe that a teaching is not good simply because it is religious; it too must be submitted to our flawed but essential capacity for moral judgment and move with us in our moral development. Rooted in sacred text and tradition, religious teachings may provide a useful counterweight to the limitations of our own cultural perspective or the fleeting appeal of passing trends, but they must accord with the best of human ethics.

In ways large and small, rabbinic anthropology and philosophy are foundational to my outlook. For example, rabbinic texts imagine two competing inclinations inside each of us, the inclination toward evil (*yetzer hara*) and a good inclination (*yetzer tov*). The remarkable aspect of this mythology is that both are indispensable. In one Talmudic passage, the rabbis imagine "capturing" the yetzer hara. The yetzer warns that if it is killed, the world will come to an end. Prudently, the rabbis lock it up rather than destroy it. After three days they discover, to their dismay, that no hen has laid an egg since the yetzer hara's incarceration. It is a complex narrative with many possibilities for interpretation, but I delight in the insight that even our pleasure-seeking and self-serving instincts (represented here by the sexual and reproductive actions leading a hen to lay an egg) are necessary parts of existence. Ultimately, it is up to us to direct them all toward service of the Most High.[12] As it relates to this project, the tale reaffirms my intuition that our role in redemption is not dependent on vanquishing some onto-logical evil but rather on learning how to engage all aspects of our human-ity in making wise choices, cognizant of their impact on the world. More broadly, I am committed to the profound dialectical engagement in rabbinic thought, drawn to understand ideas by exploring them in tension with com-peting concepts, values, and priorities. Long study of rabbinic texts surely influences the fundamental shape and method of this project.

I am also a religious pluralist. I believe that religions are diverse lan-guages by which we come to experience the transcendent aspects of our universe, to explore our essential purpose, and to express the teachings that can help us embody it. Our brains are wired to learn religion as they are wired to absorb language. They are all translations of something ineffable, and one is not inherently superior to another. In fact, the polyphonic cho-rus is part of the beauty of human experience. My pluralist commitment includes an equal embrace of secular humanism and other lifestances that do not fit the classic understanding of religion but nonetheless have lan-guage to articulate transcendence, purpose, and an ethical path for living. With grace and patience, we learn to appreciate another's language and talk together about matters great and small. Ideally, the conversation helps us to hear and speak our own tradition with greater clarity and appreciation. The goal is not to persuade others that our religion is superior but to live our own lives in faithfulness with its highest teachings.

Lastly, I am a creature of the Western, secularized academy. When I engage the study of scriptures, I understand them all as human documents. Although I sometimes employ conventional language that suggests a cer-tain event or quote rendered in the text is historically accurate (e.g., Jesus said, God instructed), it is presented "as if," recognizing the profound ways in which the authors strive to capture and convey their experience of the divine. At the same time, I refuse to hold historical criticism as the litmus test for responsible exegesis, since the religious traditions developed their own rigorously critical tools. Premodern interpretation has much to teach about how to read scripture.

While I can find support within religious teachings for liberal democracy, intellectual freedom, human rights, and gender equality, my commitments likely derive just as much from secular Western culture. By secular, I do not mean a space devoid of religious voices and influence. Secularism, despite those who decry it as the enemy of religion, is the context in which religious ideas productively engage with other ways of thinking and knowing, and no institution has a monopoly on meaning.[13] The pursuit of meaning is a great strength of both religion and the academy, and I run in both lanes.

Within the field of religious studies, I am trained in the history of exegesis. Whatever one believes about the truth claims of religious traditions or the sources of their sacred texts, they have had and continue to have a tremendous impact on our world. Consequently, it matters a great deal what the ideas contained within are understood to mean. Both my religious tradition and this academic focus inspire me to embrace exegetical dynamism, ambiguity, and even contradiction. The study of scripture is a lifelong course in moral development, not for its tidy answers, but for the core questions of existence it brings to the fore.

NOTES

Translations—Translations of Hebrew Bible (Tanakh) are my own. New Testament passages rely on the New Revised Standard Version unless indicated otherwise. Passages from Qur'an generally utilize the translation by Abdalhaqq and Aisha Bewley, *The Noble Qur'an,* but occasionally adopt the wording of Seyyed Hossein Nasr, ed., *The Study Quran.* In these cases, I have noted *SQ* in the text.

Transliterations—Transliterations are rendered for ease of reading, using common spellings without diacritical marks.

Language—Gendered language for God is preserved if part of a quote from traditional material and otherwise avoided when possible. Nonetheless, I acknowledge that patriarchal imagery and constructs remain embedded in the discussion.

CHAPTER 1

WHAT ARE DANGEROUS RELIGIOUS IDEAS?

The terms of this study do not stay still; they shift about like restless children, depending on context and perspective. Therefore, instead of attempting a concise definition of "dangerous religious ideas," I offer reflections on each word to convey their range of meaning and to establish the premises that undergird this inquiry: Dangers cannot be isolated and surgically removed from religious life and teaching. Religion is built into the infrastructure of the human psyche and society. And religious ideas are embodied in sacred text and interpretation as well as ritual and communal life, with substantive impact on the world, thus necessitating the well-turned tools of self-critical faith. This work sets the stage for subsequent chapters, which explore specific dangers and the ways these tools have been historically employed in Judaism, Christianity, and Islam.

DANGEROUS

Religion is a potent force. It has played an essential role in history and culture, transmitting knowledge and values, shaping law and community, determining meaning and purpose. Like the power of fire or electricity, it is not predestined to be constructive or destructive. As the collective embodiment of choices that humans make—how to live, how to read, how to teach, how to engage one another—it has the potential to be wielded for good or evil. Its very power, however, makes it dangerous. The metaphor of fire is instructive: We warn our children to be careful around it and to

understand its potential for harm. We build industrial and legal safeguards
for handling it, hoping to prevent its misuse. It is known that fire sometimes rages out of control, devastating everything in its path. Although
its elemental force has been developed into diverse forms of energy, all
contain this potentially hazardous quality. Most dangerous outbreaks are
accidental, but the very existence of fire means that some people will deploy its power in deliberately destructive ways. On occasion, it will be the
action of a sociopath; more often, it will be an individual, a community,
or a nation who feels justified in using its power to achieve an ostensibly
greater objective, even though others are harmed in the process. And yet
it is impossible to imagine our world without fire. Religion is comparable
in all these ways.

Certain qualities, such as religion's claim to ultimacy, are especially
prone to abuse. It can disorient our moral compass, transforming the ethical import of hurtful words or actions. Its strong communal emphasis
can create cultures of violence that suppress moral critique; good and evil
simply get redefined.[1] A powerful nexus of religion and power makes the
words, actions, communities, and cultures of religious life of genuine consequence. Yet ambiguity creeps in because texts and traditions can be used
to justify and maintain particular power structures—or to critique them.
They may also valorize surrender in response to the divine and offer God's
favor as consolation for social or political impotence.[2] Some scholars have
attempted to discern a general rule for what makes religion dangerous, such
as its tendency to absolutism and moral certainty, its invention of artificially
scarce resources, its emphasis on obedience, or its expectation to transform
the world.[3] Because I am not persuaded that such an analysis is universally applicable, I prefer to examine specific iterations, looking for strategies
more than conclusions: how might we locate and extinguish the destructive
fires that religion can ignite?

The dangers include not only violence, but also emotional, psychological, physical, and social harm. They may be imposed directly by an individual or community, or create an oppressive culture that impairs the
well-being of those who do not accord with its values. They may be inflicted by religious or secular institutions, by legal or suspect means. They
may jump out of the book, the pulpit, the street, or one's home, or they
may linger discreetly in symbol, music, metaphors, hopes, and dreams. In

almost all of these instances, the dangers are not universally perceived. Understanding is embedded with perspective.

Gender issues provide an obvious example; some traditional communities within the Abrahamic faiths have particular practices related to women that other people may consider oppressive. Limitations on leadership, inequality in legal status, stricter requirements for modesty in clothing, restrictions on reproductive rights, and other religiously endorsed positions are often experienced as dangerous. Critics perceive that religious authority is suppressing the freedom of women and denounce it as the perpetuation of patriarchy. Yet many women *within* traditional communities affirm the value of these practices and the ideas that underlie them. Even if they seek to reform aspects of their religion, these women often perceive that the real danger lies in society's marginalization of their tradition, politicization of their bodies, and blindness to their own agency.

The perspectival dilemma contains another ripple: some dangers may be desirable. Roman orators and poets condemned the Sabbath as a pernicious idea, convinced that it undermined the ethos of productivity at the heart of Roman achievement. A plague of ignoble sloth, as Rutilius Namatianus called it. Seneca argued that it required people to waste a seventh of their lives.[4] Today, amidst another culture that tends to value people based on their achievements and productivity rather than their basic humanity, we may recognize substantial merit in challenging such a materialistic standard. Since Sabbath promises rest for servants as well as their masters, its egalitarian commitment may also have shaped early Roman suspicions. In this regard, we would surely celebrate religion's subversive power. We no longer consider the Sabbath a dangerous idea, but the polemicists were not wrong in thinking that some of the most important teachings in Hebrew Bible—like God's commitment to free a people from slavery and the command to redistribute wealth every fifty years (jubilee) to limit economic inequality—can seriously destabilize society. Dangers come in all shapes and sizes. Some we might embrace. The capacity within religious thought to imagine a world different from the one we live in—the world transformed or transcended—is surely a vital source of its power.

Given that most religious ideas are not presumed to be dangerous, I try to identify the hazards, both enticing and injurious, as the chapters of the book unfold. We examine how diverse voices within the traditions have grappled with their spiritual inheritance, the constructive and destructive sparks of religious fire.

RELIGIOUS

Religious is perhaps the most slippery of the three terms to define, or at least the most disputed. What makes an idea religious? Frequently, observers focus on the substance of religion, attempting to identify some essential shared quality. Belief in god(s) or supernatural beings is generally discarded as not universally applicable. Émile Durkheim and Mircea Eliade, for example, preferred a broader concept of "the sacred," although each applied it differently.[5] Functional definitions take a different approach, setting aside the specific content of ideas to focus instead on how religion operates in the life of the individual or social group—to explain the causes of things, for example, or to resolve deep-seated psychological needs, or to unite individuals in a moral community.

The goal of defining religion at all has been called into question. Wilfred Cantwell Smith, a preeminent scholar of comparative religion in the twentieth century, argued that the subject "religion" reifies a thing that does not exist. It is not an objective and discrete entity. His insight helped spawn critical conversation within Western scholarship about various ways that academic study of religion distorts the very subject it hopes to illuminate.[6] Tomoko Masuzawa and Richard King are among those who demonstrated how the invented category of religion was used to privilege Christianity and consign colonized cultures to the realm of the primitive.[7]

Wendy Doniger's "toolbox" approach may be most helpful here, selecting whatever tools best accomplish the task of understanding in each situation.[8] It examines substance and function, it explains and interprets, it investigates the individual mind and social structures. I count as religious anything taught or practiced as "religion," even if it lies outside the mainstream and even if its origins lie elsewhere. The complex interactions of religious ideas with historical, political, social, biological, and other factors cannot be tidily sequenced like a genome, so analysis is best served by a variety of methodological lenses. Drawing from the disciplines of anthropology, sociology, psychology, neuroscience, and evolutionary biology, this study aims for a vivid, multidimensional perspective that expands our understanding of how religious ideas impact our world. The goal is not to define religion but to discern what happens when ideas are transmitted as part of religions and to explore the complex of forces that gives religion its power. Although the discussion below gathers insights from an eclectic menu of approaches, it must be considered illustrative of diverse ways in which religion "works" rather than a comprehensive analysis of theories of religion.

Will to Pleasure, Power, and Meaning

Freud was among social scientists who believed that explaining the origins of religious experience should facilitate its end, but his more general psychological emphasis on the pleasure principle illuminates the continuing power of religion. Some aspects of religious experience are immensely pleasurable, such as the warmth of community, the beauty of ritual, the ecstasy of mystical experience, and the ubiquitous family feast. Our desire for self-gratification of this sort makes religious teachings that enable our *will to pleasure* very influential.

Alfred Adler absorbed Nietzsche's notions of our *will to power* into his psychological model and identified it as the primary human motivation. One aspect is power over others. Many animal communities demonstrate instinctive patterns of dominance and submission. Humans often insert a moral dimension that makes it particularly problematic: might equals right. In Adler's psychological analysis, however, he emphasized the *internal* struggle—a will to self-mastery more than power over others, with the goal of achieving a holistic self.[9] Many religions strike on all these cylinders. They spur self-mastery through lifelong learning, religious discipline that tames our impulses, and pursuit of the holistic human living in perfect harmony with divine instruction. They authorize power over others with hierarchical structures, instructions for communal life, and a summons to influence the course of human history.

Pursuit of these objectives does not require coercion, but religious communities have certainly proven themselves capable of it. There is a long record of state establishment of religion entailing legal and military enforcement. Religious authorities have exerted control to sustain their own truth claims, again making might equal right. Broad cultural influence can also be coercive. Western colonialism, for example, exerted an overpowering blend of forces that still shapes much of the world today. Superior military power suggested to many of the colonizers and the colonized that the victors' religion and culture were better as well, facilitating a remarkable degree of social control.

Viktor Frankl, a psychologist who imagined a productive role for religion, emphasized the *will to meaning*. He argued that human beings are forever in need of and responsible to meaning, capable of discovering it through action, through relationship with others, and through response to events in our lives. Influenced deeply by his experience in the Shoah, he noticed how personal agency allowed individuals to find purpose in the most horrendous conditions. Even suffering could be a path for unearthing meaning that is essential to our being: "We who lived in concentration camps can remember the men who walked through the huts comforting others, giving away their last piece of bread. They may have been few in number, but they offer sufficient proof that everything can be taken from a man but one thing: the last of the human freedoms—to choose one's attitude in any given set of circumstances, to choose one's own way."[10]

The Abrahamic traditions strive to endow our actions with abiding worth, holding individuals morally accountable and making us a critical part of God's unfolding plan for redemption. They present texts that have yet to be fully plumbed for their significance, and fashion rituals that transform ordinary moments into holy time, ordinary places into sacred shrines. These are indicative of religion's exceptional gift for making meaning.

Although the will to power, pleasure, and meaning were presented as competing theories of the human psyche, each arguing for primacy, their value here is cumulative. Religious teaching and experience feed all these fundamental human needs. Neither moral nor immoral in themselves, such deep psychic forces can drive the full range of human aspiration and degradation.

Human Community

Sociological theory frequently focuses on the need for human community. Émile Durkheim claimed that "nearly all the great social institutions were born in religion" and that "the idea of society is the soul of religion."[11] Moving away from anthropology's emphasis on the individual thinker, trying to make sense of the universe and then transmitting it to others, he argued that religion's primary purpose is not intellectual but social. It draws people together with a common identity, praxis, narrative, and set of values, all of which can activate the deep emotions that bind them in lasting community. His discussion of the sacred, by which he meant that which is set apart by the community, recognized that it is not always good.

Religion serves a necessary social function that can be directed toward good or evil ends.

One danger inherent in religion's tremendous capacity to fashion community is the concomitant creation of the "other" who stands outside it (discussed in part III). Since religion responds to our communal needs but does not create them, conflict with the other is neither invented by nor unique to religious life. There are economic, political, national, racial, gender, geographic, intellectual, and organizational "others," and the boundaries are often fraught. What religious thought adds to the equation is the perilous impression that God favors one group over another and takes sides based on religious affiliation. It sometimes adds the volatile idea that people's faith in this world may impact their fate in the next. On the other hand, religious texts can inspire more universal conceptions of humanity that transcend our groupishness, and a more holistic understanding of life in this universe.

Custodians of Cultural Values

Cultural systems are composed of many elements, including symbols, stories, values, laws, customs, ideas, patterns of thought, institutions, attitudes, behaviors, and worldviews. They form a circle of influence between individuals and groups, and an interlocking puzzle of constituent parts. Religion is influential here but not generally determinative. Its texts and stories provide powerful paradigms of thought and values. Its rituals fit into intricate systems of symbols that embed the sacred into every aspect of daily life. Its institutions impact laws, customs, and worldviews and are capable of transmitting values that challenge prevailing cultural perspectives. These dynamics shape culture in conscious and unconscious ways. Religion is also profoundly shaped *by* culture, however, which can be readily observed by examining how religions are transformed in diverse contexts, how texts come to mean different things, how practices and perspectives evolve. It is also evident when we investigate lived religion in its messy multiplicity.

Some observers have concluded that religion has a particularly strong association with violent aspects of human culture. Georges Khodr, for instance, commented that all warfare is metaphysical; human beings do not go to war except religiously.[12] René Girard's influential theory of mimetic desire maintained that the human instinct to imitate others is essential to how we learn and why we come into conflict. He described the violence endemic to religion as part of its effort to channel these impulses. Rituals of the scapegoat, especially, were identified as enactments of redemptive violence, with controlled expressions to cleanse the community of its murderous rivalry.[13]

Beyond the boundaries of mimetic analysis, the myth of redemptive violence remains a critical problem for religion. Walter Wink showed how this myth operates in multiple cultural vehicles, with film and television far more effective today than religious institutions in promoting its values. To those who might argue that religion is simply co-opted by earthly powers, however, he countered, "The gods are not a fictive masking of the power of the human state; *they are its actual spirituality.*" He characterized it as an ideology of domination: "The gods favor those who conquer. Conversely, whoever conquers must have the favor of the gods. This is a fail-safe theology! Religion exists to legitimate power and privilege."[14] The last statement is reductionist, ignoring the many other reasons religion exists. Yet the notion of a cosmic struggle does indeed provide a powerful spirituality for violence; its transcendent claims promote a hazardous moral certainty. With visions of an afterlife and assurances of divine purpose, theology can overpower our fear of death or deny its power.

The relationship of violence and religion is an urgent question for religious scholars. Its tension is manifest in Søren Kierkegaard's teleological suspension of the ethical, Reinhold Niebuhr's warnings about absolutizing political agendas, Regina Schwartz's emphasis on the invention of scarce resources, and Mark Juergensmeyer's analysis of cosmic war and its cultures of violence.[15] Even with the tools of cultural anthropology and thick description, however, it is impossible to map the interplay of religion with other cultural forces. Beyond the basic enigma of cause and effect, there are multiple barriers to understanding. We cannot shed our own context as we try to step into others, and it clouds how we interpret information. The fact of a written text does not determine whether or how broadly it was practiced or believed. In addition, much of culture is subliminal; sources cannot be completely self-aware or self-disclosing. Consequently, it can be more instructive to consider *correlations* rather than *causes*—even as we recognize the important role of religion in shaping values and behaviors within the web of culture.

Human Evolution

Pascal Boyer described culture as a collection of memes that serve as "copy-me" programs. Ones that copy well are most relevant to human experience, threading through multiple aspects of our lives. They shift more rapidly than genetic material and quickly adapt to new contexts as the memes spread. Religion is ubiquitous in human experience because it transmits on many frequencies key to our success as a species, and it is highly adaptive as evidenced by the diversity of religious expression.[16]

Boyer identified information and cooperation as our most foundational needs.[17] Brains must process enormous amounts of information and cue us to focus on what is most compelling. We cannot afford for every stimulus to require thorough evaluation. Some of the data overload we distill through habit. Religion helps as it directs action, identifies relationship, and establishes priorities. Emotions, which can frequently be triggered in religious experience, prompt us when to raise the stakes and focus our attention. Narrative is another vital capacity we develop to order information. Religious traditions capitalize on this, transmitting much of their substance through story. Narrative structure helps with recall, inference, interpretation, and response.

Most researchers consider religion to be an evolutionary "by-product," a social construction that utilizes cognitive abilities that had developed for other reasons.[18] Our brains are wired to apprehend and fashion order, assign meaning, and discern the significance of what was, what is, and what may follow—all clearly useful for survival. Religion makes profound use of such adaptations. Many conceptions of God, for instance, rely on our ability to think about things that are not visible, but this ability likely developed so we could learn from other people and accumulate cultural wisdom. Theologies also align with our highly attuned instinct for detecting agency and our theory of mind that allows us to understand or even anticipate the actions of others. The instinct for personalization, which presumes that anything happening around us may have relevance for our own lives, has clear value for survival, even if it is magnified and lamented as narcissism in our current age. It also underlies notions of revelation and providence, among other things, which assert that the Creator of the universe is intimately involved with our lives.[19] Even as by-products, spiritual traditions affect the ongoing adaptation of humanity.

We are generally accustomed to thinking about evolution as the survival of the fittest, eliciting associations with domination. It is true that biological development of the human brain has made us ferociously efficient competitors, a quality essential to our being and sadly reflected in the history of religion. Qualities evolved for "selfish" purposes, however, are available for unselfish use as well. Compassion and empathy are also adaptive; the evolutionary advantage of cooperation is integral to social interaction.[20] It has provided the ground rules for creating human communities, with instincts for evaluation of trust, coalitional dynamics, reciprocal altruism, and procedures for dealing with violation and restoring the community to health. Religious systems incorporate these into their foundational structures. Our instincts for morality result from this long evolutionary process as a species of cooperators, making religion easier to acquire. Although culture and experience determine the specifics of moral systems, there has likely developed a "grammar" of the moral mind, which explains how some aspects of ethics appear to be universal.[21] Natural selection prompts us to engage questions of right and wrong, to struggle with evil, and to help members of our community.

Evolutionary biology illuminates how even irrational aspects of religion are significant components of our adaptive capacities.[22] To shape our environment, we need to be able to imagine the world as different than it is. Ritual experience is particularly good at dissolving the boundary between the actual and ideal worlds. Its capacity to express and evoke emotion also cements memory and reinforces group cohesion. Even the strangest of beliefs may function to motivate members of the community to behave in ways that enhance their survival and lead to the flourishing of the group. And yet—while religion builds on life-sustaining forces in human evolution and natural selection may favor brains equipped with spiritual capacities—religion can be a leading cause of death as well. The adaptation itself is amoral; it depends on how we use it.

Neurotheology is a recently developed field that explores how religion works. For example, experiments have located the segment of the brain most affected by meditative practices, namely the parietal lobe. Because it impacts our spatial awareness and sense of boundedness, meditation enables a sense of self-transcendence.[23] The frontal lobes are understood to influence responses of willfulness and surrender; certain aspects of religious thought and practice can "fire" neurons in these regions. Although the brain places some functional restrictions on all thought processes, including how we experience religion or construct theology,[24] it is not all biologically determined. According to Malcolm Jeeves and Warren Brown, neurons do not create religions; instead, our religious training and experience shape our interpretation of neuronal activity. They wrote of an irreducible interdependence: "The spiritual dimensions of our lives are *both* firmly *embodied* and *embedded.* As *embodied,* these dimensions are not immune to the effects of changes in the brain. As *embedded,* these religious dimensions of experience, belief, and practice also sculpt our brains." Organisms actively participate in their own evolution.[25]

Distilling how religions work in individuals and in human community neither confirms religious truth claims nor reduces them to scientific phenomena without spiritual substance. This question is not of particular interest in the present study. Instead, the collection of theories suggests that the amazing staying power and ongoing relevance of religion is related to the fact that it is woven through every facet of human development and experience. Religion may reach for heaven, but it unfolds through the psychological, sociological, anthropological, evolutionary, and neurological dimensions of our being.

IDEAS

Religious experience, like all experience, must move through the mind, taking on the form of images and ideas. The Christian mystic Meister Eckhart intuited it this way: "Every time that the powers of the soul come into contact with created things, they receive the created images and likenesses from the created thing and absorb them. In this way arises the soul's knowledge of created things. . . . Does the soul want to know the nature of a stone—a horse—a man? She forms an image."[26]

Two scientists working on the nature of the brain borrowed his insight and argued that, if God exists and chooses to reach out to you, the only way to experience it is as an idea—a neurological translation of reality. "In this sense," they maintained, "both spiritual experiences and experiences of a more ordinary material nature are made real to the mind in the very same way—through the processing powers of the brain and the cognitive functions of the mind."[27]

Ideas do not stay in the mind, however; they continually translate into deeds. How does something experienced or expressed as mere thought, belief, or story come to enter the stage of action? All ideas have the potential to change people and to define the realm of the real. Religious ideas have common modes of translation that facilitate their tremendous impact on the world. We explore three of these methods here: sacred text/interpretation, ritual, and community—each with the power to actualize religion's dangers and to ward against them.

Sacred Text and Textual Interpretation

Sacred texts of the Abrahamic traditions include significant instructions regarding behaviors of the faithful: observance of holy days, business and sexual ethics, relations with people outside the community, care for the less fortunate, and more. Even though early Christianity declared its adherents "free" from many commandments of Hebrew Bible, it developed its own praxis that relies on New Testament for some of its rhythm and substance. Scriptures clearly convey the notion that religious ideas are *designed* to have an impact on the world, that God expects human beings to respond to divine instruction through action. Religious institutions build upon those textual foundations in guiding individual behaviors and communal customs; they developed substantial literatures of halakhah, *fiqh*, and canon law that translate teachings into actions.

Because scripture is considered authoritative in some measure for community members, discussions frequently involve prooftexting, grounding certain actions with explicit citation and interpretation of the text. Even those who do not believe that the texts represent unalloyed transmission of divine revelation will quote them as the source of their obligation to feed the hungry, tend to the stranger, and repent of their sins. The relationship is far from straightforward, however. Regardless of how religiously progressive or conservative one may be, prooftexting is frequently a secondary phenomenon that justifies actions determined by other social forces. Some ideas do appear to originate in scripture and translate directly into practice, but the derivative prooftexting pattern is also widespread. For example, Tanakh, New Testament, and Qur'an do not refer to abortion. There is one mention of miscarriage that results from injury to a pregnant woman in Exodus 21: if no other injury to the woman results, it is settled by payment of a fine. But people tend to begin with their conviction and then hunt for scriptural verses to support their view, making religion speak to the contemporary debate.[28] For people of faith the text remains an essential catalyst for action.

Proper observance has always depended on proper interpretation, which is why we argue so vociferously about what these texts mean.

Ritual

Religious ritual often derives from scripture, but it has its own dynamic of idea and action. A number of rituals are understood to effect change through speech. The bread becomes Jesus's body in some Christian rites of the Eucharist, for example, and a husband divorces his wife with the rituals of triple *talaq* in Sunni Islam.[29] Rituals also operate on complex symbolic planes, evoking narratives, emotions, and commitments with multiple layers of action. The specially knotted strings on the Jewish prayer shawl (tallit), for instance, symbolically represent the unity and sovereignty of God and the Jew's obligation to perform *mitzvot* (commandments). It is a ritual action to wear the tallit and, ideally, consciousness of the strings leads toward a broad array of actions in the service of God. The Muslim ritual of hajj provides another example: making the pilgrimage is one action, and each of the elaborate rituals attached to it evokes some aspect of the foundational narratives of Islam. Together, they help to cement the participant's religious identity and values, shaping future behaviors.

Prayer is another ritual category with multiple layers. It is an action in its own right, and may prompt further actions inspired by the teachings lifted up in the worship service. Because prayer can stimulate deep spiritual, emotional, and intellectual responses, its power to catalyze action is potentially quite strong—in conscious and subconscious ways. The social function of prayer is also significant: communal prayer builds cohesion within the group. Religious travelers often remark how inspiring it is to go to a worship service of their faith community in a different context and still feel at home. Relationships among worshippers who consistently share a spiritual home can be more complicated but yield even stronger bonds of connectedness. Ritual is ubiquitous in religious life because it so successfully translates idea to deed.

Community

Writing about the ways culture gets expressed, Clifford Geertz asserted that it must transform ideas into behaviors and social action.[30] He examined both the *force* and *scope* of religious culture through this lens. When he studied daily life among Muslims in Indonesia, for instance, he found that religious ideas, rituals, and customs infused every aspect. The *scope* of religious life was tremendous, although its impact on behavior could frequently be indirect, subliminal, or trivial. In contrast, the scope of Islam in Morocco was narrower but its *force* was more intense. It was not felt much in the street or the marketplace, but where it did come into play, its ideas profoundly influenced individual and communal action.[31]

The cultural influence of religion throws the movement from ideas to action across a large canvas. Fusing worldview and ethos, religious ideas can shape social and economic policy, international relations, artistic expression, learning styles, work habits, family dynamics, social customs, and more. They may be used for purely religious purpose or be co-opted by other forces, both beneficial and dangerous. Charles Selengut noted,

> Religion is such a powerful tool to motivate people to action and provide resources for social movements that it is highly useful in battling for nationalist and secular goals. Leaders of national, ethnic, and linguistic movements are aware of the ability of religious belief to motivate collective action, and they often seek to use religious language and symbols to foster and justify continuing ethnic conflict, even in situations where religion was not initially an element in the conflict.[32]

Arguing that the reverse dynamic also takes place, Hector Avalos quoted Adolf Hitler's *Mein Kampf* to demonstrate that religion inspired his hatred of the Jews even though Nazism is considered a secular totalitarianism: "Hence today I believe that I am acting in accordance with the will of the Almighty Creator; by defending myself against the Jew, I am fighting for the work of the Lord."[33] Even here, however, it is not clear whether religion is the cause or the justification.

As mentioned above, the amalgamation of influences argues for discussing correlation rather than causality. It is not possible to identify and assess each contributing cause to chart the movement of ideas to praxis. Nonetheless, the religious transition from word to deed, from thought to action, has always been central. Many forms of Christianity stress faith as primary, which might appear to deemphasize action, but the foundation of belief is still designed to shape how one behaves in the world. In bumper sticker form, this notion is articulated, "What would Jesus do?" We return to the speech of Swami Vivekananda: "Religion is realisation, not talk, nor doctrine, nor theories, however beautiful they may be. It is being and becoming, not hearing or acknowledging; it is the whole soul becoming changed into what it believes. That is religion."[34]

These are some of the theoretical underpinnings for our investigation into dangerous religious ideas. As we study particular themes, we will come to appreciate the deep roots of self-critical faith in the history of Judaism, Christianity, and Islam—necessitated by the dense warp and woof of religion in human life. With scripture, we explore how the traditions historically understood their own multiple and conflicting texts and interpretations. How have they grappled with issues of truth and doubt? What have they acknowledged about their own evolution? What role have they assigned to human beings in discerning the proper path?

PART II

SCRIPTURE

CHAPTER 2

SCRIPTURE AS A DANGEROUS RELIGIOUS IDEA

What is scripture? Dictionaries define it simply as a body of religious writings considered sacred or authoritative. This description hardly conveys the wide-ranging influence scripture has had in human affairs. As Wilfred Cantwell Smith explained, "The role of scripture in human life has been prodigious—in social organization and in individual piety, in the preservation of community patterns and in revolutionary change, and of course in art and literature and intellectual outlook." He acknowledged that the historical impact of scripture has been mixed, at times elevating the human spirit and challenging society to live up to its highest values, while in other instances serving as justification for oppression and moral blindness.[1] As such, it falls squarely into the purview of this study of dangerous religious ideas. Since many other religious ideas find articulation or validation within scripture, we take it up first.

Trying to discern what is common to scriptures across civilizations, Smith asserted that it is not a shared quality or type of text but rather the ongoing relationship between each text and a particular community. If we focus on how Jews, Christians, and Muslims relate to Bible and Qur'an, an obvious commonality is that the canonized texts are *interpreted* by the communities who deem them sacred. Arguments about meaning are recorded in the earliest layers of commentary and continue in every age. There is no reading that is not an interpretation, and some are clearly problematic; as Shakespeare noted, even "the devil can cite Scripture for his purpose."[2]

Thus, when dangers of scripture are discussed, they generally invoke or presume particular interpretations.

This chapter, however, addresses a far more fundamental problem with scripture. It is an issue of ideology and theology, not merely of hermeneutics (methods of interpretation). The *idea* of scripture is dangerous. As long as there is scripture, people will wield the word as a weapon against each other in order to justify their own biases. As long as there is scripture, we have to reckon with the painful silences of those voices left out of the canon. As long as there is scripture, some people will turn their back on other God-given ways of knowing.

Of course, scripture is not simply an idea. As described in the previous chapter, it is translated into action through exegesis, ritual, and communal embodiment. Every aspect of religion's work in the human psyche and society is evident in the relationship with scripture. We derive pleasure from its recitation, explication, and artistic representation. The words overflow with meaning and the texts have symbolic status in delineating culture and mediating divine presence.[3] Manifesting our will to power, we may deploy scripture politically—as justification for policies, as evidence for moral claims, or as an instrument of cultural imperialism.[4] Scripture's role in sustaining community testifies to its adaptive value as it lays the foundations for belief, behavior, and belonging.

SCRIPTURE'S ABIDING RELEVANCE AND AUTHORITY: DANGER AND PROMISE

The continuing relevance of Bible or Qur'an, stable in a sea of change, is undoubtedly one of its strengths. It is the sacred story that binds adherents together and shapes their purpose. As a "control" of the human experiment, scripture can test the value of new ideas and serve as a check on our less worthy desires. Its authority can push human beings to grow in goodness, to transform society toward justice—with prophets who call us to account for our moral failings, visions of communities that tend to the poor and the stranger, ontological equality between the sexes, and images of a God overflowing with love and mercy.

Yet these same scriptures appear to sanction slavery and condemn same-sex intercourse. They present a God who punishes a number of crimes with exceeding harshness. They include passages that subordinate women and incorporate hateful depictions of some who stand outside the community.[5] New religious communities frequently polemicize against established religions or peoples from whom they seek to distinguish themselves; once canonized in sacred texts, this hostility is automatically conveyed to future generations of believers long after the original conflict has ended.[6] Here, the abiding relevance of scripture transforms historical tensions into eternal enmity.

Scripture's permanence can stifle positive change. Benedict de Spinoza (1632–77), also known as Baruch, complained that people failed to distinguish between scripture's timeless, universal teachings and those that were shaped by historical context: such "promiscuous" faith could not avoid "confounding the opinions of the masses with Divine doctrines . . . and making a wrong use of scriptural authority."[7] Attitudes toward sacred text have impeded embrace of scientific thought, pluralism, and social equity. The case of slavery presents an interesting example. Tanakh, New Testament, and Qur'an did not invent slavery, but all accepted it as an institution. Passages conveying concern about the condition of slaves (Lev. 25:35–55, Deut. 23:16–17, Philemon, Qur'an 4:36) prompted many critiques regarding poor treatment in Late Antiquity and the early Islamic era, but most people presumed scripture's general sanction.[8] Those who later tried to remove the stain of slavery from the American landscape cited the Bible's passionate commitment to liberation in Exodus, its command to love the stranger, and its teaching that all human beings are created in the image of God. They maintained that scriptural texts making slavery more humane were meant as a stepping-stone toward universal emancipation—even though they could not point to a text that explicitly said so. More recently, Amina Wadud argued in similar fashion that discussion of slavery in Qur'an would never have led to its eradication in Islam, but the Qur'anic ethos of equity, justice, and human dignity catalyzed reform.[9]

This effort to distill overarching scriptural values undergirded abolitionist writings, while proslavery forces cited the Bible's explicit discussion of slavery. The latter condemned their opponents' "disregard of the authority of the word of God, a setting up of a different and higher standard of truth and duty, and a proud and confident wresting of scripture to suit their own purposes."[10] Systemic racism and the economics of slave labor undoubtedly drove opposition to change, but slavery's existence in sacred text perpetuated the oppression. It took a long time and a bloody Civil War for "new" ideas of universal emancipation to win the day. Both proslavery and antislavery arguments, however, reinforced the danger of scripture by presuming that we can find verses in the texts to prove God is on our side.

Scripture's authority is traditionally traced to God, either as human reflections of divine teaching or as God's Word itself. Within Islam, for instance, orthodox faith maintains that the angel Jibreel (Gabriel) conveyed the divine message directly to Muhammad: "Muslims believe that the Qur'an is a flawlessly reliable source of truth because it is the accurately preserved record of the words of the Living God."[11] Hebrew Bible and New Testament, which contain a broader range of material (prophecy, historical narrative, law, psalms, gospel testimony, letters) were still understood to have their source in God through a combination of revelation and inspiration. In 2 Timothy 3:16, the sacred texts are described as *theopneustos,* literally "God-breathed." Divine imprimatur also undergirds scripture's claim to abiding influence: "Because the authority of Scripture lies not in itself but in the living God to whom it points, such authority is not confined to the past but continues in the present."[12]

Consequently, the presence of an idea in scripture can override our own moral instincts, as it claims a higher law. Hebrew Bible, New Testament, and Qur'an privilege devotion to God's will over one's own, and that will is expressed through scripture. Even though there are passages that affirm the moral stature of humanity, including striking examples in Tanakh that portray individuals challenging God on ethical grounds (e.g., Job, Abraham), traditional notions of scripture frequently emphasize how our flawed instincts must be disciplined through the text. In fact, one critique Qur'an levels at Jews and Christians is that they distorted their scriptures and deified their leaders (5:13–14, 9:31). In a famous hadith, a Christian contests the idea that they worship their religious authorities; Muhammad substantiates the charge by asserting that they forbid what God permitted and permit what God forbade, setting their own authority above God's.[13]

Many claims of contemporary biblicists, like those articulated in the Chicago Statement on Biblical Inerrancy at the 1978 Summit Conference of evangelical leaders, continue to insist on scriptural ultimacy, nullifying human perspectives that contradict its teaching: "Holy Scripture, being God's own Word, written by men prepared and superintended by His Spirit, is of infallible divine authority in all matters upon which it touches; it is to be believed, as God's instruction, in all that it affirms: obeyed, as

God's command, in all that it requires; embraced, as God's pledge, in all that it promises."[14]

Are there times when a reader with this view of scripture wants to disagree on ethical grounds, but feels constrained by its overriding authority? Robert Gagnon wrote about grappling with the hurt his fealty to scripture causes in his stance against queer sexuality: "Perhaps worst of all is the knowledge that a rigorous critique of same-sex intercourse can have the unintended effect of bringing personal pain to homosexuals, some of whom are already prone to self-loathing."[15] Does he act against that compassion because he believes God demands it—even though such views cause the suffering he laments? Does he maintain a notion of Kierkegaard's "teleological suspension of the ethical," a faith that scriptural instruction which runs counter to ethical convictions has a higher purpose?[16] Or does the justification mask a preconceived bias, even an unconscious one? It is not certain whether people can be completely honest with themselves about their motivations in such a situation, but their discrimination against LGBTQ+ individuals is rationalized scripturally.

Yet it is impossible to remove the human element from scriptural teaching. Everyone reads selectively. Much of scripture's teaching is simply laid aside, and the rest is subject to uneven human attention and interpretation. Why do some people endorse the Bible's capital punishment but not its redistribution of property in the jubilee? How is it that Muslim religious scholars of differing legal schools read the same text but disagree about its provisions for criminal justice, warfare, interreligious relations, and other vital issues? There is no unmediated encounter with the Word. It must be interpreted, and we tend to do so in keeping with our own values or interests—a reflection of our will to meaning and will to power exercised through religious texts. As George Bernard Shaw famously quipped, "No man ever believes that the Bible means what it says: he is always convinced that it says what he means."

Thus one danger of scripture's ultimacy is that it takes human perspectives and grants them divine authority. Khaled Abou El Fadl described this brandishing of the Book as locking "the will of the divine will, the will of the text, into a specific determination and then presenting [it] as inevitable, final and conclusive."[17] It becomes a trump card. Feminist, queer, liberationist, and postcolonial critiques among others from the margins have illuminated how the history of interpretation emphasized certain teachings and ignored or reinterpreted others in order to perpetuate existing power structures and norms. Why were biblical and Qur'anic texts that seem to support patriarchy prominently deployed, for instance, while those showing women equal in creation, with moral courage and political and spiritual power, were not seen to have equally broad mandates?[18] Why obsess over the few verses that may address same-sex intercourse when poverty or adultery are clearly much greater concerns within scripture? These contemporary scholars' essential insights underscore the way human authority disguises itself as scriptural.

RECOGNIZING THE HUMAN ELEMENT

Jewish, Christian, and Islamic traditions have long recognized the inescapable human element in determining scripture's meaning and used it as a tool for self-critical faith. Piety does not demand that human beings forfeit their judgment but rather that they deploy it to defend against the dangers of scripture. Living in the Greco-Roman world around the turn of the Common Era and eager to show the philosophical brilliance of Torah, for example, Philo asserted that it must accord with reason: "In the poetic work of God you will not find anything mythical or fictional but the canons of truth all inscribed, which do not cause any harm."[19] Moses Maimonides (1135–1204), Ibn Tufayl and Ibn Rushd (twelfth century), and Thomas Aquinas (1225–1274), all influenced by the resurgence of Hellenistic philosophy in the Middle Ages, similarly sought to affirm divine law as the embodiment of reason and truth—not by changing what they understood to be true, but by adapting what they understood to be scripture's meaning.[20]

Early in their development, Judaism, Christianity, and Islam formalized the human extensions of scripture, which was essential to preserving scripture's relevance and proved determinative in the history of interpretation. While their teachings are assigned secondary status compared to the unique transcendence of scripture, religious authorities attached a measure of scripture's exalted status—its authority if not its sanctity—to these other sources.

Rabbinic Judaism identified its classical texts—Mishnah, Tosefta, the Palestinian and Babylonian Talmuds, and collections of midrash (redacted in the second through sixth centuries CE)—as Oral Torah, imagining that their interpretive conclusions were transmitted verbally in a chain leading back to revelation at Sinai.[21] Torah, which in its narrow sense refers to the Five Books of Moses as the perpetually privileged core of scripture, also became a referent for all of sacred learning. Since rabbinic Judaism eventually became normative for the vast majority of Jews, much of Jewish praxis today is shaped by the teachings of Oral Torah.

The Catholic Church grounded its authority in apostolic succession, tracing back to scripture, so that its councils, creeds, and canons were seen as uniquely sanctioned to advance Jesus's charge to the apostles. Catholic magisterium was considered authoritative teaching.[22] Augustine dismissed other claimants of that privilege, describing how the mandate of the Catholic Church "inaugurated in miracles, nourished by hope, augmented by love, and confirmed by her age, keeps me here. The succession of priests, from the very see of the apostle Peter, to whom the Lord, after his resurrection, gave the charge of feeding his sheep [John 21:15–17], up to the present episcopate, keeps me here."[23]

Islam established the sunna, the sayings and doings of the Prophet Muhammad, as a necessary corollary for discerning the right path after his death. Believed to be chosen by God not only to transmit the Qur'an but also to interpret and embody it according to Allah's intentions, the prophet's legacy serves as the authority for large portions of Islamic legal, theological, and popular religious traditions. The human hand in collecting these teachings is explicit, prompting a medieval version of critical textual analysis to determine the reliability of each hadith (saying) and story of the prophet's life.[24]

These later texts played a critical role in forging a path for growth and dynamism within the traditions. There are numerous examples in which their interpretative methods discerned dangers and sought to defuse them. For example:

- Rabbinic texts understood the biblical notion of "eye for an eye" as a system of restorative justice (m. B. Qam. 8, b. B. Qam. 83b): One is liable to compensate the injured party for pain, for time lost from work, for medical expenses, for any permanent loss in earning potential, and for emotional suffering. No reciprocal eye-gouging is involved.
- Catholic canon law established a means by which an unhealthy marriage could be annulled, even though New Testament teaching was

understood to demand a lifelong commitment. Since the sacrament is essentially effected by the spouses themselves (1057.1), a "defect" in the consent of one of them means that the binding power of the sacrament never took hold. At the same time, their putative marriage established their children as legitimate.[25]

- The Qur'anic verse that appears to allow husbands to strike their wives if other methods of disciplining them are not effective (4:34) was mitigated by the sunna tradition: the Prophet Muhammad never struck his own wives. There are numerous hadiths brought to bear, limiting the circumstances, delineating the rights a woman is owed by her husband, and encouraging the model of the prophet: "The best of you are those who are the best to their wives, and I am the best of you to my wives."[26]

In the contemporary context, historical-critical perspectives extend the human role to the creation of scripture itself. As human documents, the texts do not bear absolute authority, even if we imagine that they strain to discern God's will. Scholarship like the documentary hypothesis, which identifies diverse authors and contexts for the Pentateuch, highlights evolving theologies and praxis. Scriptural statements about women, same-sex intercourse, slavery, and violence are recognized as reflections of the perspectives and power dynamics of the societies that generated the texts. Rather than dictating the eternal nature of these ethics, the scriptures invite us to interrogate our own. Seen as the work of human hands, it becomes harder to wield the sacred word as a weapon to cudgel those who disagree with or are different than us.

This protection comes at a price, however, often diminishing scripture's capacity to transform. Many people begin to wonder whether these ancient books are really relevant to life today in any significant measure. Even among religious adherents who still read, study, and cite their holy books while embracing their human origins, can the Word command the spirit? While it may draw attention to our inadequate concern for the poor, for instance, can it inspire the requisite sacrifice to establish economic equity? If scripture is no longer the custodian of social ethics, then how can it effectively challenge the overweening corporatism, materialism, and militarism of the current age? The positive dangers of social critique, upending the status quo to fashion a better world, shrink once scripture is no longer seen as God's blueprint for creation. Mahatma Gandhi once commented, "You Christians look after a document containing enough dynamite to blow all civilization to pieces, turn the world upside down and bring peace to a battle-torn planet. But you treat it as though it is nothing more than a piece of literature." Its power to heal is bound up with its power to harm.

Neither traditional nor contemporary strategies provide a comprehensive solution to the dangers of scripture. Oral Torah, canon law, and the sunna were responsible for holding back progress on a range of issues and embedding the biases of their own eras within scriptural authority. Restrictions on women's leadership, for example, are largely grounded in these later teachings. Historical-critical method similarly layered one flawed source of authority on top of another. With the rise of modern scholarship in the wake of the Enlightenment, the academy became a new arbiter of truth. Scholars falsely presumed that they could stand outside history to describe objective reality, thus obscuring their own agenda and social location.[27] Displacing scripture's ultimacy did not guarantee a freer flow of ideas; arguments about correct interpretation were often fierce, with dogmatism continuing to haunt the discourse. Old ways of thinking still infected academic methodology, adding the authority of "science" to their conclusions. One example is the adaptation of anti-Jewish teaching. A significant group of Bible scholars stopped the supersessionary practice of looking for ways to draw out Christian truths encoded in Hebrew Bible; instead, they sought to identify "the origins of Christian society's present ills in the errors and superstitions of the Israelites and Jews."[28] Acknowledging the human hand in scripture does not fully dissolve the dangers.

Yet the academy also has the capacity for self-critique. Interrogating its methods and conclusions, scholars have helped to uncover how all interpretation is linked to the exercise of power. Elisabeth Schüssler Fiorenza offered these reflexive questions: "How is meaning constructed, whose interests are served, what kind of worlds are envisioned, what roles, duties, and values are advocated, which socio-political practices are legitimated?"[29]

Those who reject the historical-critical method see the threat quite differently. Although many Jews and Christians embrace scripture as a human document and preserve a sense that their Bible is a sacred text, the theory was fiercely resisted when broached in the nineteenth century. It is still seen by many adherents to be an affront to their faith. The text they believe to be the inerrant teaching of God is rejected as such, and they resent feeling that people think their attitude is obscurantist or ill-informed. Within the Muslim community, the issue is bound up with the history of Western colonialism and concerns about Orientalist approaches to Islamic studies. Although Islam developed rigorous textual-critical tools in the Middle Ages, the idea that Qur'an is also the product of human hands rather than a perfectly transmitted revelation was first broached by non-Muslim academics and was often experienced as an attack against the faith. One Muslim scholar stated his objection quite forcefully:

> The Orientalist enterprise of Qur'anic studies, whatever its other merits and services, was a project born of spite, bred in frustration and nourished by vengeance: the spite of the powerful for the powerless, the frustration of the "rational" towards the "superstitious" and the vengeance of the "orthodox" against the "non-conformist." At the greatest hour of his worldly-triumph, the Western man, coordinating the powers of the State, Church and Academia, launched his most determined assault on the citadel of Muslim faith.[30]

Whether Western historical-critical Qur'anic studies have been the witting or unwitting accomplice of colonialism, there remains a fair deal of pressure for Islamic scholarship to embrace human authorship of Qur'an in order to participate fully in academic discourse. Even though there are other tools for practicing Muslims to engage the critical conversation, many derived from Islamic tradition, the tension around this question is still palpable.[31] Nonetheless, the power of scripture need not be strangled in a problematic dichotomy between oppressive fundamentalism and academic supersessionism. Aware of the dangers, it is possible to navigate between Scylla and Charybdis by engaging more fully with the received tradition.

EXCAVATING THE TRADITIONS: DEEP ROOTS OF SELF-CRITICAL FAITH

Exploring the rich self-reflective capacity of Judaism, Christianity, and Islam, the following chapters deliberately emphasize "precritical" resources within the traditions that mitigate against the dangers of scripture's authority. They were not all derived for such a purpose, but all have served to refine the way scriptural power is wielded, even among those who feel they hold God's word in their hands. Long before the rise of historical-critical scholarship, we find woven through traditional engagements with sacred texts an awareness of multivocality in scripture and its exegesis, the provisional nature of truth and the human role in discerning the Word, epistemological humility and the role of doubt in faith, consciousness of historical change and its impact on religious meaning—each moderating the use and abuse of scripture's power.

Again, this part of the book is not about specific dangerous ideas within the sacred texts; examples of those will be addressed in subsequent sections. Having laid out the framework through which the *idea* of scripture can do harm, the next three chapters focus on the complex assortment of tools that might limit or prevent it. Different in each religion, close examination also reveals similarities. Thus, the traditions are examined independently in order to clarify the unique issues and articulations, but the methods are grouped in parallel fashion in order to highlight common ground as well. Chapter 6 then explores contemporary efforts to reckon with the power of scripture for good and ill and how they relate to the tools of self-critical faith—ending with a discussion of scripture and politics in the United States. Prescriptions of self-critical faith do not constitute a cure; the dangers remain salient. Instead, it is helpful to think of the strategies as treatments to manage the life-sustaining capacities of scripture and its life-threatening side effects, diverse parts of the inheritance of religious tradition.

CHAPTER 3

JUDAISM–THE CANONIZATION
OF CONTROVERSY

Your word is a lamp to my feet and a light to my path. (Ps. 119:105)

As Judaism became a text-centered tradition during the Second Temple period, expertise in interpretation was a source of power and prestige. Scripture was not simply to be obeyed but also studied in depth for the manifold meanings that could be discovered.[1] New possibilities seemed to grow organically from close reading of Torah, with its multiple tellings, gaps, and ambiguities. Historical-critical analysis explains how the redactors brought together diverse narrative sources and religio-political agendas from multiple time periods—but traditional exegesis discerned its own kind of multiplicity. The text itself also became an essential locus of religious experience. During the long exile that followed the destruction of the Second Temple in 70 CE, rabbinic Judaism saw Torah as the primary sign of God's ongoing covenant with Israel. Study of the text became a central part of their life of dialogue with the divine.[2] George Steiner commented on the adaptive value of this emerging theology of scripture: "Hermeneutic unendingness and survival in exile are, I believe, kindred. . . . In dispersion, the text is homeland."[3]

POLYSEMY AND PLURALISM

The earliest rabbinic texts, redacted by the Tannaim near the beginning of the third century CE, took the forms of Midrash and Mishnah. As the building blocks of Oral Torah, they canonized exegetical multiplicity and legal controversy. Midrashic collections, organized around particular books of Torah, included diverse interpretations of the same verse without determining a "correct" reading; each was separated only by the marker *davar acher*, another interpretation. Multi-layered exegesis was eventually formalized using the acronym *PaRDeS*, although each layer could contain multiple possibilities:

- *Peshat*, the contextual meaning
- *Remez*, allusions derived through various hermeneutics
- *Drash*, philosophical, theological, and ethical notions "searched out" within the text
- *Sod*, esoteric or mystical interpretations

The framework is almost an afterthought; both before and beyond its construction, rabbinic anthologies established the legitimacy of contradictory readings (e.g., Mek. Baḥodesh 7, Shirata 9).[4]

Some passages explicitly affirmed scripture's hermeneutical openness, marveling at God's ability to express multiple (even conflicting) ideas in a single utterance (Mek. Baḥodesh 9, Sifre Deut. 313),[5] and imagining that at the very moment of revelation on Mount Sinai, Israel examined each word to see how many different interpretations they could draw out. Each person received the word according to their ability.[6] Such polysemy, embracing the notion that the canonical text legitimately yields multiple meanings, can discourage oppressive enforcement of a singular interpretation. According to David Stern, "The rabbis appear to have repudiated the absolutist claims of apocalyptic fulfillment in favor of hermeneutical multiplicity." They raised the multivocality of Tanakh, which preserved diverse traditions as if they were compatible, to an exegetical ideology: "Editorial pluralism has become a condition of meaning."[7]

The Mishnah is organized thematically; while its central topics were determined by biblical teachings (e.g., Shabbat and holy days, tithes, sacrifice, civil and criminal justice), it does not frequently use scriptural exegesis to support its determinations. For our purposes, the most interesting thing about the Mishnah is that it transmits the tradition through dialectical argument, presenting sages who disagree, and majority and minority opinions. At one point, it asks the purpose of recording an opinion rejected by the rabbinic community—and gives conflicting answers to the question! The majority maintain that it serves as precedent for potentially overturning their ruling in the future (m. Ed. 1:5),[8] a view that recognizes the teachings of Oral Torah as provisional efforts to discern divine will. A sage may continue to teach according to his opinion even after he has been outvoted, as long as he does not publicly rule that others should do as he does (m. Sanh. 11:2).

There is also a poetic and powerful passage in the Tosefta, a collection of Tannaitic sayings not included in the Mishnah but redacted around the same time. In response to a question about how to (literally, *why*) learn Torah when one sage permits and another prohibits, one says clean and another unclean, it examines the various verses of God revealing divine "words" and asserts, "All the words have been given by a single Shepherd: one God created them, one Provider gave them, the Lord of all deeds, blessed be He, has spoken them. So make yourself a heart of many rooms and bring into it the words of the House of Shammai and the words of the House of Hillel, the words of those who declare unclean and the words of those who declare clean" (t. Sotah 7:12).[9]

The heart in rabbinic imagination is the seat of the mind, and "a heart of many rooms" is likely a helpful image for how to retain knowledge that does not have a single, direct answer; it does not necessarily argue for the modern pluralism we might hear in such a phrase. Further, we must acknowledge that the passage's affirmation of diverse voices is limited, representing only the community of sages and those who followed them.[10] Yet it clearly claims that all their opinions derive from God, giving divine authorization to multivocality. Rabbinic culture embraced multiple schools of thought and saw positive value in teaching the controversy.[11]

Pluralism became increasingly "thematized"—raised up as an ideological value—in the Talmuds, redacted during the Amoraic (c. 200–500 CE) and Savoraic (c. 500–600) periods. It seems especially prominent in the Babylonian context.[12] Unpacking the brief disagreements found in Mishnah and Tosefta with elaborate analysis, discussions in the Talmud tend to maintain the validity of conflicting viewpoints—grounding each one deeply in the soil of scripture—rather than resolve the argument. Local variation is affirmed by statements such as, "Each river follows its own course" (b. Hul. 57a, b. Git. 60b). Certain passages have become what Steven Fraade calls the poster children of Talmudic pluralism, including a repeated trope that identifies all the contradictory opinions from the sages as the word of the living God (b. Eruv. 13b, b. Git. 6b, y. Yevam. 1:6 [3b]). Another suggests that the argument is what substantiates Torah in the life of the community: "Had the words of Torah been given as clear-cut decisions, it would not have a leg to stand on" (y. Sanh. 4:2 [22a]). Even God is portrayed as involved in rabbinic controversy, studying the opinions of the sages, disagreeing with the heavenly academy, and occasionally deferring to the earthly one (b. B. Metz. 86a). Increasingly, the notion took hold that disagreement and difference play a uniquely important role in fulfilling the Word.

Rabbinic texts also developed a productive tension between conservatism and innovation. One example can be found in *Avot d'Rabbi Nathan*, extolling the virtues of diverse students. Some are lauded for piety, righteousness (literally fear of sin), or bringing joy to parents. The two that rise to the top of this esteemed group, however, are Rabbi Eliezer b. Hyrcanus and Rabbi Eleazar b. Arakh. The former is described as a cemented cistern that does not lose a drop, an apt metaphor for the faithful bearer of tradition. The latter is described as a flowing spring, representing the dynamic and life-giving nature of creative fidelity. In place of mechanical transmission of tradition just as one received it, it makes room for change. While there is disagreement about which of the two star pupils is *most* prized, one opinion describes Rabbi Eleazar b. Arakh as outweighing all the other sages in the world (Avot R. Nat. A 14).[13] At the same time, there appears to be appreciation for the fruitful intersections of their disparate perspectives. Rabbinic thought preserves a dynamic balance between the religious requirements for boundaries and consistency versus openness and change.

Ultimately, as Jeffrey Rubenstein noted, the rabbis "thematize dialectical argumentation and portray it as the highest form of Torah."[14] Several passages present this discourse almost like an extreme sport. One Talmudic narrative tells of Rabbi Shimon bar Yohai after emerging from a cave where he had hidden for twelve years to evade the Roman emperor's order of execution. When Rabbi Shimon's son-in-law saw his distressed physical state, he lamented his father-in-law's ordeal. Rabbi Shimon told him to rejoice instead, since he had devoted himself to Torah study during that time and could now offer twenty-four different scriptural and logical resolutions for any difficulty his son-in-law might raise (b. Shabb. 33b). Even more remarkably, the Palestinian Talmud recounts a tradition that God revealed

to Moses forty-nine arguments for demonstrating the purity of an object
and forty-nine arguments for declaring it impure. When Moses questioned
how long the community would be subject to the obvious uncertainty such
information would cause, God responded, "Follow the majority" (y. Sanh.
4:2; see b. Eruv. 13b, Num. Rab. 2:3, Midr. Ps. 12:4, Pesiq. Rab. 21). This
trope privileges the power of persuasion rather than coercion; while the
rabbis claim authority to interpret scripture, it is not absolute and their
approach to truth is ultimately ambiguous.

As later figures reflected on possible motivations behind this "unortho-
dox" approach to transmitting divine instruction, many of their suggestions
focused on pragmatic considerations. Saadia Gaon (ninth to tenth century
CE) wrote in the introduction to his commentary on Genesis that there
was often only a pretense of disagreement, in order to draw out the train of
thought more completely. In other cases, he determined that each opinion
was right for a different context, or a sage thought he heard a matter in its
entirety but in fact heard only part.[15] Some commentators argued that the
rabbis imagined dialectical engagement as the most rigorous way to distill
the truth, or saw the anthology of traditions as the most effective pedagogy.
In the fourteenth century, for example, Rabbi Abraham Akra wrote in his
Talmudic commentary: "They were all spoken by one shepherd, which
means that most times we gain a good understanding of something by
considering its negation, and we cannot understand the matter on its own
so well as by considering its negation. Therefore the Holy One, blessed be
He, sought to endow us with dissenting opinions, in order that when we
arrive at the true opinion, we will understand it thoroughly" (*Meharerei
Nemarim* 17a).[16]

A strange rabbinic ruling is explained along similar lines: If the Sanhedrin unanimously arrived at a death sentence, they would not carry it
out. Only when doubts force rigorous investigation of all possible considerations, can one arrive at the truth (*Lev Avot* on m. Avot 5:17).

It is also likely that the rabbis considered pluralism as the best strategy
for retaining community cohesion. *Lo titgodedu*: do not form factions, they
warned (b. Yevam. 13b).[17] While they still determined which opinion to
endorse as normative practice, they could present divergent teachings as
authentic embodiments of Torah. Allowing dissent kept all the parties inside the system, domesticating subversive forces to some degree and adding

legitimacy to their authority. As minority populations in the Sassanian and Roman empires, Jews struggled to resist the unceasing imperial and cultural pressures that caused communities to fracture. Perhaps the rabbis' theology of exile, which they attributed in part to baseless hatred among the diverse Jewish groups of the late Second Temple period, also pressed upon them the importance of holding the community together. They were afraid of division, not diversity.

Disagreement is not easy to manage, however, and rabbinic efforts at pluralism did not preclude oppressive wielding of scriptural authority. Although many passages within Oral Torah present an idealized form of respectful controversy, some acknowledge how fraught disputes could be. Ongoing discord between Rabbi Joshua and Rabban Gamaliel II prompted the former's public repudiation and the latter's temporary removal as head of the Sanhedrin (b. Ber. 27b–28a).[18] Rabban Gamaliel II was also responsible for the expulsion of his brother-in-law from the rabbinic community after a halakhic dispute, a move that he defended as necessary to prevent division from multiplying within Israel, but one that reportedly led to great suffering as well as his own death (b. B. Metz. 59b). As material redacted in Babylonia about the early Palestinian sages, the narratives may not be historical, but they represent ongoing anxiety about the possibility of factionalism, with a preference for tolerating diversity despite the challenges.

NATURE OF TRUTH AND HUMAN AUTHORITY

These dilemmas become more complex as we move from the practical value of pluralism to polysemy as an exegetical ideology. As Moshe Halbertal pointedly asked, "How does the canonization of controversies relate to the problem of truth in interpretation, especially when the word of God is concerned?"[19] One way of thinking about this issue is to consider what the rabbis meant when they asserted that divergent ideas are all the word of the living God. Did they mean that God intended multiple senses, either simultaneously or for different circumstances? Or were the rabbis being authorized to distill God's purposes, by which legitimate processes of interpretation could yield equally legitimate alternatives? Or is divine meaning singular, with the rabbis striving toward the single correct answer based on proper procedure? Not surprisingly, each of these possibilities can be found within Jewish tradition.

At times, the rabbis of the classical period explicitly affirmed the multi-faceted nature of scriptural truth—e.g., "Turn it over and turn it over again, for everything is within it" (m. Avot 5:22). This perspective became more pronounced in Jewish mysticism. A thirteenth-century kabbalistic commentary on the Talmud, for example, emphasized that the divine teaching by definition can lack nothing and therefore contains all possibilities of meaning, with every sage grasping a portion.[20] Rationalist legal texts picked up on the theme as well, as in Rabbi Yehiel Epstein's nineteenth-century lyrical introduction to his halakhic code:

> Truly, for one who understands things properly, all the controversies among the Tannaim, Amoraim, the Geonim and the decisors, are the words of the living God, and all are grounded in the law. And furthermore, this is the glory of our pure and holy Torah, all of which is called a melody. And the glory of the melody, the essence of its delight, is that the tones differ from each other. And one who sails the sea of the Talmud will experience the diverse delights of all these distinct voices. (*Arukh haShulkhan*)

In this way, Jewish tradition understood scriptural truth to be multiple and contextual, yielding a dynamic praxis and theology that adapted to changing circumstances.

The second possibility is represented by people like Nachmanides (thirteenth century) and his students. They held that rabbinic sages have the privilege, granted by the scriptural Author, to *constitute* the meaning of divine instruction. Some believed that God would not let them rule contrary to divine intent, but the perspective emphasized procedural authority over the fixity of truth; it left open the reality of diversity, change, and even error.[21] As twentieth-century orthodox halakhist Moshe Feinstein wrote about disagreeing with sages from the classical period, "Truth is as it seems correct to the scholar after he has studied the law properly. . . . This is indeed the true ruling, and he is required to proclaim it, even if in heaven it is really known that the true interpretation is otherwise."[22]

The most famous passage expressing this idea is found in the Babylonian Talmud; it recounts a rabbinic dispute in which Rabbi Eliezer was the lone dissenter in a decision, but various miracles suggested that God agreed with him. Each marvel was contested by the other rabbis as invalid proof for his position, with the final challenge lifted from Deuteronomy: "It is not in heaven" (Deut. 30:12). The sages thus claimed authority to determine scripture's meaning, and God's purported response was to laugh and proclaim with delight, "My children have defeated Me." It is the same passage, however, that records Rabbi Eliezer's expulsion from the rabbinic community; affirming human authority does not ensure a liberating embrace of all voices (b. B. Metz. 59b).[23]

Christine Hayes has argued that rabbinic pluralism is pragmatic, not philosophical; debate was designed to yield God's intended meaning. This brings us to the third perspective, represented by figures like Abraham ibn Daud (twelfth century), in which God's will constitutes the singular truth of scripture. He claimed that certain knowledge eroded over time due to harsh conditions and human failings; halakhic reasoning is an attempt to retrieve and reconstruct God's teaching. While his perspective limited the possibilities of multiple truths, it also acknowledged room for error in the negotiation of scripture's meaning. This line of thinking raised some concerns about rabbinic authority. Maimonides, for example, claimed that actual disagreement attached only to newly derived practices; in general, the process of rabbinic adjudication could be trusted to secure the right answer.[24] At the same time, he opened another door to limit the ultimacy of scriptural truth. Both he and his son were emphatic that revelation did not extend to all areas of knowledge; one need not defer to the rabbis in matters of medicine, science, astronomy, etc. These medieval Jewish Aristotelians affirmed truths derived from human experience and observation; they drew on threads within classic rabbinic thought that made room for other sources of knowledge.[25]

The value of human reason is well-established in the tradition, even though the rabbis knew it would sometimes be in tension with revelation. David Kraemer cited fourteen instances in the Babylonian Talmud in which a rabbinic dispute was explained by determining that one sage relied on scriptural interpretation in his decision, and one relied on reason—both legitimate ways of trying to discern truth. There are also over two hundred instances in which the rabbis suggested that the biblical text "should" be different than it is.[26] Although they generally found ways to reconcile the text with what they thought correct, they repeatedly affirmed the exercise of their God-given intellect, free will, and moral capacity. The sages also knew that proper procedure would not always yield the best answer, even if it was technically correct. In such cases, they privileged overarching values that the law was meant to embody—e.g., justice and fairness, cultivation of compassion, humility, righteousness, and peace—naming this functional emphasis as *lifnim m'shurat hadin*, beyond the letter of the law. Literally translated as "inside the line of law," the phrase implies resolutions that are not *against* the law but focus on higher principles. The rabbis imagined that God, too, sometimes set truth aside for the sake of compassion, and extolled it as a divine virtue.[27]

Ultimately, rabbinic explication of scripture is not primarily about pursuit of "truth." Describing halakhah, the rabbinic praxis developed to flesh out the values of Torah, Hayes explained: "Rabbinic literature reflects a desire to discern what is just, equitable, pious and obedient to God's will in the realm of human behavior and to do so through interpretation and debate, rather than ratiocination from first principles." Philosophy aims to describe "a uniform and eternal truth," while rabbinic Judaism addresses "the shifting conditions of human existence."[28] Reckoning with the shifting conditions of our existence embeds an ultimate contingency in the authority of Written and Oral Torah, moderating the dangers of scripture without succumbing utterly to relativism and post-modern indeterminacy.[29] It stakes out a middle ground.

ACCOUNTING FOR THE HUMAN: EPISTEMOLOGICAL HUMILITY, DOUBT, ACCOMMODATION, AND CHANGE

Jewish tradition frequently acknowledges that which we do not know. The Tannaim spoke of the end of prophecy and *ruach hakodesh* (divine inspiration), as well as elimination of the *urim* and *tumim*—diverse gifts that had enabled ancient Israel to ascertain God's will (m. Sotah 9:12, t. Sotah 13:2). Recognizing that subsequent decisions necessarily relied on the art of interpretation, they cautioned, "The prudent person sees danger and takes precautions" (Prov. 22:3). Almost every independently authored rabbinic text included an apology in the introduction (still common in academia today) for any errors contained within. Although humility did not always prevail, the rabbis valorized it and cited it as the one virtue ascribed to Moses in Torah (Num. 12:3, Deut. 34:10). As one of the preeminent Jewish scholars of the Middle Ages, Moses Maimonides was not particularly humble. But he stressed epistemological humility—the limits of human understanding—in several ways. Ferreting out a difficulty in Genesis 2, he wondered why God would not want human beings to eat from the tree of knowledge of good and evil. Would it not be of benefit, providing the necessary understanding to make moral choices? His interpretation of the narrative held that we had a superior knowledge before eating from this tree—knowledge of truth and falsity. All we have after violating the divine command is relative judgment, uncertainly grounded in personal feelings about right and wrong, contingent upon culture and context (*Guide for the Perplexed* I:2).

Maimonides also stressed epistemological humility in relation to our understanding of God's essence, claiming in *Guide for the Perplexed* (I:56–59) that we can make no true affirmative statement about the nature of the divine. The best we can do is to speak in negative terms—e.g., "God is not lacking in power." In other words, God has power but does not possess it in a way that is comparable to anything else. Along with this "negative theology," he also established an intellectual distinction between faith and certainty. He argued, for instance, that traditional and metaphysical reflection led him to affirm the creation of the universe in time, but neither creation ex nihilo nor the eternality of the universe could be demonstrably proven. His conviction was a matter of faith, not certainty (*Guide for the Perplexed* II:25).[30]

In canonizing controversy, the rabbis also made room for doubt as the counterpart rather than the enemy of faith. Even when they believed fervently in the rightness of their perspective, they could not claim absolute proof. Nachmanides, for instance, dedicated an entire treatise to contest a commentary on Alfasi but wrote in the introduction, "Every student of our Talmud knows that in a controversy between commentators, there are no incontrovertible arguments, and in most instances no absolute refutations" (*Milchamot haShem*). The Maharshal (sixteenth century) believed that no text existed without lacunae, even Torah: "Were all the heavens above scrolls and all the oceans ink, they would not suffice to expound even one passage and all the doubts arising from it."[31] A few medieval voices added more space for doubt by questioning the inerrant transmission of Torah: Abraham ibn Ezra, Judah heHasid, and David Kimhi thought that Ezra, the biblical scribe, had a hand in correcting the text.[32]

Ibn Ezra was also among those who argued that Torah speaks in the language of human beings, communicating in ways that we can understand.

When rabbis of the classical period first invoked this principle (*dibra Torah kileshon benei adam*), they generally meant that one should not overread the text, contrary to interpreters who felt every jot and tittle overflowed with meaning. Yet Ibn Ezra understood it as a hermeneutical principle of accommodation. He assumed that divine revelation was adapted to the capacity of ancient Israel to receive it, vitiating the ultimacy of scripture by opening the doorway to change. God's teaching is adjusted to "the process of intellectual, moral and even political advancement of man."[33]

This idea was already broached in the Tannaitic period, imagining that God—the Teacher of all teachers—operated differently according to context, even changing "appearances" to meet the needs of the moment. God appeared as a warrior when the Israelites were trying to escape Egypt across the sea, but as a kindly elder for the revelation at Sinai (Mek. Yitro 5). An Amoraic midrash on Leviticus suggested that sacrifice was designed as a stopgap measure to wean Israel from idolatry (Lev. Rab. 22:6). Medieval commentators expanded on these themes, pointing out how God judged people's actions according to context: eating meat was not allowed for Adam, for example, but it was for Noah—and then constrained by the conditions of *kashrut* for the people of Israel.[34] Bahya ibn Pakuda (eleventh century) and Maimonides believed that biblical anthropomorphisms were utilized to accommodate the lesser capacity of the masses in terms of abstraction. (Philo had suggested the same thing in the first century CE.) They maintained that various aspects of halakhah, even something as fundamental as the system of reward and punishment, embody pedagogical value rather than ultimate truth.[35] Interpretation of scripture is intended to evolve, potentially liberating many problematic passages and previous exegeses from the dangers of fixity and ultimacy.

There is a classic pericope at the beginning of Genesis Rabbah that illustrates the rabbis' sense of scripture as a dynamic rather than static guide: with artful rhetoric and close reading of Genesis 1:1 (and Prov. 8:30), the rabbis imagined that God created the world with Torah. The idea is presented in a parable, compared to a king who wants to build a palace. He does not construct it out of his own head, but hires an architect who fashions scrolls and wax tablets to work out the plans. Determining the referents for these figures in the parable, all three are associated with Torah: the architect is the primordial Torah as the sum of divine instruction, the scrolls represent the Five Books of Moses, and the wax tablets signify Oral

Torah—the part that is designed to be written, erased, and reinscribed differently to fit each new situation.

Scholars also acknowledged how the meaning of scripture shifts for each person, according to capacity or temperament. *Leḥem Mishneh* (sixteenth century) asserted that souls differ, inclined to strict or lenient readings of the text; thus, it is important that Torah can be expounded in forty-nine different ways to provide the teaching each person requires (comment on m. Avot 5:17). In the early twentieth century, Ahad Ha'am commented in poetic fashion: "The book exists forever, but its content is changed by life and learning. What have men not found in the Holy Scriptures from the time of Philo until the present day? . . . In the Holy Scriptures they all sought only the truth, each his own truth, and they all found what they sought, found it because they were compelled to, for if not, the truth would not be the truth and the Holy Scriptures would not be holy."[36] The tradition knows itself to be provisional because it is the bearer of multiple voices and modifications—a manifestation of historical consciousness.[37] *Mikra'ot Gedolot*, the medieval commentary that set diverse exegetes together in literary "conversation" across the generations, may reflect this kind of historical awareness as well.

Rabbinic literature also recognized the mutability of scripture in affirming the prospect of *ḥidush*, an innovative interpretation. Rashbam claimed that his grandfather Rashi (1040–1105) said he would have loved to write a whole new commentary if he had time, to incorporate all the fresh interpretations that emerge daily. Innovations with implications for observance could be slow in coming, but they were still seen as essential mechanisms for sustaining the relevance of religious instruction. Non-halakhic innovations came from all kinds of sources and were celebrated for their vibrant range and creativity. Writing in Ladino in the eighteenth century, Turkish scholar Rabbi Eliyahu haCohen made it sound like a mitzvah (divine commandment): "One should find new interpretations of the Torah . . . for just as a person is required to procreate his kind, he must procreate in Torah . . . until he innovates great and weighty matters."[38]

Rabbinic appreciation for the paradox of the eternal and eternally changing notion of Torah is perhaps best encapsulated in a Talmudic *aggadah* that imagines Moses sitting in Rabbi Akiba's classroom in the second century CE. He is completely lost and has to sit in the back (the sign of a beginner). When one of the students asks Rabbi Akiba for the source of his knowledge, however, Akiba replies, "It is from Moses on Sinai," and Moses is comforted (b. Menah. 29b). Whether meant as metaphorical transmission or an actual chain of instruction, the passage reckons with how tradition is remolded in each generation. The result may be unrecognizable to its forebears but it stands as an authentic embodiment of Torah teaching. With the meanings of scripture always in flux, we have another tool in the moderation of scriptural ultimacy.

CHAPTER 4

CHRISTIANITY—THE HUMAN EQUATION

... the knollege and practising of the worde of God, which is the light to our paths, the keye to the kingdome of heaven, our comfort in affliction, our shielde and sworde against Satan, the schoole of all wisdome, the glasse wherein we beholde Gods face, the testimonie of his favour, and the only foode and nourishment of our soules. ...

—Translators' preface to the Geneva Bible,
published in 1560, after English Protestants took refuge in
Switzerland during Queen Mary I's persecution of non-Catholics

POLYSEMY AND PLURALISM

The New Testament stands as Christianity's foundational witness to multivocality. Like the Hebrew Bible, its collection of books speaks with various voices, but it is more explicitly a synchronic portrait of diversity in the emerging Church. The eponymous books ascribed to Matthew, Mark, Luke, and John all present themselves as "the gospel according to . . . ," and they contain significant differences that attest to the subjective ways in which individuals understand religious experience and present the "worde of God." The ratification of four canonical gospels "introduces a principle of mutual correction and limitation whereby each Gospel is deprived of pre-eminence or complete validity"—working over against notions of inerrancy and ultimacy.[1]

Multiple passages reference controversy and diversity among the believers; the Jerusalem Council described in Acts 15, for example, authorizes

different ways of participating in the covenant of Jesus for Jews and Gentiles. In Romans 14:1–15:13, Paul acknowledges distinct practice and doctrine within the community and encourages followers not to quarrel over
disputed matters. As portrayed in 1 Corinthians 11:19, he is not happy about
divisions among the followers but surmises that the natural differences
might be necessary to discern the best path; the subsequent chapter discusses different ways in which each person receives the Holy Spirit, comprising interdependent parts of the body of Christ.[2]

Modern New Testament scholars repeatedly point out the texts' substantive diversity of Christologies, theologies, and ideas about the developing Church. Originally composed as autonomous perspectives, they came
into relationship as part of the canon. Regarding the two collections of epistles (Pauline and non-Pauline), Robert Wall maintained that they "form an
effective, self-correcting interplay of theological and ethical concepts," le-
gitimizing ecclesial diversity and modeling how biblical diversity enhances
the life of the church.[3] What holds the New Testament together? John
Reumann shared the humorous but telling response: "Two covers and a lot
of church traditions." Countless volumes have attempted to discern a unifying core, and the numerous suggestions (e.g., grace, justification by faith,
reconciliation, being "in Christ," covenant, love of God, promise, salvation,
shalom) constitute yet another testimony to the multivocality of scripture
and its interpretations—arguing against absolutizing the Word.[4]

The process of forming the Christian canon also traveled a pluralistic
path, albeit a bumpy and contested one. Marcion (85–160 CE) and his
followers opposed the very idea of a dual canon; they did not see the "Old"
and "New" Testaments as a continuous narrative of God's redemptive
plan. There were also disputes about which gospels should be included.
It was Irenaeus (second century) who first suggested that there were four
authentic versions. Congregations tended to have one or two that they
preferred, and selection of the four was likely a compromise.[5] Since the
discovery of ancient books at Nag Hammadi, we have become aware of
additional texts—e.g., the Gospel of Thomas, the Gospel of Philip, the
Gospel of Truth, and the Gospel to the Egyptians, that were excluded
from the canon but remained in circulation in some quarters of the Christian community.[6]

Eusebius's *Ecclesiastical History* 6.26, 7.25 (c. 325) classified the different
standing of various Christian texts in circulation—acknowledged books,

disputed books, and heretical works—but other historians and documents differed on what belonged in each category.[7] Multiple lists continued to circulate and, even after official ecclesial decisions in the latter half of the fourth century, communities did not agree. Trying to enforce uniformity, the powerful archbishop Athanasius of Alexandria sent an order in 367 to purge all apocryphal books with "heretical" tendencies. Nonetheless, prior to the dogmatic definition of the canon approved at the Council of Trent (1564), its proper limits continued to be debated.[8] The declaration at Trent was primarily a response to Protestants questioning the boundaries of scripture, but the reformers' exclusion of apocryphal books and Martin Luther's 1522 edition of the New Testament, in which texts he personally held in low regard (Hebrews, James, Jude, and Revelation) were placed at the end, all grew out of longstanding canonical controversies. To this day, the Protestant, Roman Catholic, Orthodox, and Coptic canons vary from one another.

Origen (184–253 CE) had imagined Christian heresies in a positive light. He used the term with its original Greek denotation, "choice" or perhaps "faction," to defend Christianity against a philosophical critique that viewed lack of agreement as a sign of falsehood. Origen retorted that "heresies of different kinds have never originated from any matter in which the principle involved was not important and beneficial to human life." They were necessary, emerging not from schism and strife, but from the earnest desire of intelligent individuals, "led by certain plausible reasons to discordant views" in their efforts to define Christian teaching (*Against Celsus* 3.12–13). Eventually, however, heresy came to differentiate choices that stood outside orthodox tradition, and Origen himself was accused of heresy for some of his heterodox ideas.

Many scholars ascribe the pressure to standardize faith and practice to Roman imperial culture after Christianity became the official religion of the empire; it pressed administratively for uniformity and order and moved philosophically toward Platonic universalism. Emphasizing the role that the emperor Theodosius I (ruling 379–95) played in settling the great theological debates, Charles Freeman argued that his actions were motivated by politics rather than theology: an exertion of his will to power by co-opting the power of religion.[9]

Dialectical tension between forces of pluralism and uniformity unfolded throughout Christian history, including in the understanding of scripture, where differences in interpretation could have significant implications. Based on the creation of humanity in Genesis 1, Clement of Alexandria (c. 150–215) insisted that men and women share equally in divine perfection and are to receive the same instruction; he listed numerous women (biblical and later) who were worthy of praise for learning, skill, valor, and leadership. Reading Paul's letters (see Rom. 16), he concluded that women played leadership roles in the apostolic age, serving as deacons and traveling alongside their male colleagues to spread the gospel among women (*Paed.* 1.4, 6; *Strom.* 3.6, 4.19). While the majority of Church Fathers adopted a more restrictive policy that did not allow women to preside over sacraments, teach, speak in church, etc.—also grounding their positions in exegesis (1 Cor. 14:34–35, 1 Tim. 2:11–15)—the role of women in the church was in dynamic flux for at least the first five centuries of Christian history and is again contested in the modern age.[10]

At times, this multivocality was valorized. Writing about the command to "increase and multiply" (Gen. 1:28), Augustine (354–430 CE) offered a meditation on exegesis that acknowledged its subjective nature. He understood such open-ended reading strategies to be intended by God: "Consider the verse 'In the Beginning, God made heaven and earth.' Scripture presents this truth to us in one way only, and there is only one way in which the words can be shaped by the tongue. But it may be understood in several different ways without falsification or error, because various interpretations, all of which are true in themselves, may be put upon it. The offspring of men increase and multiply in this way" (*Conf.* 13.24).[11]

The Catholic Church continued to preserve the work of numerous exegetes, including their contradictions and arguments, with new voices adding to the discourse. In the Middle Ages, the standard version of a "study" Bible was the *Glossa Ordinaria*, which set distinct interpretations from different times and places together on a single page and illuminated the polyphonic nature of scriptural verses. It reflected individual perspectives, historical contexts, and shifting emphases over time on how to read scripture.[12] (Similar to the rabbinic *Mikra'ot Gedolot*, these texts were the most frequently copied works for centuries.) Thomas Oden, the general editor of the Ancient Christian Commentary on Scripture series, has attempted to bring back this catena tradition. In his introduction he notes, "One will immediately see upon reading these selections that within the boundaries of orthodoxy . . . there are many views possible about a given text or idea and that these different views may be strongly affected by wide varieties of social environments and contexts."[13]

Such diversity did not exist without problems, however, and disputes about the contents and meaning of scripture could be intense. The Jesus movement polemicized against traditional Jewish interpretation of Hebrew Bible for its refusal to embrace Christological readings. Tertullian (160–220 CE) railed against allegorical readings, which he believed led away from the truth (*On Modesty* 9.2.3). He asserted that the Church had established the authoritative interpretation and rejected "heretical" groups laying claim to scripture at all: "Thus, not being Christians, they have acquired no right to the Christian Scriptures; and it may be very fairly said to them, 'Who are you? When and whence did you come? As you are none of mine, what have you to do with that which is mine? Indeed, Marcion, by what right do you hew my wood? By whose permission, Valentinus, are you diverting streams of my fountain? By what power Apelles, are you removing my landmarks? This is my property'" (*Prescription against Heretics* 37).[14]

What appeared to be small interpretive arguments could instigate or undergird lasting breaches. The statement attributed to Jesus, "This is my body, this is my blood" (Matt. 26.26), for instance, prompted a major disagreement between Martin Luther and Ulrich Zwingli about the nature of the Eucharist. It was perhaps the first famous dispute about what the word *is* means. Luther believed that Jesus was actually present in the bread and wine, but Zwingli maintained that the passage spoke in metaphor, that the bread and wine *signify* the presence of Christ in the world. Each marshalled additional verses to support his perspective, and they attempted mediation at Marburg—but ultimately it precipitated the establishment of separate Protestant confessions. Thus, while the diversity of interpretations could cultivate possibilities of pluralism and growth, it also prompted division. Christians regularly declared each other outside the boundaries of faith. As John Dryden quipped in his 1687 poem "The Hind and the Panther" (II:150–155),

> For did not Arius first, Socinus now
> The Son's eternal god-head disavow?
> And did not these by Gospel Texts alone
> Condemn our doctrine, and maintain their own?
> Have not all hereticks the same pretence,
> To plead the Scriptures in their own defence?

Contesting the *idea* of scripture was also fraught. The creation of Christian orthodoxy was accompanied by an anachronistic mythology that godless error—represented by anything that diverges from established dogma or praxis—entered Christianity after the apostles died. Tertullian, for instance, maintained that truth always precedes counterfeit, and the Church is charged with reestablishing the former. In the modern period as well, many Christians erroneously believe that their understanding of doctrine obtained from the beginning, erasing the pluralism of early Christianity that in fact came first and was deeply embedded in the development of Christian scripture, exegesis, theology, and institutions.[15] Esteemed scholars within the Catholic and Protestant worlds—e.g., Alfred Loisy (1857–1940) and Charles Augustus Briggs (1841–1913), were excommunicated and put on trial for heresy, respectively, for supporting historical-critical study of the Bible. Their method was believed to threaten orthodox conceptions of its authority and infallibility.

Ignoring the pervasive interpretive pluralism that characterized the history of Christianity, some fundamentalist readers presume to reason their way to scripture's single, precise meaning—mistakenly assuming that they can somehow stand outside history. Christian Smith remarked, "Without realizing it, evangelicals embraced a view of scripture that was more driven by Cartesian and generally modern preoccupations with epistemic certainty than by Scripture itself and a long Christian tradition of scriptural interpretation."[16] This type of biblicism also ignores diversity within the fundamentalist community, where many exegetes recognize that belief in a singularly perfect text does not require belief in singular perfect understanding. In a collection of essays by evangelical scholars with diverse notions about gender and sexuality in Christianity, Gordon Fee commented, "God did not choose to give us a series of timeless, non-culture-bound theological propositions to be believed and imperatives to be obeyed. Rather, he chose to speak his eternal word *this* way, in historically particular circumstances and in every kind of literary genre. By the very way God gave us this Word, he locked in the ambiguity."[17]

Polysemy and pluralism are thus persistent realities of Christian experience with scripture, even though the present review also reveals abiding tensions. Multivocality was not thematized the way it was in Jewish exegesis but, for many Christian readers in the current era, exegetical diversity takes on comparable value. Ellen Davis hailed the Bible's "inexhaustible complexity." Embracing the rabbinic instruction to turn scripture over and over, she reflected, "It is a verb one might use of turning a crystal over and over to examine its different facets, or of turning compost until it is ready for the soil. . . . Reading Scripture well is like being a master gardener, and the Bible is like soil; the thoughts of those who study it deeply grow in that medium."[18]

NATURE OF TRUTH AND HUMAN AUTHORITY

A traditional critique of postmodern reading is that it forfeits the notion of truth. As Lieven Boeve described it, "Truth is fragmented, the radical particularity and contingency of human cultures and traditions is unmasked."[19] If no interpretation can lay exclusive claim to truth, some adherents believe the result is unacceptable relativism—trapped in irreducible plurality and subjectivism. Long before postmodernity arrived on the scene, however, Christians grappled with the nature of truth. The issue is central to self-critical engagement with scripture and wards against using the sacred text as a weapon.

There have always been ontological questions about truth (what is it?) and epistemological ones (how do we know it?). In the modern age, truth is perceived exclusively as something that corresponds to external reality. Medieval Christian scholars like Anselm of Canterbury (1033–1109), however, also spoke of a thing being true when it conformed to divine intent for its creation—a teleological theory of truth that he believed would improve the study of scripture. The result could be similar to the rabbis' idea of "beyond the letter of the law" and later readers' novel interpretations, designed to privilege what they understood to be God's overarching purposes.[20] The abolitionists who invoked God's commitment to liberation and love of neighbor in order to argue against scriptural sanction of slavery, for example, saw biblical truth in this way. Addressing how we might come to know truth, Augustine argued that everything is known merely as God makes it manifest to us (*De magistro* 12.40, *Conf.* 12.25); only divine knowledge can be absolute. Aquinas sought to approach truth through dialectical argument, explicitly drawing out diverse perspectives.[21]

Spinoza's work marks the move toward modern biblical interpretation. He repudiated medieval methods that served primarily to align scripture with ecclesial dogma, claiming in his preface to *A Theologico-Political Treatise* that he would "examine the Bible afresh in a careful, impartial, and unfettered spirit." His reasoning evoked a historical positivism that asserts its own absolute authority, but also moved scripture out of the business of ultimate truth. "Henceforth the task would be less a matter of mining the texts for timeless theological doctrines (the quest for what is true) and more a matter of determining historically contextualized meanings (the quest for what was meant)."[22] More recently, Flemish philosopher Herman De Dijn asserted that religion is not really about truth in any event. Truth is a cognitive-scientific quest. Religion is about meaning, about being immersed in a particular and contingent tradition, belonging within a particular community. "Meaning is not about universal and objectifiable truth, but about 'truth-to-live-by,' unassailable and unmasterable."[23]

Other early modern voices did not abandon religious truth claims but reintroduced contingency in other ways. Existentialists and Romanticists emphasized subjectivity in our perception of truth, arguing that although God's truth may be absolute, our beliefs and knowledge cannot be. Kierkegaard (1813–1855), for example, defined truth as "objective uncertainty, held fast in an appropriation process of the most passionate inwardness," and declared it "the highest truth available for an existing person." He also focused on truth as that which is most relevant to our existence. Even if it were possible to establish the historical veracity and authentic inspiration of Holy Scriptures, without "a single little dialectical doubt," it would bring one no closer to faith—a posture that can only be approached subjectively.[24]

One also finds scattered through the history of Christian thought sources of authority other than scripture that shape the truths-to-live-by. For Catholicism, the most significant is "tradition." In the fourteenth and fifteenth centuries, tradition became understood as a distinct source of revelation, akin to Oral Torah. Where scripture was silent, God had providentially arranged for a stream of unwritten tradition going back to the apostles.[25] Although the Reformation challenged papal authority and the centrality of tradition, hoping to restore scripture to its throne, Protestant denominations also affirmed multiple ways of discerning God's truths. The Wesleyan quadrilateral, for example, identifies scripture, tradition, reason, and experience as legitimate ways of knowing.

The role of reason and experience is often framed in the language of conscience and is found in every age. Cyprian of Carthage (third century) asserted the right of an individual bishop, in conscience before God, to make up his own mind regarding the proper way to perform baptism. Luther was told to recant at the Diet of Worms in 1521, but responded, "Unless I be convinced by evidence of Scripture or by plain reason—for I do not accept the authority of the Pope or the councils alone, since it is demonstrated that they have often erred and contradicted themselves—I am bound by the Scriptures I have cited, and my conscience is captive to the Word of God."[26] Documents from the Second Vatican Council (1962–1965) affirm that in religious matters, no one should be forced to act contrary to their conscience.

Human reason and experience explicitly shape the meaning of the Bible. In the Middle Ages, *Sacra Pagina* utilized grammar, rhetoric, philosophy, and other human sciences to draw out and test the theological "truths" of sacred text. Catholic magisterium relied on the authority of the pope, the collective voice of the bishops, *consensus theologorum* (agreement of trained theologians and exegetes), and *consensus fidelium* (common belief of ordinary Christians) to constitute the meaning of the text. None were absolutely authoritative by themselves, and these distinct bodies could (and did) disagree.[27] Claims of infallibility were rare. The Council of Trent and Vatican I, the two notable exceptions, were defensive responses to the Reformation and modernity, respectively, trying to preserve the power of the Church in the world. Outside of these contexts, there was room for individual Catholic scholars to challenge Church teaching on scripture; some who did still gained the status of "Doctor of the Church."

Long before the rise of historical criticism, ancient interpreters acknowledged, "Mystery, then, was characteristic of sacred texts. God is the speaker, but humans are the writers, and multiplicity of meaning (plain and obscure) is to be expected in the discursive space between what the words humanly say and what they divinely teach."[28] Eventually this space came to accommodate critical biblical scholarship; documents such as *Divino afflanta Spiritu* (1943) allowed it, and *Dei Verbum* (1965) actively promoted it so that "the judgment of the Church may mature."

ACCOUNTING FOR THE HUMAN: EPISTEMOLOGICAL HUMILITY, DOUBT, ACCOMMODATION, AND CHANGE

While according human reason and experience a voice, Christian theology and exegesis also recognized the fallible nature of human beings. Charles Schultz offered a playful expression in a Peanuts cartoon: Charlie Brown says to Snoopy, "I hear you're writing a book on theology. I hope you have a good title." Snoopy closes his eyes and settles upon what he considers the perfect title. He types out: "Has It Ever Occurred to You That You Might Be Wrong?"

Many early thinkers like Clement, Gregory of Nyssa, John Chrysostom, Basil the Great, and John of Damascus, spoke of all that we cannot understand about God and God's purposes. It is not merely a matter of intellectual humility, but an admission that much of what we might seek to understand about the divine is simply unknowable. According to Cyril of Jerusalem (fourth century), "[W]e explain not what God is but candidly confess that we have not exact knowledge concerning Him. For in what concerns God, to confess our ignorance is the best knowledge" (*Catechetical Homilies* 6.2).[29] The most influential early expression of this idea came from Pseudo-Dionysius (sixth century), who felt even describing God through negation was too presumptuous; his apophatic theology was popular among Christian mystics.[30] It was also seen as a tool for preserving church unity within diversity. Nicholas of Cusa (fifteenth century) borrowed the term "learned ignorance" from Augustine; recognizing the limitations of human understanding made it possible to accept multiple rites and schools of Christian thought.[31]

How does this relate to the dangers of scripture? In an edited volume on learned ignorance in the Abrahamic traditions, James Heft described the resulting space for doubt as an instrument of pluralism: "An emphasis on learned ignorance, or the realization among learned people that their grasp of reality is inescapably limited, prevents all forms of fundamentalism, which assumes that believers are in perfect possession of ultimate reality. Once that illusion is fixed in believers' minds, all that remains is to force their belief on others. But Judaism, Christianity, and Islam all affirm that God alone is absolute and that all affirmations about God and God's revelation are inescapably limited."[32] Doubt also drives our continuing passion to learn. Peter Abelard, a brilliant scholastic theologian (1079–1142), wrote, "By doubting we come to inquiry, and by inquiry we perceive the truth."[33]

Jerome and Origen admitted there could be minor errors within scripture, although the idea was not broadly embraced.[34] More commonly accepted was the limitation of human language to communicate divine intent. It was enough of a truism that James Madison invoked it to argue by analogy that the laws of the new republic could not be established without ongoing debate: "When the Almighty himself condescends to address mankind in their own language, his meaning, luminous as it must be, is rendered dim and doubtful by the cloudy medium through which it is communicated."[35]

The notion of accommodation is one of the most common strategies used to dilute scriptural absolutism in the history of Christian thought. During the patristic period, it appeared in both hurtful and helpful forms. It served as a polemical device against Jewish practice, arguing as did Paul that "the law" was a pedagogue to lead people to Christ (Gal. 3:24); appropriate to the condition of the people at the time, it lured them away from idolatry and drew them from the temporal toward the eternal. It had been supplanted, however, by the coming of Jesus and justification through faith. The idea of divine commitment to speak to the human heart, adapting as necessary to time, place, and individual character, also made room for ongoing change. Origen, for instance, explained that the doctrine of salvation was presented on several levels—body, soul, and spirit—to reach individuals with different capacities for faith and reason. It allowed a spiritually gifted person to achieve the highest level of truth while protecting the masses. He also believed that the new covenant was a temporary accommodation, shifting over time with the community's spiritual capacity: Jesus's incarnation served as a revelation of the divine to guide the faithful from flesh to spirit, but the New Testament would be superseded when the people grew ready for a full realization of heavenly truth.[36] Scriptural truth is fluid if God always meets human beings where they are.

John Chrysostom (d. 407), sometimes called the doctor of condescension (*synkatabasis*) for his frequent use of accommodation, employed it in elaborating on ideas of virginity, incarnation, and other central doctrines of Christianity.[37] The Latin Fathers embraced it too, especially after the Visigoth invasion in 410 CE. According to Stephen Benin, "The idea of change and permanence, which emerges as part of the divine plan of revelation, took on enhanced meaning in a world where Rome, the very symbol and guarantor of stability, authority, and permanence, could be sacked and put to the torch."[38]

Scriptura humane loquitur, Aquinas and others taught, mirroring the Jewish maxim that Torah speaks in the language of human beings. It can highlight straightforward rather than encoded teaching, or a willingness to use imagery, expressions, and ideas that the human mind can understand even though they are imprecise. William of Auvergne (c. 1180–1249) described scripture as a divine textbook for all levels of students, with deliberate multiplicity. He used a range of metaphors: a mine with distinct veins of precious metals, a garden of delights, a wine cellar, a medicine chest, a table set with a rich assortment of different dishes where each guest finds food that appeals most.[39] Anselm of Havelberg (1100–1158) focused on change over time, insisting that "this variety is explained not on account of the mutability of an immutable God who is 'always the same and whose years shall have no end' (Ps 101:28), but on account of human infirmity, which is mutable and on account of temporal changes from age to age" (*Dialogues* 1.13.117).

These complex, dynamic conceptions of faith and scripture all mitigate against the ultimacy of the text and abuse of biblical authority. It is not simply the idea that God's teaching evolves, but a consciousness that religious truths are not eternal, that everything we might consider absolute is only provisional. Aquinas died having been rejected in ecclesial and scholastic circles; his teachings were declared unacceptable by the Franciscans. A short time later, however, he was canonized and declared a Doctor of the Church. When *Divino afflante Spiritu* (1943) reversed official Catholic attitude toward critical biblical scholarship, "the anathema and unacceptable of one age became the *doctrina communis* of another."[40] There is an old joke that relates the sure signs of a new Church teaching: First there are increasingly severe warnings against a particular idea or practice, culminating with a truly exceptional condemnation. A short while later, an authoritative statement that endorses the previously reviled opinion is promulgated, beginning with the words, "As the Church has always taught. . . ."[41]

CHAPTER 5

ISLAM—THE ROLE
OF DOUBT IN FAITH

*We have sent down the Book to you making all things clear
and as guidance and mercy and good news for the Muslims.*

—Qur'an 16:89

POLYSEMY AND PLURALISM

Considerations of multiplicity begin with the Qur'anic text itself, prompted by critical awareness that there were differences among the early written copies. According to a hadith, Muhammad asked the angel Jibreel to teach him different variants (*ahraf*, sing. *harf*) of the Qur'an until he had mastered seven (*Sahih al Bukhari* 3047). Muslim tradition views this as a divinely intended multiplicity, in which Allah conformed the transmission to fit the needs of each community. Understood to confirm the miraculous nature of the Qur'an because the fundamental meaning did not change, it allowed the Book to be revealed through "seven gates."[1]

Presented in the multifaith context of Arabia with some knowledge of Judaism and Christianity as scriptural traditions, Qur'an implies that all revelation is tailored to particular peoples: "And we have sent down the Book to you with truth, confirming and conserving the previous Books. So judge between them by what Allah has sent down and do not follow their whims and desires deviating from the Truth that has come to you. We have appointed a law and a practice for every one of you. Had Allah willed, He would have made you a single community, but He wanted to test you regarding what has come to you. So compete with each other in doing good" (5:48).

Qur'an repeatedly affirms the validity of the revelations received by Moses, the Hebrew prophets, and Jesus (e.g., 2:136, 3:84, 29:46), and various Muslim voices have expanded on this conviction in their theologies of religions. Each community was elected in its time to accept, embody, and transmit divine instruction: "Every people has a guide" (13:7). There is even a notion that the obscure Qur'anic references to "Mother of the Book" and "Preserved Tablet" refer to the eternal teaching as lodged in heaven, from which the diverse scriptures were drawn.[2] Acknowledging multiple revelations that overlap but are not identical, Qur'an appears to qualify the singular authority of any static conception of scripture.

There are also countervailing expressions, however. It became common to read passages that accused Jewish and Christian leaders of corrupting their scriptures as justification for Qur'anic supersession, claiming it alone has a pure transmission of divine instruction. Some Muslims interpret the teaching in 5:3, "This day I have perfected for you your religion, and completed My Blessing upon you, and have approved for you as religion, Submission (*islam*)" (*SQ*), to mean that Allah previously adjusted the teachings to fit particular historical contexts, but Qur'an is eternal and universal.[3]

Nevertheless, pluralistic possibilities endured. Reza Shah-Kazemi identified four principles associated with sura (chapter) 5: Qur'an is the protector of previous revelations; the plurality of revelations is divinely willed; it should stimulate healthy competition in ethical striving rather than domination; and different dogmas are inevitable, to be tolerated in the human sphere and resolved by Allah in the hereafter.[4] Islamic tradition has waxed and waned in its capacity for interreligious pluralism (to be discussed in part III), but the last of these principles shaped *intra*religious issues as well. *Irja* (deferment) emerged as a significant teaching in the eighth century, in response to a number of schisms that splintered the community, like the Sunni–Shi'a conflict and the Khawarij who rebelled against Ali. Seeking to preserve the unity of the people, it taught that judgment belongs to God and opposed accusing each other of unbelief based on disputes about theology or praxis.[5] The Murjite sect who emphasized this principle of deferment was, ironically, eventually declared heretical. Nonetheless, *irja* left its mark in more liberal schools of Islamic thought and stimulated tolerance for interpretive disagreements.

Many aspects of interpretive diversity in Islam are familiar from the review of Judaism and Christianity. Numerous hadiths speak of distinct layers of meaning in each verse, with Qur'anic notions of exoteric and esoteric exegesis that resemble the traditions of Judaism's PaRDeS and Christianity's Quadriga.[6] Perceiving the text as fathomless admits that no one has the last word. In addition, traditional commentators were forthright about disagreement in interpretation amongst themselves. One hadith asserts, "The differences of opinion among the learned within my community are a sign of Allah's grace."[7] There is a sub-genre of commentary, *tafsir al-muqarin*, which focuses specifically on comparative exegesis. It presents the range of meanings distilled from a verse, often drawn from different schools of law, and acknowledges the diverse theology and praxis that result. Even commentaries without this explicit purpose frequently cite opposing opinions, maintaining confidence in their own position but treating the others with respect; it is considered an important characteristic of Islamic intellectual tradition.[8]

While passionate disagreement sometimes meant that such courtesy was observed in the breach, a mystical approach typified by Ibn Arabi (1165–1240) imagined that they were all correct: "Every sense (*wajh*) which is supported by any verse in God's Speech (*kalam*)—whether it is the Qur'an, the Torah, the Psalms, the Gospel, or the Scripture—in the view of anyone who knows that language is intended by God in the case of that interpreter. For His knowledge encompasses all senses. . . . Hence no man of knowledge can declare wrong an interpretation which is supported by the word."[9]

The Qur'an itself states that clear judgments comprise the core of the Book, but there are passages that are open to interpretation (3:7). Additional variables—such as whether an *aya* is to be understood literally or metaphorically, applied generally or read very narrowly, seen as teaching explicitly or implicitly, in qualified fashion or unconditionally—all multiply the possibilities of meaning.[10] When are women included if they are not specifically mentioned? Is the condemnation of drinking alcohol (59:7) a censure or a prohibition, contextually limited or broadly applied? Are the descriptions of paradise to be understood literally or as metaphors for intellectual and ethereal delights? Qur'anic hermeneutics established rules for interpretation, but still exegetes did not always agree.

Early development of the Islamic sciences further compounded multivocality by identifying diverse approaches to understanding divine instruction. Both Sunni and Shi'a tradition maintained that Qur'an and sunna are the two fundamental sources of legislation. Other methods were confirmed and contested to varying degrees, including consensus (*ijma*), juristic preference (*istihsan*), public interest (*masalih mursalah*), precedent/status quo (*istishab*), and independent reasoning (*ijtihad*), which is generally thought to include analogy (*qiyas*) and personal opinion (*ra'y*).[11] Sufism added inspiration from God to the list, often privileging it over historical tradition. In the words of Bayazid Bistami (804–874), "You take your knowledge dead from the dead, but I take my knowledge from the Living One who does not die."[12]

The geographic spread of the rapidly expanding empire, absorbing a broad range of unique cultures, also catalyzed diversity. Custom varied according to place, with veneration of saints in Morocco, pilgrimage to local sacred stones as a substitute for the hajj in Southeast Asia, and other heterodox practices.[13] The remarkable variety of Muslim life and thought prompted eighteenth-century Indian theologian Shah Wali Allah to compose *An Evenhanded Elucidation of the Causes of Disagreement*, "an intellectual history that explained how the single message delivered by the Prophet Muhammad in Arabia had resulted in the stunning plurality and dissonance of the Muslim intellectual landscape."[14] Amidst this diverse, transnational *ummah*, scripture was clearly used to persuade, coerce, and control—but there remained a developing pluralism. Between the first and fourth Islamic centuries, nineteen schools of legal opinion emerged. Even narrowing our focus to the four schools that eventually comprised Sunni orthodoxy, Islam's unique approach to multiplicity formalized legal pluralism: all judgments made by qualified jurists and adopted by any of the legal schools were regarded as equally correct. When the Abbasid caliph proposed making Imam Malik's code the single basis for law throughout the empire, the scholar refused, explaining that each region had forged its own path.[15]

Nevertheless, the ultimacy of scripture and shariah could not be compromised. Jonathan Brown described the way Islamic tradition navigated this tension:

> The undeniable diversity of the schools of law presented a potential challenge to the ulama [Muslim scholarly guild], who all believed that the Shariah was the unified law of God. They explained this inconsistency by upholding the unity of the Shariah as the idea of God's law, while acknowledging that humans will necessarily come to different understandings of

fiqh, or the actual law as derived and applied in this world. Although scholars from different *madhhabs* [legal schools] would argue and write spirited
polemics against one another, they recognized each other's legitimacy.[16]

While fiqh translated the claims of scripture to regulate daily life for
Muslims and those living in the empire, legal pluralism provided a measure
of agency. In areas where there were multiple schools, a person could declare
affiliation with a specific madhhab to secure a desired ruling. The differences could be significant. In the case of women, Hanafi courts empowered
women to testify in almost all legal matters. Muhammad ibn Tumart (c.
1080–1130), the Mehdi of Muslim Spain, was committed to gender equality
in family law and maintained that those who disagreed had misinterpreted
the Qur'an.[17] Some Hanbali and Shafi'i jurists argued there was precedent
for female prayer leadership and preaching. According to Ibn Arabi, there
was no scriptural restriction on women leading prayer, and those who ruled
otherwise need not be heeded. There have always been such countervoices
within Islamic tradition resisting the patriarchal consensus that gradually
restricted women's rights; they illuminate the importance of multivocality
in understanding scripture.[18]

The pluralist approach was frequently embraced as a pragmatic appeal
for peaceful coexistence, but sometimes multiple interpretations were affirmed in recognition of the human potential for error. Hanafi scholar Abu
Hafs Nasafi (twelfth century) grudgingly admitted, "Our school is correct
with the possibility of error, and another school is in error with the possibility of being correct."[19] Giants of the tradition promoted a hermeneutic of
grace; al-Ghazali, for instance, taught that one should have a good opinion
of all people and seek in any scholar's instruction a positive interpretation.[20]
The range of opinion could also be celebrated as a sign of the vibrancy,
creativity, and intellectual rigor of Islam.

Yet there were also efforts to contain the diversity as Sunni and Shi'a
orthodoxies took hold. Around the eleventh century, religious leaders became far more concerned about *bid'a* (heretical innovation in religion); they
promulgated official understanding of sacred texts and marginalized dissent.[21] This constriction of tradition included coercive measures enacted by
both the ulama and the state. Scriptural authority was linked to imperial
authority in the command to fashion a just society, making it difficult to
tease apart the dangers of religious and political forces.[22]

Recent history has complicated the dialectic between pluralism and orthodoxy. Secularism heightened the tensions between those who had confidence in human reason and those who insisted that only revealed knowledge is secure. Modernism's historical positivism empowered those who claimed unique possession of scriptural truth and sought to enshrine their perspective in social practices; they suppressed Islam's long tradition of multiple commentaries and legal debate.[23] In the 1990s, Egyptian scholar Nasr Abu Zayd complained about ideologues who monopolized "the right to understand, comment, do exegesis and interpretation, as if they alone could transmit from God"—a critique that contributed to his being declared an apostate.[24] Jonathan Brown has argued that scripture became more fragile in the modern period, threatened by the rise of secular reason and science as ultimate arbiters of truth: "At these moments of epistemological rupture, approaches to scripture that had never previously been controversial in and of themselves can overstep the new lines demarcating treason to the rump canonical community." Comparing it to the Council of Trent in 1546 that anathematized longstanding questions about biblical unity after the rise of Protestantism, he identified a similar narrowing in Islam's understanding of sacred text.[25]

We should not overread these trends to project a unidirectional hardening of tradition, since historical circumstances nurtured diverse movements. Yet it is important to recognize the outsized influence that colonialism had on the suppression of pluralism—even if some of the consequences were unforeseen. One example was fostering the rise of Wahhabi Islam. Ibn Abd al-Wahhab challenged the Ottoman Empire's claim to represent Sunni tradition and argued that their policy of religious tolerance allowed heresy to flourish; the zeal of his followers was harnessed by Ibn Saud to legitimate territorial expansion in the Arabian Peninsula. Ottoman forces were able to keep the rebellion contained until the demise of the empire after World War I. Backed by the British, Ibn Saud established Saudi Arabia under the banner of restrictive Wahhabi Islam, with spreading global influence fueled by petro-dollars. Contemporary fundamentalists are not the first to wield scriptural authority in oppressive fashion, but traditional institutions that historically limited their influence no longer have the power they once did.[26]

Many contemporary Muslim reformers also argue that the history of colonialism makes it more difficult to reclaim the pluralist tradition of Islam's past. It has become tainted with notions of Western influence even though consideration of textual ambiguity, multivocality, and the politics of reading are all native to Islamic thought. Nonetheless, these scholars have chosen to engage tradition in its fullest sense rather than as a synonym for orthodoxy. They embrace what Mohamed Arkoun calls "exhaustive tradition"—the full collection of diverse customs, schools of law, institutions, exegeses, and theologies that are part of their religious inheritance.[27]

NATURE OF TRUTH AND HUMAN AUTHORITY

Part of that inheritance is the storehouse of medieval Islamic philosophy, which helped to preserve the wisdom of the Greeks and made room for non-revelatory knowledge. Although the Mutazilites and *falsafa* seemed prepared to subject theological doctrine to the test of reason, the distinction between religious and philosophical truth was generally closely guarded. When Ibn al-Haytham (Alhazen, 965–1040) wrote that "truths are immersed in uncertainties," he was speaking about philosophical and scientific truths derived in the human sphere: "The seeker after the truth is not one who studies the writings of the ancients and, following his natural disposition, puts his trust in them, but rather the one who suspects his faith in them and questions what he gathers from them, the one who submits to argument and demonstration."[28] Conversely, that which was established under scriptural teaching was divine in origin, perfect and immutable— separate from what reason was permitted to debate and decide. Although Qur'an insists that humanity listen, be aware, reflect, penetrate, understand, and meditate to discern the meaning of Allah's teachings, the theology of salvation posited that the divine intellect guaranteed the outcome, making scriptural truth absolute.[29]

Yet Sufi philosophy resisted such certainty; adherents believed that human beings were generally witness to the outwardness of things, perceiving truths that were in constant motion and confusion. Although they accepted non-Sufi ways of cognition as true within the limits of the intellect, they sought out the essential truth with inner sight and heart, to see things *in God.* This perspective made law, as an intellectual structure, penultimate to the individual's experience of the divine.[30] As a result, Sufi piety was more invested in the personal model of the sheikh, and its constructions of scriptural authority tended to be less rigid.[31]

The human role in ascertaining truth spurred an animated discourse. Islam's concept of *fitra* asserts that Allah endowed humanity with innate

capacities for reason and moral cognition. If this ethical voice is independent of scripture, it can serve as a check on presumptions of ultimacy,
but the nature of fitra was contested. Although most Sunni thinkers, influenced by Asharite theology, denied that human reason could discern
right or wrong outside of God's revelation, Mutazilite and Shi'a theologians affirmed that it could: moral agency is a gift and burden that God
bestows in fulfillment of divine justice. Both perspectives are compatible
with what Abdulaziz Sachedina called "the complex portrait of humanity
presented by the Qur'an"—God controls all of creation at the same time
that human beings are endowed with the capacity to know the truth and
choose the good.[32]

Certain principles of Islamic law carved out space for human authority.
One was the notion that the formal obligations commanded in sacred texts
are few, designed to give adherents the freedom to exercise their autonomous and communal judgments in many matters, especially those that do
not involve one's obligations to God. Consequently, areas governed by the
certainty of divine truth were limited. A second principle is the "ease of
obligations," making exceptions to rules when they were too onerous or
when they collided with other values. Human reason was thus required to
determine whether circumstances made something lawful that normally
would not be (e.g., eating during Ramadan because of illness), or set aside
a command (e.g., declining to "enjoin right and forbid wrong" in order to
preserve peace).[33] These precepts empowered adherents to define the foundational values of scripture.

Another tool of human judgment that could balance the authority of
scripture was the exercise of independent reasoning (ijtihad). Malik's *Mu-
watta* (eighth century CE), typical of early Islamic legal discourse, clearly
employed it—along with a mix of Qur'anic exegesis, hadiths, rulings of the
Companions, and practice of the Medina ulama.[34] After the four Sunni
schools were effectively canonized, however, many authorities set ijtihad
out of bounds as no longer necessary and too likely to distort the revelation
over time. Received tradition prevailed, and reasoning was formally limited
to efforts at reconciliation, to discover and explicate the rationality of the
tradition. Yet Muhammad Iqbal (1877–1938) claimed that "the closing of the
door of *ijtihad* is pure fiction suggested partly by the crystallization of legal
thought in Islam, and partly by that intellectual laziness which, especially
in the period of spiritual decay, turns great thinkers into idols." He detailed

ways in which independent reasoning continued to play a role in exegesis and law. He also cited a fourteenth-century scholar who challenged the premise that early teachers had a purer perspective; on the contrary, cumulative tradition with its careful compilations of commentary and instruction provided later scholars with superior resources for self-critical faith.[35]

ACCOUNTING FOR THE HUMAN: EPISTEMOLOGICAL HUMILITY, DOUBT, ACCOMMODATION, AND CHANGE

The human role in shaping the authoritative texts of the hadith literature is broadly acknowledged. Recognizing how political conflicts, sectarian bias, and even the sincere desire to guide the people led to the fabrication of hadiths, medieval scholars began a premodern exercise in textual criticism. While some anthologies sought to collect as many sayings as possible, those that became more authoritative sought out reliable chains of transmission and widely repeated teachings consistent with the overall prophetic message; they flagged sayings that were considered suspect. Some hadiths that fell into the latter category were still transmitted, however, and cited when nothing else spoke to the issue at hand. The evident human role and the dubious authenticity of some sources, along with the diversity of exegetical and legal opinion, helped make room for doubt in Islamic tradition.[36]

Intisar Rabb wrote about its acknowledged place in religious law, explaining that "Muslim jurists collectively *canonized*, *textualized*, and *generalized* an Islamic doctrine of doubt rooted in early judicial practice." There is foundational doubt, given what she calls "the indeterminate nature of the sources"—the fact that there are numerous situations Qur'an does not address. There is substantive, procedural, and interpretive doubt, fed by textual ambiguity and legal pluralism. "Muslims across time have conceived of God as the sole Legislator, and of implementing His law (as expounded by the Prophet) as their sacred duty. In other words, Islam was a tradition that promoted a core idea of *divine legislative supremacy*. Yet the nuance with which medieval Muslim jurists approached that ideal is shrouded in a history not of certainty, but of doubt."[37]

Countervoices exist, such as the modern Wahhabi sect that effaces doubt by imagining that pristine Islam can be recreated through strict literal interpretation of Qur'an and precedent of the Prophet, unsullied by later tradition.[38] But classical Islamic jurisprudence grappled with doubt in a straightforward way in its application of scripture, acknowledging that the system is mostly built on probability or presumption rather than certainty, a key distinction in Islamic thought.[39]

Within theology, the recognition of epistemological humility could similarly "qualify" the imposition of scripture. As in Judaism and Christianity, Muslim belief embraced God as the Ultimate Absolute, beyond full comprehension by human beings.[40] Mutazilite, Shi'a, and Sufi Islam emphasized that much of what we affirm about God can be approximated only in the negative—a premise they saw poetically supported by the *shahada*, which begins with a negative/positive assertion: "There is no God but Allah. . . ." Neither legal doubt nor *via negativa* precluded fervent argument or conflict among those who disagreed, but they created a foundation for dealing in convictions more than absolute truths.

The strongest premodern foundation in Islam for deflecting the dangers of scriptural ultimacy is a tradition of contextualism. It takes several forms, some of which can present their own problems, but together they fashioned an interpretive process by which Muslims adapted their understanding of sacred texts and resulting praxis to changing circumstances. One is a principle of gradualism. There are three different instructions related to drinking alcohol, for example: a warning that it is sinful (albeit with some benefits, 2:219), a limitation (not to pray while drunk, 4:43), and an outright prohibition (5:90). Rather than view these contradictory verses as an error, they are seen as a mercy, gradually weaning the people from drinking wine.[41]

There is an account that Omar (also known as Umar II), the Ummayad caliph from 717–720 CE, used this example to dampen his son's zeal to impose immediately all the strictures of shariah "for the sake of the truth." Omar reportedly replied, "Do not hasten my son; God dispraised wine twice in the Qur'an before He forbade it in the third time. I fear to enforce truth on the people once and for all lest they refuse it, and a tumult would result."[42] Evoking the notion of accommodation, early works frequently cited the maxim, "We have been commanded to speak to people according to their minds' abilities."[43]

Tradition holds that the Qur'an was revealed to Muhammad over twenty-three years, forming the foundation of a contextual approach. So a second aspect of scriptural fluidity is the concept of *naskh*, by which a verse may be abrogated by one revealed later. There are other ways to reconcile apparent contradiction, however, so religious scholars have not always agreed about which verses have been abrogated and what the criteria should be.[44] Some arguments have extremely high stakes. Since "the verse of the sword" that commands slaying idolaters wherever you find them (9:5) was ostensibly revealed late in the Prophet's life, many authorities claimed that it cancelled out earlier verses urging peaceful coexistence. While most of the (over one hundred) conciliatory passages come from the Meccan period when the Muslim community was struggling to survive, the ninth sura is from the later Medinan period, when Muhammad and his followers were growing in strength and securing territory.[45] These historical contexts were considered sufficiently divergent to warrant updated instructions. So momentous was the geographic-political shift, in fact, that the Muslim calendar begins in this year of the *hijra*, the migration to Medina (then called Yathrib) in 622 CE.

Still, the claim that the "verse of the sword" overrides more conciliatory passages is contested, as is the supersessionist claim that Qur'an abrogates previous revelations (including the Jewish and Christian Bibles, to be discussed in part III). Countervoices point to literary and historical context in order to *contain* the scriptural authorization of violence and exclusivism.[46] Whether invoked for good or ill, *naskh* contributes to the consciousness of an evolving tradition. In fact, Sufi jurist al-Shar'ani (c. 1492–1565) thought it did not go far enough; he saw the four main Sunni legal schools as one great school with a purposefully broad, dynamic range of positions and thought that abrogation unnecessarily restricted the interpretive plurality that God intended.[47]

Qur'an is not presented in chronological order, so Islamic scholarship tried to establish the occasions of revelation (*asbab al-nuzul*): What was happening in the world when each passage was taught to Muhammad? These determined not only which verses came later but also informed interpretations, clarified the relationship of adjacent verses, and grounded the text in the life of the Prophet.[48] The context of revelation did not always limit the message to those particular circumstances, but understanding the occasion that gave rise to each prophetic experience could aid later believers in appropriately applying the word to their own time and place.[49]

Consciousness of historical context has always inserted a dynamic dimension into Islamic engagement with scripture. Long before al-Wahidi composed the first well-known collection of *asbab al-nuzul* in the eleventh century, Umar, the second "rightly guided caliph" (583–644 CE), adjusted religious praxis in light of shifting circumstances. He suspended the *hudud* punishments for theft in a year of drought, recognizing how scarcity drove people to desperation. Since hudud punishments are those explicitly commanded in Qur'an as the harsh consequence for violations considered trespasses against Allah and the public order, he overrode scriptural authority. He also redirected the charity which had been distributed to Medinan tribes who had not yet accepted Islam, asserting that Qur'anic instruction and Muhammad's practice in this matter were intended to garner support at the beginning and were no longer appropriate. Other Companions of the Prophet protested his adaptations, but he prevailed.[50] More recently, the religious leader of the 1979 Iranian revolution, Ayatollah Khomeini (not exactly a progressive, but a Twelver Shi'ite for whom ijtihad constituted a religious obligation), made adjustments for the modern context, allowing things like music, chess, and the presence of women on television and radio. When others objected, he said, "I feel it necessary to express my despair about your understanding of the divine injunctions and that of the [Shi'i] traditions. . . . The way you interpret the traditions, the new civilization should be destroyed and the people should live in shackles or live forever in the desert."[51]

Although the question of innovation has always been challenging in Muslim societies, with concerns about changes that might be heretical (bid'a), mainstream Sunni and Shi'a religious scholars have cultivated multiple interpretive methods to authorize alterations to the canonical tradition.[52] There is also a historical commitment to revivification (*tajdid*) and the pursuit of knowledge, even foreign knowledge. As one common saying goes, "Foreign knowledge is the lost camel of the believer."[53] Islam's elaborate discursive tradition has tried to preserve the traditional authority of scripture while also minimizing the dangers of rigidity and absolutism. It is a "pious devotion to the immutable texts," alongside a never-ending critical engagement with changing circumstances.[54] The current visibility of more dogmatic voices should not obscure the substantial box of tools provided within Islamic tradition to defuse the dangers of scripture.

CHAPTER 6

SCRIPTURE IN THE
CONTEMPORARY CONTEXT

L ike religion as a whole, scripture is bound up with power—the power to
define, to lead, to set boundaries and to make meaning. These are driving forces for our species. While they can be beneficial, we do not always pursue their loftiest purposes. Elisabeth Schüssler Fiorenza's remarks about the Christian Bible can be applied to all sacred scriptures: "Because of the all-too-human need to use the bible in an imperialistic way for bolstering our identity over and against that of others, because of our need for using the bible as a security-blanket, as an avenue for controlling the divine, or as a means of possessing revelatory knowledge as an exclusive privilege, we are ever tempted to build up securing walls and to keep out those who are not like us."[1] Yet the same power of scripture also serves to form the compassionate connection of communal identity, to anchor faith in an uncertain world, to inspire righteousness, to apprehend the divine, to tear down walls that divide us, to imagine a better world. How do we cultivate its constructive force without unleashing its power to oppress and destroy?

The faithful do not want to discard the *idea* of scripture, so one common strategy is the conscious and unconscious editing we do to make a better "Good Book." Selections for public recitation and formal lectionaries do some of the work, selective memory some more. Christians often forget that Jesus is portrayed casting out demons, vilifying his enemies, or threatening damnation, focusing instead on his inspired ministry to the "least of these" (Matt. 25, which also contains the oft-forgotten threat of age-long punishment). Many Muslims living in multifaith contexts, even some who

have memorized multiple suras of Qur'an, are surprised to learn about negative statements made regarding Jews and Christians in Muhammad's time.
Most Bible readers can tell you the story of Esther—up through chapter 8—
but they conveniently overlook that the book ends in a bloody retribution of
the Jews upon their would-be attackers. Never mind that it is an invented
tale; the text records a mighty celebration of this literary slaughter. There is
also conscious omission: when I used to study the weekly Torah portion at
Stanford Hillel, people just stopped showing up for Leviticus because they
disliked its preoccupation with sacrifice and ritual purity.

We can pretend those parts aren't there. Yet the Israeli poet Yehuda
Amichai shared a compelling insight regarding our attempts at a "Reader's
Digest" version of scripture. As he recounted in one of his poems, he *tried*
to edit the Hebrew Bible:

> *I've filtered out of the Book of Esther the residue*
> *of vulgar joy, and out of the Book of Jeremiah*
> *the howl of pain in the guts. And out of the*
> *Song of Songs the endless search for love,*
> *and out of the Book of Genesis the dreams*
> *and Cain, and out of Ecclesiastes*
> *the despair and out of the Book of Job—Job.*
> *And from what was left over I pasted for myself a new Bible.*
> *Now I live censored and pasted and limited and in peace.*[2]

What was he trying to convey? Basically, he took out everything
that was ethically objectionable, emotionally unbearable, or intellectually
suspect—and there was not much left. A text that does not reckon with
unmerited suffering and choking despair cannot speak to the human condition. A text that cannot imagine fratricide and genocide alongside liberation and holiness is more attractive, but it cannot tell the whole human
story. It would leave us "censored and pasted and limited." It is not really
possible to excise the difficult texts in any event because—as long as there
is scripture, someone will seize upon their message to wield their power.

Scripture is not a Boy Scout manual, my rabbinic mentor Arnold Jacob
Wolf used to say. It does not lay out in easy steps God's path of goodness. It
is not to be read as a guidebook with all the answers. It has the *questions*. It
is a syllabus for a lifelong course in advanced ethics. Contradictions within

the text, the multiplicity of interpretations, the clash with contemporary values—all these irritations are designed to create dialectical tension. We read closely, consider carefully, consult history, rub the sore spots, and we produce from the irritating grains of sand precious pearls of scriptural instruction. We cannot simply spiritualize or ignore all the tough parts because that is where the ethical work really happens—texts as tools of moral development. This tension prompts the self-critical faith found in principles like Judaism's "beyond the letter of the law," or more broadly, Gandhi's assertion: "As soon as we lose the moral basis, we cease to be religious; there is no such thing as religion overriding morality." It begins by recognizing the dangers embedded in scriptures' very existence.

BUILDING ON TRADITION

Tradition, which always recognized the complexity of its scriptural inheritance, opted to interpret the text rather than dismember or discard it. Many contemporary efforts to preserve the transformative power of scripture while protecting against the hazards in fact correlate with strategies honed in the histories of Judaism, Christianity, and Islam. Jewish scholars glorify the tradition's multivocality; Christian authors point to the diversity of text and tradition to argue that "no single interpretation of Christianity can be conclusive and complete."[3] Muslim exegetes emphasize historical context to reshape Qur'anic teaching for the modern age. In preparing the volume *Learned Ignorance* (mentioned in chapter 4), the editors gathered Jewish, Christian, and Muslim scholars to explore how intellectual humility could disarm scriptural and religious intolerance. An even broader assortment of religious traditions was represented in collaborating on *The Myth of Religious Superiority*, where there was general consensus that ultimate truth is beyond the scope of complete human understanding.[4]

Even the academy's insistence on historical-critical analysis builds upon traditional close reading practices and recognition of apparent contradictions in the texts. Particularity, contextualization, and a sense of how interpretive communities are key in the construction of scripture's meaning all have ancient roots as well, now echoed within contemporary perspectives. Scholars challenge modernism's intoxication with universal truths. Marjorie Suchocki's theological pluralism, for example, rests on the notion that truths do not have to be universal to be compelling to a particular community; God's word can have normative authority for a self-defined group in place of absolute authority.[5] Increasingly aware that no one is exempt from contextual biases in exegesis, many researchers recognize how impossible it is to distinguish what Elisabeth Schüssler Fiorenza elegantly called "the script" from "the Scripture"—what within our sacred texts and traditions is culturally influenced or historically limited, versus what is divine and eternal. Such discernment is itself culturally conditioned.[6]

There is also a growing fondness for multivocality and indeterminacy, with a conviction that "human civilization has a stake in plural readings."[7] In Christian thought, still dominant in Western discourse, polyphony is becoming a fundamental principle of contemporary religious ethics.[8] Today, Christian exegetes and theologians frequently write explicitly from within specified contexts and identified lenses—e.g., scriptural reflection that incorporates Latin American or African American liberation theology, Confucian- or other Eastern-inflected spiritual perspectives, womanist/feminist/mujerista interpretation, queer or postcolonial theory. These scholars continue to discover diverse meanings through previously marginalized voices, and to challenge old assumptions of objectivity, scientific certainty, and the fixity of truth. There are ongoing debates about whether such readings demonstrate what the Catholic Church has called "creative fidelity," and some would not even claim to stand within the framework of tradition—but they are faithful attempts to sow in the soil of scripture.[9]

However radical the reading, it belongs to the ongoing construction project of scriptural meaning. Exegetes in the Abrahamic traditions historically accepted the teachings of their ancestors but also felt free to depart from them. Describing the open-ended character of Qur'anic exegesis, Jane Dammen McAuliffe noted how generations received their scriptural inheritance: "There are instances of influence and points of confluence. There are also disjunctions or disruptions and even . . . wholescale rejection of the accumulated consequences of centuries of exegetical activity. Yet the conversation continues, the tug of the text persists and the desire for intellectual engagement with the divine word remains irresistible."[10] Their own teachings subsequently became a part of the tradition. In the words of Jonathan Brown, "Tradition . . . is built by generations of devout scholars, who shape it to fit or fight the world of their day, their learned wraiths incorporated into its edifice."[11]

Such pervasive interpretive pluralism is indeed a powerful tool to dissipate the dangers of scriptural ultimacy, and a significant portion of this section explored its premodern constructions. Even theological conservatives who express concerns about relativism, worrying that interpretive pluralism forfeits the idea of religious truth, should recognize that sacred texts have always prompted multiple, often conflicting interpretations.[12] The ideology that undergirds scriptural literalism is a modern invention that is out of step with the way that religious communities have read scripture in the past. People can hold to their truths, but the tradition of self-critical faith should press them to look hard at the impact of their convictions in the world. Teachings of humility make urgent the ever-present religious question that even Snoopy understood: "Has It Ever Occurred to You That You Might Be Wrong?"[13]

Yet there are legitimate concerns that contemporary claims of scriptural polysemy stake out their own ideological territory, with a tendency to view non-plural orientations to exegesis as intellectually or ethically substandard. Interpretive pluralism is hard to embody if it becomes a new absolute so it, too, requires critical self-reflection.[14] The obverse concern is equally challenging: interpretive pluralism is no guarantee that the power of scripture will not be used to subjugate. Accommodating all possibilities of meaning allows harmful interpretations to flourish as well, leading Paul Ricoeur to raise a compelling conundrum about tolerating ideas we believe to be wrong: "If liberty implies a right to error, how avoid pouring intolerance into indifference, and how prevent indifference from transforming itself into a tolerance towards the wrong done to others, in particular to the most fragile?"[15] Tolerance does not require indifference, of course. One can affirm the multiplicity of scriptural interpretations and still actively combat ideas that appall,[16] but this approach both mitigates and perpetuates the dangers of scripture.

SCRIPTURE AND POLITICS

Differences in the way we read sacred texts continue to matter because interpretation is a political act. It has implications for the ways in which we construct society, the rules we establish for living together, and the world we try to create. It was true for the efforts of the Israelites to fashion a covenantal community, for the followers of Jesus to teach in the shadow of empire, and for the Muslim community to institute its schools of law. It remained true even when scriptural authority began to be challenged. At the same time that Spinoza leveled his critique about people making "promiscuous" use of biblical authority, he was bound up in Dutch political disputes, masterfully finding biblical texts to vindicate Republican policies and undermine the Calvinist party "with a barrage of sacred missiles."[17] Scripture still gets deployed as a trump card in political debate.

Every interpretation is arguably political—in the academy, the congregation, and the public square—because it relates to the exercise of power. Elisabeth Schüssler Fiorenza's questions again come to mind: "How is meaning constructed, whose interests are served, what kind of worlds are envisioned, what roles, duties, and values are advocated, which socio-political practices are legitimated?" Ideologies that undergird interpretation are perhaps most evident in today's highly polarized public square, which connects scripture and politics in diverse ways. It is also a space in which the dangers of scripture show. This chapter concludes with a partial review of the uses of Bible and Qur'an in contemporary American politics in order to mark the hazards, and to examine whether the tools of tradition do or can provide a measure of protection, or even improve public discourse more generally. Most of the examples relate to Christianity, given its predominance in the US public square, but the forces at work impact us all.

Scripture frequently enters the political arena as an icon, as when a Torah scroll is carried to a protest march with the implicit message that the sacred text supports the cause. More often, the iconic power of scripture is used to assert identity. For example, the Museum of the Bible in Washington, DC, funded by the conservative CEO of Hobby Lobby, makes a statement about the centrality of the Bible in American identity by establishing itself three blocks from the United States Capitol Building. Sometimes governmental entities are directly involved, complicating the power dynamics of iconic gestures. When Ronald Reagan declared 1983 the "Year of the Bible," he proclaimed, "Of the many influences that have shaped the United States of America into a distinctive Nation and people, none may be said to be more fundamental and enduring than the Bible."[18] The president spoke as if the Bible's role was always a unifying one, forging a common sense of purpose and inspiring the abolition of slavery based on its teaching of love for neighbor. He made no mention of religious diversity, choosing to reassert the Christian biblical heritage amidst the country's rapidly changing demographics. Politically, it served as a mythos of social harmony and a powerful symbol for members of the "religious right" who had supported him.

Yet the use of religious symbols in governmental hands and on public lands has been controversial, repeatedly challenged in Supreme Court cases.[19] When deployed for clear ideological and theological purpose, the courts have generally ruled against them. For example, the former chief justice of the Alabama Supreme Court, Roy Moore, stated at his swearing in, "God's law will be publicly acknowledged in our court" and installed a monument of the Ten Commandments in the lobby of the state judicial building.[20] It was viewed by many as an unconstitutional effort to establish state religion. After several lawyers filed suit, a federal court ruled that the monument must be removed. Moore was eventually removed as well for refusing to comply with the court order.

The appearance of *some* scripture in the public square need not raise a constitutional issue to stir up controversy. When Rep. Keith Ellison used Jefferson's copy of Qur'an for his private ceremonial oath of office in 2007, he was affirming his identities as both Muslim and American—but various pundits and leaders of the Islamophobia industry presented the move as unpatriotic.[21] In 2010, a radical church in Gainesville, Florida, advocated burning the Qur'an to commemorate the September 11, 2001, attacks. Other groups responded by advocating "Read the Qur'an" day instead and by donating a copy of the text to the Afghan army for every one that was burned. Iconic uses of scripture almost always involve messages about who does and does not belong.

Sometimes candidates use scripture to demonstrate spiritual bona fides to religious voters. This exercise often backfires, as they get the verse wrong or apply it in clumsy ways.[22] Aside from promulgating poor understanding of sacred texts, the main danger here is that politicians feel it is required even though there is officially no religious test for public office. Religious and political leaders also cite passages as prooftexts, hoping to use scripture's moral authority to advance their policy position. At times, the strategy is so naked that the agenda is exposed and becomes part of the conversation. When Jeff Sessions was serving as Attorney General, for example, he invoked the New Testament to justify separation of families when asylum seekers and other undocumented migrants were picked up trying to cross the border. "I would cite you to the Apostle Paul and his clear and wise command in Romans 13, to obey the laws of the government because God has ordained the government for his purposes," he opined during a speech to law enforcement officers.[23] Legal experts cried foul, since there was no

law authorizing the separation of families and the administration was actually looking for a way to circumvent the rule that families with children
could not be incarcerated for more than twenty days. Historians quickly
noted that it was a favorite verse of British loyalists during the Revolutionary War and of slaveholders in the antebellum South.[24] Theologians
argued that he missed the biblical context of trying to avert a nationalist
revolt against Rome; he also neglected the conclusion in which Paul asserts
that love is the fulfillment of the law because it does no harm to neighbor
(13:10), as well as the broader scriptural commitment to the stranger in your
gates. Interfaith activists worried what furor would arise in conservative
Christian quarters (and beyond) if a US official tried to cite the Vedas,
Confucius, or the Qur'an that way. Defenders of the separation between
religion and state claimed there was no place for such arguments in public
policy discussions. There were others, however, who thought it was fair
game since many religious leaders were vocal about the ethical implications
of the policy, citing scripture to demonstrate its profound commitment to
the stranger.

My own response exemplified the joke about the rabbi who listens to
two contradictory positions in an argument and agrees with both of them.
An observer points out how illogical that is, and the rabbi says, "You're
right too!" I thought that the verse, for all its problems, captured something
important in Paul's dilemma of acquiescing in the rule of law even when it
violated his conscience—although Sessions suggested no such complexity.
It is also a summons to radical discipleship and could be read as a sign to
keep religion out of politics, but he did not interpret it that way either.
Rather, Sessions cited it as a prooftext to defend against criticism from "our
church friends," and it rightly stoked robust public discussion.

More fraught are the broad, sustained debates about same-sex love, en-
vironmentalism, and a host of other political issues, with competing scriptural verses drawn to support the different sides just as they did in the
case of slavery during the antebellum period. These arguments represent
conflicting worldviews. For some individuals, the sacred texts shape their
perspective; for others, they reflect and re-inspire convictions that are fashioned by other forces. Usually, it is a combination of the two. The positive
and negative potential of scripture is evident as it motivates people to work
for change. It has helped to catalyze entire movements across the political
spectrum, including social gospel, temperance, civil rights, anti-abortion,

and the Poor People's Campaign. Yet, as people generally cite sacred texts to insist that God is on their side and often portray their opponents as soulless and selfish, the dangers of ultimacy abide.

It sounds naïve to suggest that we make our "heart of many rooms," as taught in the Toseftu, in order to appreciate conflicting claims—or that we see differences of opinion as a sign of God's grace, as taught in the Hadith. It is difficult to grant Origen's premise that, in our most urgent disagreements, we all seek to benefit human life and that people are "led by certain plausible reasons to discordant views"—when the arguments of the other side seem only to magnify the dangers of scripture. Yet the religious traditions have taught that we gain a better understanding by considering the negation as well. Embracing a learned ignorance, where no one is in perfect possession of ultimate reality, we might recognize the need for each other's voices to raise questions that would not occur to us. We can cultivate what Intisar Rabb called "the doctrine of doubt." As Abelard taught, doubting will lead to deeper inquiry, which can guide us in our collective decisions.

To admit the embedded ambiguity of scripture, to accept Nachmanides's insight that there are no incontrovertible arguments, to apply al-Ghazali's hermeneutic of grace, or to allow for Kierkegaard's "objective uncertainty" even while we articulate our highest truths, would certainly change the conversation. Instead of prooftexting to win an argument, people would share how their reading of scripture connects them to this world. These are the truths-to-live-by—not absolutes—where every adherent is free to discover the core of meaning as they see it. In Ahad Ha'am's words, "For if not, the truth would not be the truth and the Holy Scriptures would not be holy."[25] Wayne Meeks's thesis that we require moral confidence, the conviction necessary to act on our beliefs—not moral certainty—is foreshadowed in the three traditions as they grappled with the limits of faith and knowledge.[26] These principles can moderate the use and abuse of scripture's power today and improve public discourse more broadly.

PART III

CHOSENNESS AND ELECTION, SUPERSESSION AND SALVATION

CHAPTER 7

A MATRIX OF DANGEROUS RELIGIOUS IDEAS

Peoples in the ancient Near East had special relationships with their tribal gods; in essence, each was "chosen." The Philistines were favored by Dagon and the Moabites by Chemosh. Initially formed by this model, Israelite religion had to grapple with the profound implications of its developing monotheism on such a relationship. If Yahweh is indeed the God of *all* the world, what then does it mean to choose a nation? There is no simple answer; Tanakh records multiple perspectives on the significance of election and God's relationship to other peoples, while also wrestling with its impact on how humans relate to each other.

Within New Testament, too, there is an evolving understanding of chosenness. It moves between "We are Israel also" and "We are Israel instead," as the authors fashioned the criteria and consequences of belonging. Hellenistic influence reshaped the formation of identity, with religion less rigidly attached to nationality. As with philosophical schools, individuals could navigate a religious path based on compatible praxis and perspective, not simply the people among whom they were born or dwelled.[1] To be chosen, then, came to mean affirming the singular mission of Jesus in the service of the one God. Election to eternal salvation—a concept foreign to Tanakh—became central within Christian thought, but it is not the only possibility explored within the gospels and epistles.

The language of chosenness in Qur'an is most often attached to individuals whom Allah reportedly favored and guided in the generations before Muhammad (Abraham, Isaac, Jacob, Ishmael, Elisha, etc.). In the

Prophet's time, however, those who submitted to God's will as conveyed by Muhammad as the final messenger—Muslims—became the elect. Faithful embrace of his teaching could earn a place in the heavenly gardens and save one from the fire. "They are the people guided by their Lord; they are the successful" (*f-l-ḥ*, 2:5). Qur'an transmits *ayat* that seem to affirm the salvific capacity of previous revelations—even presenting religious pluralism as a key component of Allah's redemptive plan—but other passages are stridently supersessionary.

As assertions of election were increasingly contested, these competing religious claims played out in governance, public affairs, art, scriptural exegesis, and other literature with substantial consequences. Yet chosenness does not mean the same thing in each tradition, nor does it have a single significance within any one of them. Particular interpretations become normative, but never static. Even the questions it raises shift in response to historical context. In the modern age, moral implications have moved to the forefront: Why would the God of all humanity choose some and not others? How has presumption of such status justified wrongdoing? What about the "unchosen?" The idea seems dangerous. Two of its most prominent problems can be categorized as conquest and the evaluation of difference.

CONQUEST

"The biblical idea of election is the ultimate anti-humanist idea," Jeremy Cott asserted in a critique that posits conquest as the primary expression of chosenness.[2] He identified the issue as one of scarcity. Limited availability of land, resources, and power has been a source of human conflict throughout time. Religion magnifies the potential for violence by offering divine justification to take these essentials by any means necessary, and by inventing new forms of scarcity—one treasured people, one path to God or to salvation.[3] Historical examples abound that illuminate the dangerous linkage of conquest and election, and it is not uncommon for peoples to imagine that God takes their side in battle. Anticipating war with the Canaanites, Deuteronomy 9:3 states: "Know now that YHWH your God is the one who passes before you, a devouring fire. God will wipe them out and subdue them before you so that you may quickly dispossess and destroy them, as YHWH has told you." Centuries later, dramatic early successes in building the Islamic empire were interpreted to vindicate the singular truth of Islam. According to Tim Winter,

> Islam could claim to have outmoded Judaism by the sheer fact of its triumph: as Freud cynically put it, "Allah showed himself far more grateful to his chosen people than Yahweh did to his." And in respect of Christianity, it was assumed that the absorption of the great patriarchal cities of Antioch, Alexandria and others into the Muslim world could never have been allowed by a God who did not regard Christianity as obsolete. . . . Jerusalem's Islamic monuments yield an allegory of supersession which is no less deliberate than that of St. Peter's Basilica and the other signs of Christian mastery of the once-pagan capital of Rome.[4]

Conquest can be conceived in spiritual as well as political terms. Western colonialism was motivated by desire for dominance and material gain, but facilitated by aspirations to "convert the heathen" and a sense of entitlement as God's elect. The world convulses still from the subsequent transformation and decimation of subject populations and cultures. Each example reveals the insidious power of rationalization that election provides: Gerónimo de Mendieta, a sixteenth-century Franciscan commissioned to write a "History of the Indian Church" in Mexico, believed Spain was chosen to lead the final conversion of the world. Having expelled Jews and Muslims from the Iberian peninsula, the Spanish set out to the New World to convert the "last" pagans and usher in the kingdom of God. Cortés was his Moses, liberating the Native Americans from demonic powers and winning more souls for Christ than Luther had taken from the Catholic Church.[5] John Cotton invoked 2 Samuel 7:10 in a sermon for Puritan voyagers to the New World in 1630: "Moreover I will appoint a place for my people Israel, and I will plant them, that they may dwell in a place of their owne, and move no more; neither shall the sonnes of wickednesse afflict them any more."[6] A sense of being God's chosen people provided consolation for their suffering at the hands of Anglican authorities, and clear title to the land they were going to occupy.

Despite the evocative biblical summons to love the stranger because we were strangers in the land of Egypt (Lev. 19:34, Deut. 10:19), experiences of persecution offer no protection from becoming a persecutor. A more common human response is to emulate the violence inflicted upon us and release the torrent of resentments that accumulate under subjugation. As Musa Dube pointed out, the Israelites suffered under numerous empires and the early Christians under Roman oppression, yet both developed their own theologies of conquest, operating under claims of chosenness.[7] Conquest is not intrinsic to chosenness, however. In the following chapters we will read of countervoices, both historical and contemporary, that work to decouple them. Thickly entwined with political agendas and embedded in the "will to power," justification of conquest is an intractable problem of election, but it is a byproduct.

DIFFERENCE

Ultimately, the fulcrum of election is the identification and evaluation of difference. Conquest cannot be justified without formulating a distinction between us and them. Establishing a chosen people simultaneously creates peoples who are not; an in-group constructs an out-group, potentially leading to discrimination, persecution, and violence. Thus, the consequences of election are bound up with attitudes toward the other in religious traditions.

Difference is a pervasive element in human existence. It is a building block of the way we think, as is poetically illuminated by the biblical creation narrative that envisions God creating the universe through distillation of difference: night is separated from day, water from land, etc. (Gen. 1). More simply, we can examine how *Sesame Street* uses the sorting song "One of These Things (Is Not Like the Others)" to teach basic cognitive skills. Difference is how we learn, how meaning is made possible, and how we understand our relationship to the rest of the world.[8] It is significant, not only to the issue of chosenness, but to the religious project as a whole—integral to identity, faith, and practice. We can mark difference without viewing it as evidence of inequality, but humans frequently conflate the two. Research in social identity theory has demonstrated that group membership, even if arbitrarily assigned, provokes favoritism for members and discrimination against those outside.[9] Religious ideas such as election and salvation are certainly prone to burden distinction with dangerous baggage. Consider Rousseau's argument that democracies must affirm multiple paths to salvation: "It is impossible to live at peace with people whom one believes are damned. To love them would be to hate God who punishes them. They must absolutely be either brought into the faith or tormented."[10]

Navigating difference is further complicated because it is constructed by those who hold power in society. William Scott Green noted, "A society does not simply discover its others, it fabricates them by selecting, isolating, and emphasizing an aspect of another people's life and making it symbolize their difference."[11] The ones with power get to define themselves—and to define others as their (inferior) opposite. In this social structure, deviant is the other of normal, alien the other of citizen, criminal the other of law-abiding, animal the other of human, woman the other of man, black the other of white. Assertion of dominance *depends on* the creation of an "other," so self and other are mutually constituted.[12] It is ironic that the most similar is often set up as one's opposite. There is no creature on earth as similar to man as woman, for example, and yet she is his "other." It is this proximate other that stimulates the greatest anxiety: "While difference or 'otherness' may be perceived as being either like-us or not-like-us, it becomes most problematic when it is too-much-like-us or when it claims to be-us. It is here that the real urgency of theories of the other emerges, called forth not so much by a requirement to place difference, but rather by an effort to situate ourselves."[13]

As a consequence, struggles for the power to define self and other within the religious "family" of Abraham, Sarah, and Hagar can be especially fraught. Jews, Christians, and Muslims are often the most proximate others—geographically, historically, and religiously—and they have depicted each other so as to define themselves. An honest reckoning with the dangers of election must investigate historical instances of "othering" within Judaism, Christianity, and Islam—and the ways in which they can still infect relationships between people of different religious traditions. The catalysts may be social, economic, and political concerns, but conflicts are often constructed around cultural identities. Religious values, beliefs, and narratives give them meaning, frequently framed by a moral binary of good and evil.[14]

The following chapters explore these dynamics in greater detail within each tradition, but several examples here serve to elucidate the unique ways in which religion shapes the problem. While there is an unfortunate tendency to collapse the polysemic scriptural teachings into one voice, the sacred texts do include passages with troubling views of difference that are animated by ideas of election. In the Tanakh, Canaanites and Amalekites are to be obliterated; no one is considered innocent. A number of

New Testament texts present "the Jews" as a singular and malevolent entity: blind to the meaning of their own scripture, responsible for the death of Jesus, cast off by God for their sinfulness, children of the devil. Qur'an repeatedly denigrates pagans, Jews, and Christians.

This rhetoric is polemical, used to strengthen group identity and to demonstrate why they are God's elect. Nonetheless, the demonization of the other in sacred texts breeds abiding hostility because these biases do not remain isolated on the page. One of the hallmarks of "successful" scriptural religions is a hermeneutic that makes the text eternally relevant, so the images become archetypal in our religious imagination. Time and again, for example, Amalekites stand in for the demonized other: Protestant re-formers identified the Catholic Church as this eternal enemy, Luther and his student Johannes Brenz invoked it against the Jews, many American colonists cast Native Americans in the role, and some ultranationalist Is-raeli settlers see Palestinians as the Amalekites of today.[15] Always, the bib-lical association assigns transcendent significance and kindles deep-seated emotion. Always, the identification justifies what might otherwise be seen as immoral action against them—killing, deportation, occupation, legal discrimination—because they stand over against God's elect.

There have been interpreters, past and present, who sought to limit hostile passages within their historical context. Modern readers frequently invoke such strategies to circumscribe the potential dangers. Farid Esack, for example, has struggled with a number of troubling ayat (including those that vilify some Jews as apes and pigs) and lamented the way they continue to poison conceptions of non-Muslims. After recounting the tension that arose between the communities in Muhammad's lifetime when most Jews did not embrace his prophetic status and some stood against him in early conflicts, he concluded, "Historicizing the text is probably the only way that the text itself can be saved in a world where we understand a bit more about a) the insidiousness of attributing to any historical community—and all communities—ahistorical characteristics of praise or opprobrium, and b) the interconnectedness of all forms of life and the fact that the diminish-ing of any species really spells the diminishing of all species."[16]

Even without violence and demonization of the other, the concept of chosenness is fraught. It can encourage chauvinism (you are good, but we are better) and division (you are all right, but association with you may draw me away from the chosen path). Families have been ripped apart by imagining that one of their own will be going to hell for abandoning the path of the elect. Interreligious understanding is undermined by suspicions that people want to persuade everyone that their faith is superior, or that they stand closer to God's own truth.

Yet election also provides the traditions with valuable sustenance, helping to fashion the boundaries of community and solidify its glue. Beyond the raw survival advantage of a strong group identity, it instills a sense of purpose among adherents. God has a stake in their embodiment of the divine promise and supports their endeavors. Chosenness strikes on all the cylinders discussed in chapter 1 that give religion its power. Critiques are weakened to the extent that they fail to reckon with its positive potential or reduce the meaning of election to something singular.

To grapple with the very real problems, then, we begin with an exploration of chosenness in the scriptural material. The theme is so pervasive and polysemous that this review cannot be comprehensive, but it demonstrates a range of thought that broadens the possibilities of meaning. Dangerous ideas are embedded there, but so are contrapuntal voices that suggest different understandings of and insights about the hazards of election illuminated within the texts themselves. Then, selecting from historical layers of interpretation, the discussion concentrates on issues of conquest and difference. How were the scriptural texts understood, and which ones came to dominate the religious imagination? What happened as the dangers became alive, wielded through erasure, discrimination, demonization, oppression, or warfare? How do recent representations still echo older tropes, revealing how complicated it is to expunge religious bias? Some examples manifest the problems and others diminish them, demonstrating the longstanding capacity within religious traditions to uncover their own weaknesses and to transmit multiple and even opposing ideas. There are voices that reject conquest and writings that acknowledge the fundamental humanity, equality, and value of religious others. These redemptive readings plant seeds for more fruitful possibilities of meaning.

Each tradition is treated in its own chapter. Because we should not allow the dangers of election to determine its meaning, each chapter concludes with focal points of chosenness that indicate its positive religious value and enduring significance—not unalloyed blessings, but capable of nurturing worthy aspirations and profound ideas, addressing a compelling range of human needs. Since even these powerful teachings cannot erase the threats of conquest and othering, however, the final chapter of the section examines how they continue to play out in the public square.

Two caveats are in order: (1) Since the subject would require a book-length study to provide a thorough review of a single religious tradition, the history is necessarily selective. It presents a series of exegetical snapshots. Like any anthology of material, the selection itself is an interpretation and my reading of it comprises only one of many possibilities. (2) Although the details in each tradition are obviously unique, the challenges they present are shared. The snapshots are designed to convey urgency in dealing with the dangers and to excavate strategies for containment, not to judge one faith or another.

We can neither wish chosenness away nor permanently purify the concept of its poisonous elements. Despite the real harm inspired by history's living out of election, these ideas are deeply embedded in the sociological, philosophical, psychological, and political dimensions of our being. But we can identify the dangers and the benefits, recognize the common burden, and recover the strength of alternative readings—including those that demonstrate the self-critical foundations of faith—as we reckon with the place of dangerous religious ideas in the construction of the human.

CHAPTER 8

CHOSENNESS IN JUDAISM

TANAKH

Hebrew Bible presents many layers of meaning in chosenness, and also recognizes its dangerous potential. The book of Genesis makes evident the problem of God's choosing immediately after it wrestles with the problem of humans' choosing. We are barely out of Eden when Cain and Abel each offer a sacrifice, but God pays heed only to Abel's offering. Although no reason is given, I had students who were certain that the text must somewhere indicate Cain offers second-rate produce. Why? It is an interpretation that goes back to late antiquity, a close reading of the biblical text that states, "In the course of time Cain brought an offering to YHWH from the fruit of the soil, and Abel also brought some of the fatty parts of the firstlings of his flock" (Gen. 4:3–4). Wanting to believe that God's choice has some rationale, we may determine that Abel offers choice cuts of meat. So he brings the best stuff, while Cain just brings stuff.[1] We could just as easily detect that Cain initiates the offering, however, and Abel seems merely to copy his brother. In fact, the text never states that Abel is bringing "an offering to YHWH"; perhaps it is an empty gesture. We do not read it that way because we prefer that God's choice make sense.

Tanakh, however, is more interested in how human beings respond to God choosing. That is what occupies the bulk of the chapter. God exhorts Cain to control his urge to sin and asks, "Why are you angry, and why is your face fallen?" (Gen. 4:6b). Written on Cain's face is the pain of feeling "unchosen" and, when he murders Abel, we see the terrible weight of his resentment. Long before any mention of the singular covenant with Israel, the Hebrew Bible illuminates the human conundrum of God choosing.[2]

Echoes of rivalry for divine favor play out through the narratives of Genesis. With Jacob and Esau, Torah illustrates how pursuit of election can prompt unjust behavior, but we also glimpse the possibility of forgiveness rather than fratricide (Gen. 25, 27, 32–33). In the Joseph novella, chosenness enables the divine plan for blessing to unfold. After Joseph's dramatic reconciliation with his aggrieved brothers, the covenantal promise is for the first time transmitted to all the siblings, and they become the putative ancestors of the twelve tribes. Joseph as the chosen one, invisibly guided and protected by God, saves the Egyptians and his own people from a prolonged famine in the region. Blessing flows between and among the households of creation . . . until a Pharaoh arises who "does not know Joseph" and he identifies the Israelites as a threat (Gen. 37–50, Exod. 1:8–11).[3]

The election of Abram (renamed "Abraham" in Gen. 17:5) explicitly invokes this notion of mutual blessing. Called at the outset without explanation, he is promised: "I will make of you a great nation, and I will bless you; I will make your name great, and you shall be a blessing. I will bless those who bless you, and one who curses you I will damn; and all the families of the earth shall be blessed through you" (Gen. 12:2–3). Immediately following the passage, however, Abram is forced to leave the land due to famine and his life is endangered. He is childless for many years, learns that his descendants will be enslaved for centuries, and undergoes numerous trials. Clearly, we are not meant to interpret election as a life of ease.[4] Neither is it a mark of superiority. Although Genesis 18:19 suggests that God singles Abraham out so "he may charge his children and his household after him to keep the way of YHWH by doing what is right and just," Genesis commonly presents God's favor as an act of grace. Abraham is simply a friend of God.[5]

One does not need to be elect to elicit divine favor and have an essential role in God's plan for creation. The story of Noah presents "a theology that places all people in a relationship of grace and accountability with God," with divine commitments and commandments in the wake of the Flood.[6] Ishmael provides a more detailed example: twice God promises to make of him a great nation (Gen. 17:20, 21:18), and he becomes the father of twelve tribes just as Jacob does. Ishmael carries the sign of the covenant (circumcision), and repeatedly the text mentions God's blessing upon him. Yet Tanakh does not present him as an ancestor of the "chosen people."

The chosenness of the people Israel is generally tightly bound with the covenant at Sinai: "Now then, if you will hearken well to My voice and keep

My covenant, you shall be to Me a special treasure among all the peoples. Indeed, all the earth is Mine, but you shall be to Me a kingdom of priests and a holy nation" (Exod. 19:5–6a).[7] This is the language of aspiration, nurturing a special relationship with God by creating a national religious life devoted to divine service. Revelation at Sinai follows, and Torah becomes central to the Jewish understanding of election. Often compared to ancient Near Eastern suzerain–vassal treaties, the Sinaitic covenant entails obligations for each party. The Israelites are commanded to live by the teachings of Torah; God's reciprocal blessing is both abstract and concrete, with commitments of love, favor, glory, fertility, health, and security (Exod. 23:25–6, Deut. 7:12–15, 26:16–19, 28:1–11). This theology permeates much of Torah, and many of the metaphors that evoke close relationship between God and Israel similarly entail mutual obligation—parent and child, husband and wife, shepherd and sheep, master and servant—although the people do not always hold up their end of the bargain.[8] They are warned that violation will incur punishment, but the relationship abides (Lev. 26, Deut. 30:1–5, 1 Sam. 12:22, 2 Sam. 7:8–16, Ps. 105:7–10, Neh. 9).[9] Both the covenant of divine friendship and the covenant of Torah remain vital in Tanakh. In the synthesis of love and commandment, chosenness is still an unearned gift, but intimacy breeds high expectations.

Although some critics have identified Jewish chosenness with racism because it is linked to a people rather than a faith, it does not fit the vast majority of biblical evidence. "One of the hardest points of biblical thought to understand is the concept of peoplehood, which is familial and natural without being racial and biologistic."[10] The textual portrait of the people of Israel has included since its exodus from Egypt a "mixed multitude" (Exod. 12:38), and individuals not born into the community continue to join it.[11] Deuteronomy 23:8–9 speaks about Edomites and Egyptians becoming part of the "assembly of the Lord," a type of national legislature, in the third generation. It is perhaps most comparable to modern national identity, where residency eventually earns full citizenship even while ethnic origins remain a part of one's identity.[12] Over time, the "chosen people" grew even more multiethnic and multinational.

Parts of Tanakh express concerns about intermarriage and treaties with resident Canaanites who might lead the community toward idolatry (Exod. 34:15–16), but a desire to preserve the integrity of one's culture is not necessarily malevolent. Unfortunately the language of Ezra, when he rebukes the

Jews for intermarrying and mixing "the holy seed" (9:1), introduces racist overtones.[13] One can view his perspective as an outlier, and identify the book of Ruth (likely redacted around the same time) as a contemporaneous countervoice since its Moabite heroine becomes the ancestress of King David. Nonetheless, Ezra's imagery provides a glancing biblical foundation for those who want to read into chosenness a genetic foundation.

The people of Israel is a "group," and with every group, from teenage cliques to the rise of nations, there is a risk of developing exclusivist strains. Aware of this danger, the prophets teach in numerous ways that election does not provide exclusive title to divine concern. Amos proclaims God's relationship with every nation: "Children of Israel, are you not just like the Ethiopians to Me, declares YHWH. Did I not bring Israel up from the land of Egypt, but also Philistines from Caphtor and Arameans from Kir" (9:7)? The prophet conventionally identified as Third Isaiah insists that foreigners who attach themselves to God and observe the covenant have equal status and equal claim to the spiritual inheritance; he presents the Temple as "a house of prayer for all peoples" (Isa. 56:3–8). The book of Jonah portrays a Hebrew prophet being sent to Nineveh, capital of the conquering Assyrian empire, to save them from God's judgment; he struggles with the mission, but God tries to teach him about divine compassion for the whole of creation. Micah announces a pluralistic vision for God's multitude of nations: "And they shall beat their swords into plowshares and their spears into pruning hooks. Nation shall not take up sword against nation; they shall never again train for war. Rather, every man shall sit under his grapevine or fig tree with no one to make him afraid. . . . For all the peoples walk each in the name of its gods; we will walk in the name of YHWH our God forever and ever" (Mic. 4:3–5).

The prophets also recognize the temptations of complacency, chauvinism, and parochialism that can accompany chosenness, and warn the people against them. Amos 3, in calling the nation to account for its failures, declares that chosenness entails additional liability rather than special privilege. Jeremiah, standing in the Temple gates, rails against invoking God's presence in Jerusalem as if it is a divine talisman that protects the people even while they perpetrate injustice (7:3–11). The nation is reminded time and again that its election entails living in faithfulness with the covenant, including manifest concern for the widow, orphan, and stranger. Jeremy

Cott called the theology of the stranger an "anti-election" theology.[14] It might better be construed as the necessary corollary of election, a rule for how to conceive of and engage the other to prevent marginalization and abuse.

After the Temple is destroyed, the prophets focus more on reassuring a devastated people that God's special love for them abides (e.g., Jer. 31, Isa. 43:1–4, 44:1–5). Second Isaiah helps the exiles find purpose in their suffering and claims they can become a light unto the nations (ch. 42). Yet chosenness carries risk for the chosen, a dynamic highlighted in Tanakh's "Diaspora literature." The book of Esther, composed in exile, provides a literary demonstration of how easy it is to demonize difference; Haman persuades King Ahasuerus to order the annihilation of the Jews by claiming that their unique practices prove they do not obey the king's laws (Esther 3.8).[15] Second Isaiah, portraying Israel as the suffering servant (e.g., 52:3–53:12), laments how God's elect suffer for their faithfulness. Indeed, Jewish adherence to the covenant has frequently been villainized, prompting oppressive legislation and violence.

Today, we are far more conscious of the dangers that election poses for those *outside* the covenanted group, including suppression and conquest. These are evident in Deuteronomy 7. After establishing that God's choice of Israel is not based on size or might but rather fulfillment of a promise to the patriarchs, the nation is asked to show comparable loyalty to God by refusing to intermarry with the Canaanites and by excising every remnant of pagan worship in the land: "Tear down their altars, smash their pillars, cut down their sacred posts, and burn their graven images with fire. For you are a people holy to YHWH your God: YHWH your God chose you to be His treasured people from among all the peoples on the face of the earth" (7:5–6). Never mind that the purge is never executed. Living today in a pluralistic society, we see it as xenophobia and religious persecution— even though our own age is also poisoned by Islamophobia, religious hate crimes, and destruction of other people's sacred sites.

Some rabbinic texts and contemporary scholars understand the biblical text to authorize war only as a divine prerogative, forbidden unless God specifically commands it.[16] Yet Torah sanctions violence to advance the cause of the elect. Instructions for conquest include slaughtering every Canaanite in the heart of the land (Deut. 20:16) along with more "generous" terms for outlying areas. There, the Israelites are commanded first to sue for peace and to attack only if they are refused, at which point they are told to kill all the men and take the women, children, and property as spoils of war (vv. 10–14). Although biblical and archaeological evidence indicates that this brutal vision was not implemented and Canaanite presence continued in the land, Tanakh fails to grapple with the moral implications of its charge.[17] References to the iniquity of the Canaanites (Gen. 15:16, Deut. 9:4–6, Lev. 18:24, 20:23) are designed primarily as a cautionary tale for Israel not to repeat their errors. To the extent that they also serve as justification for the extirpation of the Canaanites, they merely compound the ethical dilemma—as if sin can earn such a fate.

Nonetheless, it is worth noting that the biblical account dooms the Canaanites because their iniquity has angered God, not because they are "not chosen."[18] Although God takes the side of the Israelites in fulfillment of the promises of election, the world is not divided among the elect and the damned. Joel Kaminsky has suggested we recognize three categories in Tanakh: the elect, the non-elect, and the anti-elect. Only the last of these (Canaanites and Amalekites) are condemned.[19] The non-elect, like Ishmael, have key roles in the divine economy—and all stand in relationship with God.

The conquest tradition is not as central in Tanakh as some critics suggest; one can also derive a strong peace tradition from the text.[20] But the promise of a homeland is linked to election tracing back to Abraham, so it cannot be completely marginalized either. Our reading must be grounded in the historical context of the Deuteronomistic redaction: during the Israelite monarchy of the eighth to seventh century BCE, gods regularly took sides and proscription of enemy populations was common practice. Intense exposure to cosmopolitan Assyrian culture—impacting Israelite art, economy, and religious life—likely prompted fervent opposition in an effort to stem the tide of cultural assimilation.[21] Bearing these facts in mind neither eliminates the dangerous linkage of conquest and election nor definitively conscribes its influence, but we can learn to recognize the volatile mix of self-preservation, rationalization, and religion that justifies aggression.

Ultimately, Tanakh presents the story of one family-cum-nation, called to stand in special relationship with its God, Creator of the universe and Redeemer of all humanity. Jewish tradition grapples with its complex understandings of chosenness—both the dangers and the possibilities.

CIRCUMSCRIBING CONQUEST AND NAVIGATING DIFFERENCE

While some early rabbis supported military resistance against the Roman Empire, rabbinic texts from the classical period were redacted during a time of political powerlessness. After the destruction of the Temple in 70 CE, the decimation of diaspora communities in 115–117, and the brutal crushing of the Bar Kochba revolt in 135, the futility of fighting the Roman Empire by force of arms was clear. Rabbinic literature developed ideas that mark a different course, including:

- The catastrophes of the first and second centuries fell upon the Jews as a consequence of their sins; the path to restoration is through repentance and renewed commitment to religious observance.
- God will at the proper time lead the people home and punish the nations who oppressed Israel.
- War is associated with human wickedness, and peace is valorized.
- The warrior is transformed into a heroic master of Torah and its interpretation, trained in intellectual combat and spiritual virtuosity. Torah is the glory of Israel.[22]

Although the sages provided prooftexts for their teachings and saw them as an authentic development of biblical religion, they overlaid their own values to privilege what they saw as overarching scriptural principles.[23] Rabbinic culture was sensitized to imperial oppression and valued non-violence in fashioning a politics of exile. Conquest began to be uncoupled from chosenness.

These ideas are well-attested, but the literature spans such a broad reach of time and space—with great historical shifts and a multitude of voices—that it is problematic to deal in generalizations. Rabbinic texts do not present a uniformly pacifist ethos, and the sages imagined a time of restoration in which Jews would again hold political power. Focusing on rabbinic strategies that circumscribe biblical instructions about conquest, one move of great significance is the division of war into two categories, commanded and discretionary. "Joshua's wars of conquest everyone agrees are obligatory," one passage asserts, "while the wars of the House of David for territorial expansion everyone agrees are discretionary" (b. Sotah 44b; see also y. Sotah 8:1). The discussion leaves open whether later conquest of the land could ever be considered a commanded war, but halakhah isolates the Deuteronomic directive for conquest—not applicable to the general conduct of war.[24]

The rabbis also attempted to constrain some of the most pernicious instructions related to the Canaanites. They insisted that the emperor Sennacherib mixed up all the peoples when the Assyrians conquered territory and exiled residents from their lands, so there are no longer any nations to which the proscription applies (m. Yad. 4:4, b. Ber. 28a, b. Yoma 54a). In addition, they asserted that the Canaanites of history were spared if they abandoned their immoral practices (Sifre Deut. 202, t. Sotah 8:7, b. Sotah 35b), and terms of peace were offered in every instance (Lev. Rab. 17:6, y. Shev 6:1 (36c); Deut Rab. 5:13–14).[25] Using their standard hermeneutics of close reading and creative exegesis, the sages established a foundation to contain the teaching of conquest.

Chosenness became much more tied to difference. As an often-beleaguered religious minority from late antiquity into the modern era, Jews both embody the other and have constructed non-Jews as "other" in their literature and religious imagination. Demonstrating the abiding chosenness of the Jews became a strategy for survival. Often more concerned about elevating the chosen than denigrating others, various texts convey images of ethical, intellectual, or spiritual superiority. For example, one repeated trope presents arguments that end with the rabbinic sages persuading their non-Jewish interlocutors of the wisdom of Torah, the God who gave it, and the rabbinic tradition that interprets it. Jews had been without political autonomy or Temple for centuries by the time these texts were redacted, but they imagined victory for the chosen through a contest of wisdom.[26]

In the ongoing construction of self and other, polemical texts tried to discredit supersessionary claims in order to sustain Jewish faith in the face of physical, economic, political, and spiritual pressure to convert. A midrash on Song of Songs, for example, presents a parable in which the straw, chaff, and stubble each claim that the land was sown for its sake. The wheat tells them to await harvest, and they will learn the truth. Chaff is scattered to the wind, the straw cast on the floor, the stubble burned, and the wheat is gathered into stacks where everyone kisses it. So it is, according to the midrash, with the nations of the world: each claims to be Israel, but it will become clear at the end of days that the Jews still hold this mantle and the world was created for their sake (Song Rab. 7:3(3)).[27]

Typical of Jewish literature's multivocality, texts cite various tradents with diverse ideas about non-Jews, seemingly dependent on personal temperament, experience, and historical context. The examples here, drawn from the Babylonian Talmud and Tannaitic traditions that fed into it, should be considered illustrative rather than a comprehensive presentation of what the Talmud "says." Also, attributions are not necessarily reliable, so it is more appropriate to identify literary portraits instead of historical figures, but it is fair to assume that they approximate the range of opinion that existed within the community.[28] Rabbi Eliezer b. Hyrcanus, for instance, reportedly rejected the idea that righteous Gentiles have a share in the world to come, but Rabbi Joshua affirmed it (t. Sanh. 13:2, b. Sanh. 105a). The sages endorsed Rabbi Joshua's opinion.[29]

A mishnaic passage maintained that idolaters lack basic moral standards: "Do not lodge cattle at the inns of idolaters because they are suspected of bestiality. A woman should not be alone with them because they are suspected of sexual immorality. A man should not be alone with them because they are suspected of shedding blood" (m. Sanh. 2:1). While it did not speak of chosenness, the passage implied that the covenanted community is more trustworthy. Yet Jewish texts also discerned a universal standard of righteousness that obtained among Gentiles, traceable to God's covenant with Noah. It is found as early as the book of Jubilees (7:20), then developed more fully within Talmud as a set of seven Noahide laws.[30] Non-Jews who abided by a comparable moral code were entitled to protection and aid as "strangers" (b. Avod. Zar. 64b). The community was also instructed to support their poor, visit their sick, and bury their deceased "for the sake of peace" (b. Git. 61a).

Hostility toward non-Jews sometimes appeared in the liturgy. There was a line within the Aleinu prayer claiming that other peoples bow down to emptiness and pray to a god who will not save. It was occasionally self-censored, then officially censored by Catholic authorities. In the Amidah sequence of prayers, repeated three times a day in traditional rabbinic practice, there was a malediction. Its earliest extant versions (c. ninth century) expressed enmity toward Karaites, Christians, and others, calling on God to destroy the insolent.[31] It stood in contrast to the blessing that followed it, seeking mercy for the righteous, the household of Israel.

Expressions of antipathy were most often bound up with the people's historical experience of suffering, and thus became more widespread in the medieval period. In Jewish chronicles penned in the wake of the Crusades, for example, the chosen ones were repeatedly contrasted with the venomous attackers, urged on by a satanic Pope to "come to the tomb of the crucified one, a rotting corpse that cannot avail and cannot save."[32] Yet the suffering also stood as a sign of special intimacy. In the idiom of Jewish poetry from Askhenaz, the beloved son is wed to his bride (God) in holy sacrifice: "Young men went forth, each from his room/ to sanctify the Great Name, for today He tests His chosen ones."[33] After the Jews of Blois were massacred in response to a blood libel in 1171, Rabbi Hillel b. Jacob wrote,

> *And when it was said, "Bring them out to the fire,"*
> *They rejoiced together as a bride at the bridal canopy*
> *"It is for us to praise," they recited, their souls filled with longing.*

"It is for us to praise" is the beginning of the Aleinu prayer, which emphasizes the unique destiny of the Jewish people in their singular commitment to worship God.[34]

While Christian texts highlighted the suffering of the Jews as evidence of divine condemnation, Jewish texts interpreted it as evidence of God's special concern. Martyrdom's prominence in evincing the role of the chosen, however, did not lessen the sense of incredulity at their fate. Shlomo bar Shimshon wrote after the First Crusade, "Why have you abandoned your nation, Israel, to derision, contempt, and humiliation, to be consumed by nations impure as swine—this very people whom You chose to be the elect of all the nations?"[35]

Co-construction of self and other is also evident in the polemical medieval literature called *Toledot Yeshu* (The Life Story of Jesus), containing parodies of Jesus's life and death. These works portrayed Yeshu as the bastard son of an adulteress, deriding ideas of the virgin birth, incarnation, and ascension. His reputed miracles were reduced to magic tricks and illicit use of the divine name, with Judas as the hero of the tale.[36] David Biale argued that this was not simply a biting satire, but effectively a counterhistory, a literature of protest that transvalued the Christian narrative. For example, it cast Paul and Simon Peter as infiltrators sent by the rabbis; in order to prevent Judaism from being corrupted, they persuaded Jesus's followers to divorce themselves from it. "The strategy of the text is to reverse the sense of Jewish powerlessness in the face of Christian enmity by arguing that the Jews really control Christian history after all."[37] Such polemic did not constitute the *meaning* of chosenness, but it reinforced the distinction between the elect community and the world outside, and contested the idea that God's chosen people may have been cast aside.

Medieval polemical literature also reflected older tropes that implicitly invoked chosenness by praising the morality, piety, and education of the Jews—with some interesting additions. In Joseph Kimchi's *Sefer haBerit* (The Book of the Covenant, twelfth-century Spain/Provence), he criticized Christians for failing to "observe the law of Grace" and for violence amongst themselves. He accused them of bowing down to images, encouraging immodesty among women, swindling travelers, working on holy days—and in each instance, the Jews represented the righteous foil for their behavior. He belittled Christianity for being a noncritical faith, putting into the mouth of the Christian interlocutor, "Whoever wishes to have faith should not scrutinize the words of Jesus." In response, the Jewish character challenged, "Why do you not subject your belief to reason in an honest manner? [Scripture] speaks to a mature man, one who knows how to scrutinize his faith so that he does not err."[38] Such a statement is wonderful for its embrace of self-critical faith, but simultaneously troubling for its portrait of the "other." In the fourteenth century, Simon b. Tzemach Duran authored *Keshet uMagen* (Bow and Shield), with arguments against both Christianity and Islam. Rather than portray Jesus in a negative light, he offered a Jewish version of his life and death, insisting that his followers perverted his intent; it was another effort at counterhistory. Over against Islam, he disparaged the hajj as pagan, contested Muhammad's status as a prophet, and refuted Muslim charges against Judaism involving textual distortion and abrogation. Qur'an, he stated, is full of confusion—a weak imitation of Torah.[39] Each of his critiques served to strengthen Jewish faith and identity.

The Middle Ages also produced a small but potentially poisonous strain of thought that saw election effected through biological difference between Jews and Gentiles. Yehuda haLevi (1075–1141, Spain) believed that only those born Jewish can achieve prophecy; they are a "different level of species of creation, a species angelic in nature"—the chosen of all humanity.[40] The Zohar, a mystical midrash, took the notion of genetic difference to a frightening extreme: Israel alone is imbued with the divine image; the spirit that dwells among the nations derives from *sitra achra* (literally "the other side"), the side of impurity or the cosmic demonic (1:20b (122)).

There were important countervoices. The prominent rabbinic leader, Saadia Gaon (c. 882–942, Egypt and Baghdad), warned the people not to misconstrue the idea of Israel as God's special possession; all nations belong to God and Israel's election does not imply exclusion of others.[41] Saadia's concerns were likely philosophical rather than rooted in love for neighbor; he was resistant to any limitations placed on the infinite God. Yet some medieval sages advocated a greater sense of mutuality with non-Jews. Menachem Meiri (1249–c. 1315, Provence), for example, rejected Talmudic laws that discriminated between Jews and non-Jews, arguing that the religions of his day were not to be categorized with pagan practices of antiquity. He taught that all people who sincerely profess an ethical religion are part of a greater spiritual Israel.[42]

One often finds ambivalence within the tradition, even within the thought of a single author. Moses Maimonides specifically rejected the idea that chosenness is biologically determined. He insisted that Jews become a nation of priests only through knowledge of God; obedience to Torah leads to virtue.[43] He also believed that Muslims and Christians play a significant role in God's redemptive plan, preparing "the whole world to worship God with one accord." Yet in the same text, he lamented the enormous harm wrought by Christianity: "Can there be a greater stumbling block than Christianity? All the prophets spoke of the Messiah as the redeemer of Israel and their savior who would gather their dispersed and strengthen their observance of the commandments. In contrast, Christianity causes Jews to be slain by the sword, their remnants to be scattered and dishonored, the Torah to be altered, and the majority of the world to err and serve a god other than YHWH."[44]

Maimonides exhibited conflicting responses to his Muslim milieu as well. On one hand, he was heavily influenced by Islamic theology, philosophy, and science. On the other, he was motivated by the forced conversion of Yemenite Jews to Islam to engage in polemic, saying Islam was invented by a madman.[45] Bewailing severe oppression and rebutting teachings used to attract Jews, he emphasized the preeminence of Judaism: "Remember that ours is the true and authentic Divine religion, revealed to us through Moses. . . . As Scripture says, *Only the Lord had a delight in thy fathers to love them and He chose their seed after them, even you above all peoples*" (Deut. 10:15).[46]

VIRTUES OF CHOSENNESS: A PLACE FOR PARTICULARITY, GOD'S ABIDING LOVE, A LIFE OF TORAH

From this complex and multivocal tradition, Judaism emphasizes three themes that communicate the continuing appeal and positive value of chosenness. It creates space for particularity, affirms God's abiding love, and inspires commitment to Torah. The first of these has historically been more controversial than it sounds. Reviewing the history of the concept, Walter Brueggemann concluded, "Indeed, one can make the case that the long, brutal history of anti-Semitism in Western culture is the venomous attempt to eradicate that claim of particularity upon which the Bible stands or falls."[47] According to Jonathan Sacks, Western culture has staged a continuous assault on particularism that can be traced back to Plato, with his world of forms where what is real and true must be universal and timeless.[48] It became more insidious once Kant explicitly tied the universal principle to morality as well; these two giants of Western philosophical tradition helped to shape Enlightenment notions that goodness, ethics, and truth must be universal. Kant also argued that Christianity "from the beginning bore within it the germ and the principle of the objective unity of the true and universal religious faith."[49] Consequently, modernity's history of religions was tendentiously scripted as a hierarchical progression from tribal to national to universal—leading many scholars and religious leaders to denigrate Judaism for its particular concern with the story of the Jewish people.[50]

Christianity and Islam were exalted for their universal aspirations even though, from a Jewish perspective, a desire to convert the world seems imperialistic. Sacks has described Tanakh as an anti-Platonic work. Moving from the universal to the particular, it begins with creation of the world and stories of humanity; these culminate in the Tower of Babel, where a unified purpose leads only to totalitarian pursuit of power. So God creates difference. Jewish particularity, bolstered by claims of chosenness, can defend the dignity of difference for all.[51]

Particularism is neither exclusivism nor parochialism. Moses Mendelssohn (1729–1786), an early voice of Jewish modernity, noted that the revelation on Sinai did not proclaim a universal philosophical truth. Instead, "I am YHWH your God who took you out of Egypt" (Exod. 20:2) evokes a particular relationship. "Judaism boasts of no exclusive revelation of eternal truths that are indispensable to salvation."[52] All peoples can discern such things in their own way. Torah merely conveys the story of one people with its God and how they endeavor to live into that relationship.

Jewish voices have largely echoed the approach of Tanakh, affirming both God's universal concern and a distinct role for the Jewish people. Philo put Judaism in conversation with Hellenistic philosophy, identifying as "Israel" all those who pursue knowledge of God through a philosophical quest. He maintained that Torah accorded with the best teachings of righteousness among the nations, yet it was also a particular expression as revealed to and embodied by the Jewish people.[53] Philo believed Jews had special merit, consecrated above the nations to serve as their "priests" (Exod. 19)—a chauvinistic view, but one that sought universal benefit to Israel's election.[54]

Modern expressions frequently emphasized the idea of chosenness as a mission to help the world. Kaufmann Kohler thought Judaism should "be the bearer of the most lofty truths of religion among mankind."[55] Leo Baeck (1873–1956) and other neo-Kantian Jewish thinkers focused on election as responsibility toward others, lived out through the people's experience of revelation: "The idea of election has as its unconditional correlation the idea of humanity."[56] While these claims risk presenting one's own people as an ethical or spiritual vanguard, they emphasize the crucial mutuality of blessing tracing back to Abraham.

Still, critics of Jewish particularism linked it negatively to the idea of chosenness. Ernest Jones, a Welsh psychologist, wrote in 1945, "Everything points to the fact that the basic lesson for the non-assimilation of the Jews is to be found in the peculiarly exclusive and arrogant nature of their religious beliefs, including that of having a special relationship with the divinity."[57] While such arguments are frequently a cover for antisemitism, they have been deeply woven into the cultural fabric of the West. It is only in the postmodern era that there has been broader appreciation for the value of difference, with its manifold particularisms. In turn, there is room for Jewish conceptions of chosenness that affirm the unique but not exclusive dimensions of Israel's relationship with God. Numerous Jewish and Christian scholars since the 1990s have written new analyses that preserve Jewish particularity within a pluralist, egalitarian perspective. Irving Greenberg, a modern orthodox rabbi, provides one example: "The chosen-people concept expresses the Jews' experience of being singled out by God's love. . . . If one has truly tasted the experience, one would be reluctant to lose that feeling by dissolving back into the mass. . . . Nor is the process reserved for us to the exclusion of everyone else. God's love—God's redemptive love—which is the basis of chosenness, is never the monopoly of any one people. . . . That cannot take away my unique experience or my feeling of uniqueness."[58]

The experience of God's abiding love is so central that it comprises a distinct focus of chosenness throughout Jewish tradition. Talmudic expressions abound: one passage proclaimed that Israel is so beloved, the Holy One went into exile with them (b. Meg. 29a).[59] Another professed, "You have made Me the unique object of your love in the world, and I make you the unique object of My love in the world" (b. Hag. 3a–b), bringing 1 Chronicles 17:21 as evidence: "Who is like Your people Israel, a nation unique on the earth?" The next verse continues: "You have established Your people Israel as Your very own forever, and You, YHWH, have become their God." As exile stretched into centuries and critics alleged that the Jews' suffering was a sign of God's rejection, rabbinic texts stressed the eternal nature of Israel's status regardless of appearances. Many Jews came to see their distinctive fate as evidence of God's election, both in their adversity and in their remarkable survival. The suffering of the nation was sometimes interpreted as punishment for transgression or chastisements of love, but it did not represent a permanent rupture in the relationship with God. "Even though the people sinned, they are still called Israel" (b. Sanh. 44a).[60] Historical trauma heightened the importance of chosenness within Jewish imagination, but God's love had always felt essential to the people's existence. The prophet Hosea understood it as the shield against utter destruction: "I fell in love with Israel when he was still a child. . . . How can I give you up, Ephraim? How can I surrender you, O Israel? . . . I have had a change of heart, all My tenderness is stirred" (Hosea 11:1, 8).

While this intensity of God's love is experienced as singular, the tradition affirms God's enduring affection for Israel alongside God's universal concern. Often they are viewed as interdependent. Commenting on the verse, "A land which YHWH your God looks after" (Deut. 11:12), an early rabbinic text asked: Does not God care for all the lands? The answer is that the special concern God has for the land of Israel is the catalyst of divine concern for all lands,[61] as God's special love for the people of Israel serves as the foundation of God's love for all of humanity (Sifre Deut. 40). Ethnocentric but not exclusive, the notion is echoed by R. Kendall Soulen, a contemporary Christian theologian: "The unsubstitutability of God's love for Israel is the guarantee of God's love toward all persons, elect and non-elect. The distinction between Jew and Gentile—far from indicating a limit or imperfection of God's love—testifies to God's willingness to engage all creation on the basis of divine passion."[62]

It is Torah study and praxis, however, that comprise the primary ground of election. Spread throughout rabbinic literature are teachings such as these: Why did the Blessed Holy One choose them? Because all the nations rejected Torah and refused to accept it, but Israel gladly chose the Blessed Holy One and His Torah" (Num. Rab. 14:10). "You captured My heart with one of your eyes" (Song 4:9), when you stood before Me at Mount Sinai and said, "All that YHWH has said, we will do and we will hearken" (Exod. 24:7, Song Rab. 4:21). It is not expected that the translation to human action will be perfect; atonement is built into the system and Yom Kippur is on the calendar every year. God's gracious initiative of love, however, can inspire the nation to become worthy through its living out and living into the divine instruction.

Jewish liturgy is explicit in linking Torah and chosenness. In one blessing, God's love is demonstrated through the revelation of Torah and commandments to the people; its conclusion states simply, "Blessed are You Adonai, who has chosen His people Israel in love." Another, recited before the public recitation of scripture, praises God for choosing the Jewish people by giving them Torah. Jewish embodiment of Torah's teachings is what makes the Jews special.

Torah is not perceived merely as an obligation, but also as a life-sustaining gift, a notion beautifully expressed in a parable that portrays Israel as a queen whose husband (i.e., God) has gone away to a distant land. The king's extended absence causes the neighbor-ladies (i.e., the other nations) to torment the queen by insisting that he is never coming back. Although sometimes driven to despair, she seeks comfort by reading her marriage contract (i.e., Torah). When the king eventually returns and expresses wonder that she had waited, she tells him about the power of the marriage contract to sustain her. Similarly, when the Jews read from the Torah, they are reassured by God's promise to make them fruitful, to maintain the covenant, to always walk among them. When redemption dawns, God will be amazed that they remained faithful and they will reply, "Master of the Universe, were it not for Your Torah which You gave to us, the nations would have annihilated us long ago" (Lam. Rab. 3).[63]

The sages believed that Torah study and observance were not only for the sake of Israel. They taught that Jews' embrace of Torah "made peace between God and the world," and is essential to the divine plan for creation (Song Rab. 7:1, Ruth Rab. Prol. 1). In the creation myth of sixteenth-century Lurianic kabbalah, every fulfillment of a mitzvah redeems a divine spark, helping to repair our fractured world—providing sacred purpose to minute acts of daily life.[64] As with the first call of Abraham, Israel's election is bound up with blessing for all the peoples of the earth, demonstrating both ethnocentricity and universal concern.

The sages also taught that Torah was given in the wilderness so that none could lay exclusive claim, and it was revealed in seventy languages so all could understand (Mek. Bahodesh 1). Midrashim that tell how God shopped the Torah to other nations first, but gave it to Israel because they said yes, reveal how Israel chose God as much as God chose Israel (Mek. Bahodesh 5, Sifre Deut. 343). Such an interpretation is simultaneously humble in claiming no intrinsic merit for the nation, and partisan in asserting they were the only ones willing to accept the obligations. Trying to be clever with intertextual associations, the authors unfortunately disparage other nations in supplying the reasons they refused. Again, construction of self is bound up with our conception of others, and no interpretation of chosenness is immune to the dangers of evaluating difference. Yet a different text imagines that Israel said yes only because God held Mt. Sinai over their heads, threatening to drop it on them if they refused (b. Avod. Zar. 2b). And another explains that God will surely be angrier at the one who accepts and does not follow through (Exod. Rab. 27:9), maintaining the posture of prophetic critique that spurs continual self-reflection and improvement.

Though not immune to bias and abuse, these memes of chosenness—a place for particularity, reassurance of God's abiding love, and a life of Torah—copy well throughout the history of Judaism. They provide meaning and pleasure, they help define a community, they shape some of Jewish civilization's founding values, and they conform to the multiple adaptations in our brain that sustain religious faith and practice.

CHAPTER 9

ELECTION IN CHRISTIANITY

NEW TESTAMENT

Within the New Testament we see a scriptural shift toward soteriological understanding of election and a more binary perspective—but these texts, too, are multivoiced. They incorporate many themes from Tanakh related to chosenness: (near) death of the beloved son, Davidic kingship, suffering on account of election, and the call to live righteously in covenantal faithfulness with God and the teachings of Torah.[1] Some elect individuals, like Mary, simply find favor with God (Luke 1:30). Jesus is especially marked as chosen (Luke 9:35), and a voice from heaven announces at his baptism, "You are My Son, whom I love" (Mark 1:11 NIV). Like the servant of God mentioned in Isaiah (Matt. 12:18ff), like the seed of Abraham (Gal. 3:16), his election represents God's initiative of love toward humanity and the world.

New contexts and new ideas, however, created the chemistry for metamorphosis. In his outreach to the Gentiles, Paul problematized the emphasis on Torah observance. Apocalyptic expectations and developing ideas regarding the afterlife, common to several expressions of Judaism in the late Second Temple period, profoundly impacted the young community of Jesus's disciples, as did Platonic hierarchies of the spiritual over the material world.[2] Early in the Jesus movement, election became powerfully linked to spiritual salvation. Salvation in Hebrew Bible generally refers to physical rescue (*yeshua*, available to all), and some New Testament texts do not specify its significance. When Paul writes to the church in Thessaloniki (2:13), "But we must always give thanks to God for you, brothers and sisters beloved by the Lord, because God chose you as the first fruits for salvation through sanctification by the Spirit and through belief in the truth," he does not define salvation (*soteria*). The passage in Ephesians 1:3–14 is similarly indefinite. Other texts, however, link salvation explicitly to the gift of eternal life, sometimes with an intimation of predestination. In Acts, Paul and Barnabas invoke Isaiah's charge to be a light to the nations as authorization for their conversionary mission: "For so the Lord has commanded us, saying, 'I have set you to be a light for the Gentiles, so that you may bring salvation to the ends of the earth.' When the Gentiles heard this, they were glad and praised the word of the Lord; and as many as had been destined for eternal life became believers" (13:47–8). With this emphasis, election addresses the crisis of human finitude.

While endowing election with different meaning, the New Testament still frames it in familiar terms, especially by claiming the mantle of Israel. In Romans 4, Paul proclaims, "It depends on faith, in order that the promise may rest on grace and be guaranteed to all [Abraham's] descendants, not only to the adherents of the law but also to those who share the faith of Abraham" (4:16). He is building the case for being elect without the Sinaitic covenant, since Abraham's special relationship with God preceded revelation of Torah, and he affirms that "the promise" is both for Jews and for all the followers of Jesus. Further along in Romans, Paul asserts the seemingly paradoxical beliefs that salvation is exclusively through faith in Jesus—and that the Jews are beloved regarding election, for the gifts of God are irrevocable (Rom. 9–11).[3] Yet Hebrews 8:13 mentions "a new covenant" and states that "God has made the first one obsolete. And what is obsolete and growing old will soon disappear." Mark 16:16 (generally considered a late addition) also announces a supersessionist doctrine: "Whoever believes and is baptized will be saved, but whoever does not believe will be condemned." What appears in some New Testament texts as a defensive posture, arguing for the legitimacy of its community's interpretation and observance, is wielded offensively in other passages to claim that those who accept Jesus as Christ are the true Israel. *They* are the chosen ones.

Many texts can be interpreted in diverse ways—e.g.,: "There is no longer Jew or Greek, there is no longer slave or free, there is no longer male and female; for all of you are one in Christ Jesus. And if you belong to Christ, then you are Abraham's offspring, heirs according to the promise" (Gal. 3:28–29). Modern Christians may receive Paul's teaching here as a liberative vision of equality, flattening differences that lead to conflict. Jews, on the other hand, often experience it as an attempt to erase Judaism.[4] Most likely, it was an appeal to Christian unity, not meant to indicate much of substance about the remainder of the Jewish community or the world. A similar concern lies behind Colossians 3; enfolding diverse identities into the body of the church leads to the compelling verse, "As God's chosen ones, holy and beloved, clothe yourselves with compassion, kindness, humility, meekness and patience" (Col. 3:12).[5]

The core of the New Testament canon witnesses to that moment in history when Christianity still understood itself as a type of Judaism and religious identities were very much in flux. Internal conflicts coarsened the discourse of difference.[6] In Galatians 4, for example, there is an allegory identifying those who embrace the Sinai covenant as Ishmael—in other words as children of the servant-wife Hagar, enslaved by their observance of Torah. Isaac, the "biological ancestor" of the Jews, represents instead the followers of Jesus, heir to the promise. Presumably Paul intends to discourage this Gentile community from thinking they must observe Jewish practices. In fleshing out the parable, however, he appears to strip Jews who reject Jesus of their election: "What does Scripture say? Cast out the slave woman and her son, for the son of the slave shall not inherit with the son of the free woman" (Gal. 4:30).[7]

While the Jesus movement differed from other Second Temple Judaisms by removing the mitzvot as an obligation of chosenness, attitudes toward "the Law" in New Testament are not universally negative.[8] After all, Jesus was an observant Jew. Luke 2 emphasizes how Mary and Joseph followed Torah instructions for circumcision and purification. Various passages portray the importance of just practice (James 2:18–26, Matt. 25's parable of the sheep and the goats). Even the famous verse in 2 Corinthians 3:6, "for the letter kills, but the spirit gives life," so often cited as a critique of legalism, can be understood to refer only to overly literal reading or observance that ignores spiritual intention.[9] The Apostolic Council made clear that the easing of required observance was designed to simplify the path for pagan converts (Acts 15). Yet Paul appears to develop a negative attitude toward the *nomos*, and his Epistle to the Galatians later became foundational for portraying the covenant of Torah—which the Jews believed gave meaning to their chosenness—as a prison and a curse (see 3:10–12, 19, 23). Thick in imagery from Tanakh, 1 Peter identifies the law as the cause of the Jews' fall and transfers the status of the elect to Jesus's scattered followers, giving them courage in the face of Roman persecution: "They stumble because they disobey the word, as they were destined to do. But you are a chosen race, a royal priesthood, a holy nation, God's own people, in order that you may proclaim the mighty acts of him who called you out of darkness into his marvelous light. Once you were not a people, but now you are God's people" (2:8–10).[10]

At times, New Testament appears to limit access to God as well as salvation.[11] When Ephesians 2:11–22 speaks of both Jew and Gentile having access to the Father by one spirit, it means through the particular path of Christianity. In John 14:6, Jesus announces, "I am the way, and the truth, and the life. No one comes to the Father except through me." Some contemporary commentators interpret it to mean that Jesus controls access but one need not be Christian to know God, or that Jesus simply seeks to reassure his disciples who were anxious about his imminent departure. Like Jesus's teaching in Matthew 7:7—"Knock and the door shall be opened for you"—it signals God's commitment to make a path for the faithful.[12] Yet the verse in John is frequently interpreted as an exclusivist theology of religions, and John 15 speaks of Jesus as the true vine and God as the vine-grower: anyone who does not abide in Christ is thrown away like a barren branch, tossed into the fire and burned. 2 Thessalonians 1:6–9 also claims that those who do not know God and obey the gospel of Jesus will suffer eternal destruction.[13] Such passages reduce Kaminsky's "three categories" (elect, non-elect, and anti-elect) to two.

Competing with other streams of Judaism for converts made it critical to demonstrate the superiority of the new covenant and the efficacy of its election.[14] Polemic was an effective tool to undermine those who made contradictory claims, stimulating ferocious denunciation of the unconverted Jewish community.[15] Pharisees receive particular rebuke, as in the seven woes of Matthew 23. Like Tanakh's polemic against the Canaanites, New Testament's assault on the Pharisees reveals the special hostility provoked when delineating an other who is too-much-like-us.[16] The disciple circle surrounding Jesus and the proto-rabbinic community of Pharisees each presented a reform platform that sought to distill essential religious values through close reading of scripture and the charism of their leaders. Yet all "the Jews" were vilified: according to the Gospel of John, Jesus calls them children of the devil, not of God (8:43–4). In Acts 7, Stephen testifies

before the Sanhedrin that the children of Israel repeatedly rebelled against
Moses. He claims they are stiff-necked, uncircumcised of heart, always opposing the Holy Spirit, and that they persecuted the prophets, killed John
the Baptist, and betrayed Jesus to the Roman authorities. Several of these
charges are repeated in 1 Thessalonians, which then concludes: "The wrath
of God has come upon them at last" (2:16).[17] The early Christian community, still struggling against Roman oppression, could not have known how
devastating this rhetoric of othering would become after they held the reins
of imperial power.

Many condemnations of the Jews within New Testament draw from
self-critical portions of Tanakh, but read with a "schism of judgment and
promise." Rosemary Radford Ruether lamented, "By applying prophetic
judgment to 'the Jews' and messianic hope to 'the Church,' Christianity
deprived the Jews of their future. They also denied to the Jews the record
of their greatest moral accomplishment, the breakthrough from ideological
religion to self-critical faith. By the same token, the Church deprived itself
of the tradition of prophetic self-criticism. . . . Prophetic faith was converted into self-glorification and uncritical self-sanctification."[18]

Although the schism deepened over time, there *are* important cautionary notes to the emerging church communities within New Testament. Paul warns followers, for instance, not to be arrogant as inheritors of
election; they too might lose it (Rom. 11:20–21). Jesus teaches against self-
righteousness (Matt. 7:1–5); James counsels against presumptions of divine favoritism and critiques selfish ambition disguised as religious leadership (2:1–13, 3:1–18). These warnings echo the concerns of the prophets in
Tanakh as vital articulations of self-critical faith. There are also more embracing universalist messages, as in 1 Timothy 4:10: "We have put our hope
in the Living God, who is the savior of all men and especially of those who
believe." The diversity of voices leads to intense debates about Christian
theology and leaves open inclusive possibilities for reading.

While New Testament displays substantial problems with difference,
conquest is less of an issue: the entire collection is composed and redacted
when the elect wield no political power. In fact, the historical context of
imperial Rome stimulates religious teachings of peace and prophetic critique of oppression. Jesus's parables can be read as subversive challenges
to unmask the destructive dynamics of domination.[19] The beatitudes in
Matthew 5 and the tribute to love in 1 Corinthians 13 challenge Roman

hegemony by proclaiming the spiritual power of the poor and the meek. They glorify righteousness and kindness rather than conquest: "Blessed are the poor in spirit, for theirs is the kingdom of heaven. . . . Blessed are the meek, for they will inherit the earth. Blessed are those who hunger and thirst for righteousness, for they will be filled. Blessed are the merciful, for they will receive mercy" (Matt. 5:3–7).

It would be a mistake to imagine there is no embrace of redemptive violence in New Testament, but it generally relates to the chosen ones as victims—crucifixion in the gospels and martyrdom in the book of Acts. As Calvin Roetzel commented, "The *modus vivendi* of the elect is suffering."[20] While imagery in Ephesians 6:10–17 depicts victorious combat, it is a *spiritual* battle. Even Jesus's ominous word that he has come not to bring peace but a sword reads as rhetorical violence (Matt. 10.34). Conquest is eschatological, especially as expressed in the book of Revelation's martial discourse.[21] It is not until Christianity becomes the religion of empire that the dangerous potion of conquest and election begins to seethe.

THE DEEPENING OF DIFFERENCE

In the history of Christian exegesis, we see that the ultimate fate of the unchosen was a critical issue for the early Church. Clement of Alexandria, Origen, and Gregory of Nyssa posited that everyone can be restored to friendship with God (*apokatastasis*); punishment may endure for a long time, but God is victorious over sin and death. All will finally share in the grace of salvation—conscribing the dangerous ramifications of election.[22] Even Cyprian's (third century) classic statement, *extra ecclesium nulla salus* (outside of the church, no salvation), did not originally mean to exclude non-Christians from divine grace; rather, it was directed as a chastisement to Christians who refused to submit to the bishops' authority. While the idea of universal salvation enjoyed popularity for a time, many came to believe that it compromised divine justice and the centrality of faith. It was ruled contrary to Church doctrine at the Council of Constantinople in 543. There nonetheless remained a tradition of *apokatastasis* throughout the history of Christian thought, especially among mystics and more broadly since the Renaissance.[23] Self-critical voices like that of St. Isaac the Syrian (seventh century) also limited the dangers of election in other ways; he asserted that the idea of eternal punishment is incompatible with a loving God, and encouraged compassion for all humanity regardless of faith.[24]

Another argument addressed the merits of election. Augustine explained: they were not chosen because of their goodness (either demonstrated or foreseen by God), because they could not be good if they were not chosen. They were not chosen because they believed, because they could not believe if they were not chosen. Grace is not grace if we maintain the priority of merit.[25] Calvin echoed this concept of unconditional election, accentuating divine glory rather than the vindication of one human being over another—dampening tendencies toward chauvinism.

Yet there are also examples that illustrate election's dangerous division between us and them. Damage was often done by erasure, taking over the status and scripture of the Jewish community. Church Fathers consistently reinforced the notion that Christians had become God's elect: "True spiritual Israel," Justin Martyr (100–165 CE) called "those who have been led to God by this crucified Christ."[26] Magnifying hermeneutics evident within the gospels and epistles, they saw Jesus prefigured everywhere in the "Old" Testament: he is the seed of Abraham, recipient of the divine promise.[27] He is Isaac, the beloved son bound for sacrifice.[28] He is Moses, extending his arms like a cross to prevail against Amalek.[29] He is Isaiah's suffering servant, chosen by God.[30] The commandments were also understood as figures that presage the coming of Christ. Circumcision, for instance, was read as a symbol for removing one's fleshly nature, fulfilled in Jesus's resurrection that allows the elect to transcend physical existence.[31]

Exegetes believed the church was similarly prefigured to highlight her chosen status, and began to read "carnal" Israel (the original biblical community identified in New Testament as the Jews) as a type, a foil for the spiritual Israel that arose in Jesus's wake.[32] The church is signified by Abel, with the preferred offering of faith—rather than Cain, who represents the Jews with their earthly observances.[33] She is the family of Noah, saved by water and wood, just as Christians are saved by the waters of baptism and the wood of the cross.[34] Typological exegesis is extensive in patristic literature, and Church Fathers frequently portrayed the Jews with their minds veiled because they did not find intimations of Christian gospel in their own scripture.[35] (Nonetheless, Ephraem, Origen, Jerome, and others hired Jewish teachers for text study.) In remaking the story of Israel into the story of Jesus and his followers, the interpreters authenticated their identity as God's chosen people.

This theology of replacement, also known as supersession, had a tremendous impact on Jews and Judaism.[36] It was Augustine who provided a theological rationale to explain the continuation of Judaism after the gospel theoretically rendered the Jewish covenant obsolete. He affirmed that God chose Israel and gave them the law for their benefit. Yet Jews remain in what Augustine viewed as a fossilized form in order to serve as witnesses to the truth of Christianity; they must live in misery to demonstrate that there is no salvation without Christ. Viewed as Cain, they are punished for their crime and doomed to exile, but also protected by God with the "mark" of their continued observance. For this precarious role, he found the perfect prooftext: "Slay them not, lest My people forget; scatter them in Your might" (Ps. 59:12).[37] As Augustine's strategy became normative, it promoted a certain tolerance but it also painted Jews as the quintessential other, whose fate was dangerously woven into the narrative of Christian vindication. The post-Nicene Church Fathers saw confirmation of divine election in their ascendancy to empire, and they required the Jews' suffering to prove it as well.

Polemical literature dealing with Judaism included a growing list of calumnious accusations that came to be known as the teaching of contempt.[38] David Nirenberg identified "the vast stockpiles of anti-Jewish stereotypes" as "the product of conflicts between Christians, conflicts in which each party strove to claim the mantle of 'true Israel' for itself, and to clothe the other in the robe of 'Jew.'" The figures were rhetorical rather than real Jews. Denigrating them and their faith with fervor became a demonstration of credibility; as Erasmus and Luther quipped during a much later sectarian struggle, "If hatred of Jews makes the Christian, then we are all plenty Christian."[39]

The tone of anti-Jewish discourse grew more strident once Christianity was officially recognized within the Roman Empire, and subsequently became the religion of the state. Adversus Judaeos, John Chrysostom's series of sermons delivered in Antioch in 386–387 CE, painted a particularly hateful portrait. Challenging Christians who seemed attached to elements of Jewish practice and worship, he called the synagogue a dwelling of demons (also a theater, a whorehouse, a den of thieves, and haunt of wild animals) and later declared Jewish souls full of demons also. He identified Jews as "the common disgrace and infection of the whole world" and urged Christians not to exchange even a simple greeting with them in the marketplace.

Within the first sermon alone, he accused them of overpowering lust, plundering, covetousness, abandonment of the poor, theft, dishonesty in business, and more. He deemed them ready for slaughter, citing the end of a parable in Luke 19:27: "As for these enemies of mine who did not want me to be king over them—bring them here and slaughter them in my presence." Scholars contextualize his remarks within the increasingly fervent drive for Christian unity and the genre of *psogos*, a no-holds-barred polemical style. Unfortunately, however, accusations like these became staples in the history of antisemitism, eventually bursting the bounds of Christianity to infect other cultures as well.

Hostility did not remain in the verbal realm. There were physical assaults and discriminatory legislation, including restrictions against Jews proselytizing, intermarrying, owning slaves, building new synagogues, practicing law, serving in the imperial administration, testifying against a Christian, receiving public honor, or holding office.[40] Some of these disabilities extended to all individuals who were not Christian according to current orthodoxy, but Jews served as the essential Other for construction of the elect Christian self. In later periods, persecution grew to include prohibitions against owning land, exclusion from many trades, forced disputations, public burnings of the Talmud, identifying garb, ghettoization, expulsions, libels, and pogroms.

The precise relationship between rhetorical and actual violence, or polemic and discriminatory legislation, is difficult to discern. This study assumes only that which is in direct evidence: the images were used to justify actions against the "other." The edict of expulsion from Spain in 1492, for example, claimed that Jews and Judaizing corrupted the faith of the elect.[41] As Jerusha Rhodes observed, "While there is not always a necessary connection between negative depictions of religious "others" and intolerant actions, at the very least negative depictions can be used as fuel for already kindled fires."[42]

After the rise of Islam, there was a new enemy, one with universal theological and imperial ambitions to rival Christendom's. According to Muslim sources, the encounter did not begin this way. Early biographies of Muhammad record him dispatching a group of followers to take refuge from Quraysh persecution by going to the Christian king in Abyssinia. The monarch was particularly impressed by Qur'an's teaching about Jesus and offered them protection.[43] Christian records address a slightly later period, penned by those in the East who lived in territory captured by advancing Muslim armies. Having perceived Christian conquest as a sign of divine election, they grappled with the theological implications of a rapidly growing Islamic empire. The first instinct was self-critical, a temporary scourge meant to purify the Christian community, or a sign of the imminent apocalypse.[44] Then Christian leaders began composing apologetics to defend their scripture and doctrine against charges of *taḥrif* (textual or interpretive distortion), idolatry, and irrationality.

There was also substantial production of polemic. John of Damascus (676–749) contested the religion of the "Ishmaelites" as another in the long line of Christian heresies, a forerunner to the Antichrist.[45] The ninth-century Risâlat al-Kindi defended doctrines challenged by Islam, such as the Trinity, and presented Muhammad as an oversexed, materialistic idolater who enriched himself through trade, raiding, and marriage to a wealthy patron. He claimed that Muhammad pretended to be a prophet in order to rule over his tribe, and that Qur'an was a product of satanic law composed by Muhammad. Rites such as washing before prayer and fasting during Ramadan were presented as useless efforts to purify the body while the soul remained corrupt.[46] Again, self and other were mutually constructed; each critique was designed to highlight the superiority of Christian scripture, theology, and praxis. Such works were written for Christian readers to confirm their status as God's elect, even as they were subject to Muslim rule. "Denigration of the other can be used to defend one's own intellectual construction of the world."[47]

It is evident in art as well. Leaving aside images that demonized Muslims and Jews as monstrous or damned,[48] we examine instead the beautiful and disturbing statuary of the thirteenth-century Strasbourg Cathedral. The Church is represented by a noble woman, staff and chalice in her hands, crown upon her head, looking boldly into the future. The Synagogue is also a woman, but she holds a broken spear, the tablets of divine instruction hanging limply at her side. She is gazing down—or she would be, except that she is blindfolded. Gentler variations still deployed Synagoga to reveal Ecclesia's destiny. An ivory tablet from the Bamberg Cathedral (c. 870) shows a crowned Synagoga seated in front of the Temple, with the earth in her hands. There is no humiliation, yet Ecclesia steps up to take possession of the office and rank of her predecessor as determined in Christian salvation history. A window in the abbey church of St.

Denis (twelfth century) illuminates an eschatological Concordia confirming Christian election: Jesus stands with arms outstretched so that his body
becomes a cross, one hand on the head of the Church and the other on the
head of the Synagogue, having removed her blindfold.[49]

There were relatively sympathetic portrayals of Jews and Muslims that
humanized the "other," like Peter Abelard's poignant lament set into the
mouth of a Jew: "Whoever thinks that we shall receive no reward for continuing to bear so much suffering through our loyalty to God must imagine
that God is extremely cruel. Indeed, there is no people which has ever
been known or even believed to have suffered so much for God . . . and it
should be granted that there can be no rust of sin which is not burnt up in
the furnace of this affliction. . . . Nowhere but heaven may we enter safely"
(*Dialogue of a Philosopher with a Jew and a Christian*).[50]

In a sermon on Susannah, Abelard admired the Jewish people's commitment to teaching sacred texts to all their sons, showing up Christian
devotion.[51] James the Conqueror, a central figure in the thirteenth-century
Reconquista to establish Castilian rule over the Iberian Peninsula, expressed admiration for the "Saracens" and promised to protect their religious freedom; he also refused the order of Pope Clement IV to expel Jews
and Muslims. Still bound up with Christian election, these actions formed
the backdrop of his self-portrait as a righteous crusader for the true faith.[52]
An Italian Dominican friar, Riccoldo da Montecroce (1242–1320), admitted
how the gardens, architecture, wealth, and learning of Baghdad enthralled
him—yet he was distraught that God would allow Saracen subjugation of
God's elect.[53]

And the dangers of othering continue to lurk, easily redeployed. In
1523, Martin Luther composed an essay, "That Jesus Christ Was Born a
Jew," arguing that Jews had not converted in large numbers because they
were treated poorly and shown only a popish mockery of Christianity: "If
I had been a Jew and had seen such dolts and blockheads govern and teach
the Christian faith, I would sooner have become a hog than a Christian.
They have dealt with the Jews as if they were dogs rather than human beings; they have done little else than deride them and seize their property."[54]
When Jews failed to embrace Luther's reformed tradition, however, he
composed *On the Jews and Their Lies* (1543).[55] Abandoning the evangelical
project with the Jews, Luther advocated "merciful severity": burning down
their homes and synagogues and stripping them of legal protections.

SPIRITUAL AND PHYSICAL CONQUEST

The implications of empire shaped Christianity's development from the outset. As Catherine Keller commented, "Whether colonized or colonizing, Christianity has not existed in abstraction from empire. There is no pre-colonial Christianity."[56] Before it became the religion of Rome, before it was even a licit religion, it began to contemplate a different sort of conquest. Hellenism's universalist philosophy helped solidify its vision of a single universal faith: the community was elected to bring the whole world to God through Christ.[57] Pagan polemicists skewered Christianity for its global pretensions, given its late and provincial origins, carried along by "poor country bumpkins" (Porphyry's late third-century *Against the Christians*). They invoked what is currently called "the scandal of particularity." If Christ is the way of salvation, what about all those souls who perished before his arrival, and those in the far reaches of the empire? How can God leave so many people out?

The idea of spiritual conquest developed in early Christian literature. Origen (182–254 CE) and Eusebius (263–339 CE), for instance, argued that Christ's "wonderful sojourn among men synchronized with Rome's attainment of the acme of power" (Eusebius, *Demonstration of the Gospel* 3.7) so that the apostles could successfully reach and convert a broad swath of humanity. "How else was it possible for the Gospel doctrine of peace, which does not permit men to take vengeance even upon enemies, to prevail throughout the world . . . ?" (Origen, *Against Celsus* 2.30). This distinction between spiritual and military conquest was important. Prominent voices in the early church questioned Christian involvement in imperial warfare due to its entanglement with Roman army religion and the shedding of blood. Election required a different path.[58] Although scholars no longer maintain that the pre-Constantine church represented a uniformly pacifist tradition, there is a significant record of ethical and theological struggle with religiously inspired political conquest.[59]

The seesaw of power between pagans and Christians in the centuries before and after Constantine left behind a discourse rife with irony and the seeds of contemporary pluralist argument, in which each side challenged the imposition of spiritual and physical domination. When Christians were being persecuted, Lactantius (240–320) wrote a passionate brief for freedom of religious conscience, challenging the pagan authorities' claim that they sought to promote Christian welfare: "Do they then strive to effect this by conversation, or by giving some reason? By no means; rather, they endeavor to effect it by force and tortures. O wonderful and blind infatuation! It is thought that there is a bad mind in those who endeavor to preserve their faith, but a good one in executioners." He proclaimed that "nothing is so much a matter of free-will as religion." Without it, religion ceases to exist (*Divine Institutes* 5.19).

As Christianity gradually became the official religion of the Roman Empire, however, the tables were turned. Pagan arguments that religious diversity should be tolerated because humans cannot attain perfect truth by a single road—and that human diversity is testimony to God's desire for multiplicity—mostly fell on deaf ears.[60] Evangelism readily translated to the political and military realms. "Christianity did not invent Roman universalism," admitted Alexei Sivertsev. But by combining it with Tanakh's messianic universalism and early Christian apocalyptic expectations, "Late Antique Christianity succeeded in producing a comprehensive and coherent ideological framework that tied together the destiny of imperial Rome with that of Christ's *kerygma*."[61] Election was linked to conquest as religious and political leaders imagined seizing the whole world for Christ.

Beginning in the fourth century, there were state-sponsored and independent persecutions of non-Christians. Pagan worship was banned, its vestiges in imperial functions were erased, and temples were razed.[62] When a group of monks plundered the home of a pagan magnate their leader, Shenoute (388–466), declared, "There is no crime for those who have Christ."[63] There were synagogue burnings, assaults and forced conversions—even though Judaism officially remained a licit religion. In 418 CE, Severus of Minorca sent a letter to his fellow bishops urging that they follow his lead in attacking Jewish communities "so the whole breadth of the earth might be ablaze with the flame of love" and consume the Jewish "forest of unbelief."[64] Thinkers like Ambrose and Augustine constructed a "just war theory" that authorized violence to advance the purposes of religion.[65] Election's capacity for self-justification makes it more menacing.

There were also voices that complicated Christian thinking about conquest. Sulpicius Severus (363–425) and Paulinus of Nola (359–431) continued to express concern about military service, even in a Christian army. Canon law prohibited clergy from becoming soldiers and vice versa, and there were significant rites of penance for shedding blood no matter what the cause.[66] While imperial legislation often magnified restrictions on non-Christians,

emperors also had a stake in political and economic stability, so they sometimes rescinded or declined to enforce oppressive measures. In 598 CE,
Pope Gregory I declared papal protection against forced conversion of Jews
and wanton destruction of synagogues. When protections were violated,
regional church officials sometimes mitigated the violence. As the Crusaders of 1096 viciously attacked Jewish communities along the Rhine and
Danube en route to the Holy Land, for example, Bishop John in Speyer
and Archbishop Ruthard in Mainz took steps to protect the local Jewish
populations. Appalled by the wanton violence, Pope Calixtus II issued another protective order for the Jews (c. 1120), forbidding forced conversion,
physical harm, confiscation of property, and the disturbing of festivals or
cemeteries. During the Second Crusade (1145–1149), Bernard of Clairvaux
issued letters condemning attacks against the Jews in Rhineland communities and even visited the region in part to stem the virulently anti-Jewish
preaching of the monk Ralph.[67]

The Crusades represented the Christian empire's most dramatic engagement in physical conquest. Monastic orders were militarized, including
not only the Knights Templar but also some that were originally founded
to address poverty and illness. As usual, religion was not the only factor
in justifying conquest: economic and political fears, images of physical
violation, and demonizing the enemy all stimulated desire for battle. Sides
were drawn by religious division, however, and rhetoric evoked strains of
chosenness to motivate the troops. Pope Urban II issued a call to arms at
Clermont (1095), reportedly addressing the Catholic Franks as a "race beloved and chosen by God." He argued that the Crusade was a holy war, commanded by Christ, capable of remitting sins and guaranteeing salvation.[68]

Medieval Christian voices that questioned the sanctity of religious violence were rare. Even exceptional figures such as Francis of Assisi (1182–
1226), recognized for his expansive compassion for all of God's creatures,
supported the Crusades.[69] A dramatic exception was Nicholas of Cusa
(1401–1464), describing his vision after the fall of Constantinople in 1453:
"The King of heaven and earth stated that the sad news of the groans of the
oppressed had been brought to him from this world's realm: because of religion many take up arms against each other and by their power either force
men to renounce their long-practiced tradition or inflict death on them.
There were many bearers of these lamentations from all the earth."[70] It is
an outstanding example of self-critical religious perspective, even though

his sensitivity to the suffering did not change the geopolitical realities. It was only forty years later that Pope Alexander VI issued *Inter caetera*, with its doctrine of discovery to legitimate Catholic claims to lands occupied by non-Christians.

DISTILLING THE VALUES OF ELECTION: GOD'S INITIATIVE OF LOVE AND EMULATING CHRIST

Despite the evident difficulties, election prompts compelling themes within Christian thought—just as we saw with Jewish ideas of chosenness. One is its emphasis on God's faithful effort toward restoration and reconciliation. Growing out of dynamic and multivocal possibilities, the now-familiar doctrine was framed by Augustine: Adam and Eve's sin in the garden transformed human nature, causing every person to be born in a depraved state, a *massa damnata* (condemned crowd). It is God's grace to save the elect, available through faith in Jesus as Christ, enabling these individuals to attain eternal life. The controversial question of who is saved tends to obscure the fundamental notion that election represents God's continuing initiative of love. By drawing sin and salvation into the concept of election, Christianity addresses two existential human crises—our failings and our finitude—with faith in God's ongoing efforts to help us overcome them.

Those who see orthodox teachings around sin and salvation as rife with their own problems may discover more elastic conceptions in Christian tradition than they imagine. When Irenaeus introduced the concept of original sin, he did not interpret Genesis 3 as a cosmic fall and did not believe that humanity was stripped of its moral freedom as a result of Adam's sin.[71] He, Clement of Alexandria, and others who debated the Gnostics specifically challenged the inevitability of sin, choosing instead to emphasize human freedom and moral responsibility. Building controversy surrounding the teachings of Pelagius, however, prompted the Councils of Carthage (418) and Orange (529) to confirm the Augustinian teaching of original sin as the orthodox position.[72] Even so, the Eastern Church developed the theology in less absolute terms, and the Roman Catholic Church recorded countervoices. Abelard's commentary on Romans, for instance, maintained that humanity inherits Adam's punishment of mortality, but not a state of sinfulness.[73] Whether sin is seen as something one does or a condition into which one is born, Jesus's incarnation represents God's continuous effort to make forgiveness possible: "In him we have redemption through his blood, the forgiveness of sins, in accordance with the riches of God's grace" (Eph. 1:7 NIV).

The linkage of salvation to election need not focus on who gets a ticket to heaven. Brock and Parker argued that many Church Fathers considered multiple aspects of "paradise"—material and spiritual, personal and collective, awaited and fulfilled—including the flourishing of God's creation.[74] Themes of communal and historical salvation, traceable within New Testament and early Christian writings, only slowly gave way to an emphasis on individual and spiritual possibilities. And still God's concern for the redemption of history could not be wholly obscured.

Even in the modern age, when individualistic, otherworldly concepts seem predominant, numerous Christian theologians resisted the trend by reclaiming the life-affirming, historically embedded notions of salvation history and focusing on collective redemption. Albrecht Ritschl (1822–1889) rejected the idea that God chooses particular individuals for salvation.[75] Karl Barth identified the covenant with Israel as the beginning of God's work as consummator of creation, working with humanity through the textures of history to advance God's purposes.[76] Numerous Christian voices today affirm theologically pluralist ideas of salvation, persuaded that God's initiative of love for creation has no bounds.[77]

A second essential theme is identification with the incarnate and crucified Christ. Candida Moss described it as a "web of mimetic practices that writers and church leaders sought to inculcate in their audiences and congregations."[78] Origen, for instance, wrote in his commentary on Romans 6:11 of being "dead to sin" and "alive to God" in imitation of Christ, through wisdom, peace, righteousness, and sanctification. Other Church Fathers invoked the model of Jesus to promote diverse virtues such as patience and obedience (Tertullian, "On Patience," ch. 3–4), or forgiveness (Chrysostom, "Homily 17 on Ephesians"). For early Christians, often persecuted by the Roman Empire, suffering became the mode of identification most evocative of election. Allusions to suffering of the elect community in New Testament developed in patristic literature into a thick discourse of martyrology, where the chosen most fully emulate the salvific sacrifice of Jesus by offering up their lives for their faith.[79]

Christian art frequently depicts martyrs and holy men in the pose of the Crucified One. Peter Brown noted, "This identified him not only with the sufferings of Christ, but also with the unmoved constancy of his election and the certainty of his triumph."[80] Subverting the idea of martyrs as victims, Christianity sought to signal victory over persecutors and over death itself. In "The Martyrdom of Polycarp," for example, Polycarp was reportedly impervious to the flames so the executioner stabbed him; a dove flew out from his body, along with blood that extinguished the fire, "and all the crowd marveled that there was such a difference between the unbelievers and the elect."[81] Glorification of these martyrs at times made the lure of self-sacrifice too strong, and Church Fathers had to caution their followers not to seek out death. More broadly, the contemporary theologian Jürgen Moltmann warned, "The cross is not and cannot be loved."[82] Jesus's crucifixion represented a courageous facing of suffering and confrontation with death, but not its celebration.

After Christianity became magnified rather than marginalized by imperial power, the sacrificial posture of the elect became more of an *intra*faith issue, but it remained linked to chosenness and the imitation of Christ. Anabaptists in colonial America provide a rather late example: frequently persecuted by established Christian authorities, they viewed their status in eschatological terms that rendered their suffering purposeful: "Even though persecution and martyrdom should not be actively sought and would never merit salvation, they were regarded as prominent signs of election and the surest way of 'imitating' Christ."[83]

While contemporary aspirations to emulate Jesus often focus more on his tending to "the least of these" (Matt. 25), suffering is still recognized as a risk of discipleship. Dietrich Bonhoeffer asserted that the quest for truth in societies that lie, or for goodness in cultures that reward duplicity, necessarily entails suffering, which discipleship endows with meaning.[84] James Cone's liberation theology focuses on the election of the African American community, chosen not to imitate Christ in redemptive suffering, but to take on the responsibility of freedom—willing to stand against all things that oppose liberation. It involves suffering because it requires a confrontation with evil, but suffering is not its purpose. Noting that Hebrew Bible devotes enormous attention to freeing the Israelites from slavery and to protecting vulnerable persons, he claimed that "God's election of Israel and incarnation in Christ reveal that the liberation of the oppressed is a part of the innermost nature of God. Liberation is not an afterthought, but the essence of divine activity."[85] The elect are called to reflect this commitment in their very being.

Even refined concepts of election cannot permanently rid themselves of dangerous dross, but themes emerge from historical Christian tradition that work against ideas of conquest and othering. Divine grace can inspire humility. Mission, evangelism, and witness can be reimagined so that they are no longer bound to imposing Western or Christian dominance. Some leaders have argued that mission "ought primarily to mean being resolutely but sensitively Christian in the presence of others; evangelism ought basically to mean responding, when asked, why Christians believe and act as they do; witnessing ought most fundamentally to mean the living of a compassionate Christian life."[86] One can identify with Christ, not in judgment but in goodness. Conviction of God's redemptive power can expand one's vision of salvation, communal as well as individual, invested in this world and the next, and resisting division of the world into the saved and the damned. Chosenness thus becomes a central paradigm for imagining God in ongoing relationship with the world and inspires the elect toward a divinely ordained purpose.

CHAPTER 10

DIVINE GUIDANCE IN ISLAM

QUR'AN

Similar to the New Testament, Qur'an presents itself as a fulfillment and continuation of previous revelations. Qur'an 46:12, for example, asserts that it confirms the book of Moses in an Arabic tongue. Passages explicitly affirm Allah's election of significant figures from Jewish and Christian scriptures, frequently describing some meritorious quality as they are singled out for divine favor and guidance: "And we bestowed upon him [Abraham] Isaac and Jacob, each We guided [*h-d-y*]. And We guided Noah before, and among his progeny David, Solomon, Job, Joseph, Moses and Aaron—thus do We recompense the virtuous. And Zachariah, John, Jesus, and Elias— each was among the righteous. And Ishmael, Elisha, Jonah and Lot—each We favored [*f-d-l*] above the worlds. And from their fathers, and their progeny and their brethren, We chose [*j-b-y*] them and guided them unto a straight path" (6:84–87 *SQ*). Guidance is key—as when Allah chooses and guides Adam after he sins, suggesting that election expresses God's decision to set him on a particular path (20:122). God's instruction is itself a sign of favor: "Allah augments those who are guided by giving them greater guidance" (19:76).[1]

Other dimensions of election are familiar from earlier scriptures, as when Abraham is described as a friend (*khalil*) of God (4:125), or it is acknowledged that adherents may suffer on account of their faith (85:1–11). This concern was most acute during the Meccan period, when the newly forming Muslim community was persecuted by tribal authorities. Qur'an invokes historical tribulations of earlier elect individuals—Noah, Abraham,

Joseph, Jesus, and others—as a source of solace and strength.[2] The chosenness of the people Israel is mentioned a number of times in Qur'an, generally connected to the revelation of Torah; blessings of land, prophets and divine favor become reminders of their ongoing obligation to obedience, as well as calls for faith in Muhammad as the seal of the prophets (2:40–47, 121–124; 5:19–21; 17:104–108). Summonses to the Muslim community similarly involve covenant and commandment: "Truly God commands justice, virtue, and giving to kinsfolk, and He forbids indecency, wrong, and rebelliousness. . . . Fulfill the pact of God when you have pledged it" (16:90–91 *SQ*).

Allah may reward faithful submission with material provision, aid in conflict, forgiveness of sins and other blessings. *Falah*, a broad promise of success that appears frequently (2:5, 3:104, 5:35, 22:77–78, 23:1–11, 30:38), can indicate flourishing in this world and the next. Although a promise of afterlife is not the singular consequence of election, images of paradise are infused throughout Qur'an: "For those who believe and do right actions, We will admit them into Gardens with rivers flowing under them, remaining in them timelessly, forever and ever" (4:57). One may be "saved" from the fires of hell (19:72, 39:71, 61:10–14, 70:14), but salvation (*najat*) has a semantic range closer to that found in Tanakh; it does not connote salvation from sin. It is also important to note that chosenness does not automatically earn one a spot in the Garden: divine freedom remains absolute. Allah's grace is abundant but there is often a provisional word regarding expectations of reward: "Obey Allah and the Messenger so that hopefully you will gain mercy" (3:132; see also 6:155, 28:67, 48:14).

Collectively, the passages paint election as Allah's commitment to guide an individual or group toward righteous faithfulness, providing an opportunity to attain success, God's favor, and promise of eternal reward. It does not appear to be limited to one religious group. Repeated rebelliousness can prompt Allah to break off such providential guidance (e.g., 46:10), however, and the Peoples of the Book are portrayed as prime examples. While Qur'an affirms the authenticity of Jewish, Christian, and other monotheistic revelations (2:136, 3:84), it charges that religious leaders have distorted them with their own teaching (*tahrif*) and their scriptures do not correctly represent divine will.[3] In addition, the communities fail to uphold their covenantal commitments (2:75–78, 3:75–79, 4:44–52, 5:12–15). Islam stakes its supersessionary claim on this ground; its sacred text represents God's continuing efforts to guide the peoples by offering a new revelation that purportedly transmits divine teaching without error. Those who embrace it are described as models of superior behavior: "You are the best nation ever to be produced before mankind. You enjoin the right, forbid the wrong and believe in Allah" (3:110). Those who honor and aid "the unlettered Prophet" are the ones who will have success (7:157).

The hermeneutic of abrogation (*naskh*) is also important in considering Muslim supersessionism: "Whenever we abrogate an ayat or cause it to be forgotten, We bring one better than it or equal to it. Do you not know that Allah has power over all things?" (2:106). One of the core prooftexts for *naskh*, this verse is sometimes understood to refer to the displacement of a previous message (i.e., scripture) or religion, not simply a previously revealed instruction to Muhammad. The implications and extent of abrogation, however, have been continuously debated within Muslim discourse.[4]

Although several passages position the Muslim community as the new elect, there are also interpretations that question such an assumption. For example, most commentators understood 5:3 to affirm Islam as the one true path: "This day I have perfected for you your religion, and completed My Blessing upon you, and have approved for you as religion, Submission (Islam)" (*SQ*). Yet al-Tabari (838–923) read *islam* here simply as submission of one's heart to the principle of Divine Oneness.[5] Similarly, the standard reading of 3:85 identified Islam as the only faith acceptable to God. Since the occasion of this revelation ostensibly addresses the departure of a small group of followers who abandoned Islam, however, some commentators limited the warning to Muslims who become apostates. Others again read *islam* as submission to God rather than one particular religion.[6]

Certain indictments of religious others are, like Tanakh's mention of the Canaanites' sinfulness, likely intended as a cautionary tale for the elect community.[7] Qur'an demonstrates its capacity for self-critique, censuring followers who are guilty of self-righteous judgment, slander, letting others carry the burden of warfare, and showy piety without basic human decency (49, 107, 24:11–20, 4:94–5). In the language of chosenness, it recognizes that not all Muslims are worthy (35:32). Maulana Muhammad Ali's commentary elaborated: "It is thus made clear that when a community is spoken of as being *a chosen community*, all members of it are not alike. It is chosen because of those who are foremost in the doing of good, whose example the others should try to follow."[8] Nonetheless, Muslims are never condemned with the same ferocity as non-Muslims. Numerous passages that inveigh against Christians, Jews, and pagans effect a dangerously derogatory image of the "other."

Members of the Muslim community are cautioned not to make friends with Christians and Jews (5:51–2), likely a warning against relying on them for protection or support. Borrowing motifs from Christian polemics, Qur'an states that God grew angry with the Jews because they rejected His signs, killed the prophets,[9] rebelled, and violated limits (2:61). Some of the restrictive laws given through Moses are presented as a consequence of the people's wrongdoing (4:160–1); when they then broke the covenant, God cursed them and hardened their hearts (5:13). The text claims that many Jews are untrustworthy (5:13, 62–63; 3:75), and some so angered Allah that He turned them into monkeys and pigs (5:60).[10] Christians, too, come under withering critique, for their deification of Jesus and notion of Trinity, for intrareligious conflict, for corruption of the gospel, and for failure to uphold Jesus's teaching (4:171–173; 5:14, 68, 72–77). Qur'an also accuses Christians and Jews of idolatrous association of non-divine beings with Allah (*shirk*, 9:30–31)—a transgression that Allah will not forgive (4:48, 5:72).[11] This last charge is more frequently aimed at the prevailing polytheism of the Arabian context. Pagan practices are considered immoral; the pathos-filled condemnation of female infanticide, set in the mouth of a murdered babe on the Day of Judgment, presents a particularly powerful indictment (81:1–14; cf. 16:57–9).

Although Qur'anic objections to paganism were more absolute than its critique of Peoples of the Book, Judaism and Christianity posed particular challenges for the emergence of a new monotheistic tradition that claimed to stand as their successor. The text acknowledges that Jews and Christians will continue to believe in the adequacy or superiority of their own traditions and warns Muslims not to follow those paths (2:120). It alleges that existing monotheistic communities might be jealous because Allah is investing in redemptive work outside their institutions (4:51–54). They argue about who inherits the legacy of Abraham, even though he "was neither a Jew nor a Christian, but a man of pure natural belief (*hanif*)—one who submits (*muslim*) [to God]" (3:67). Evocative of Paul's reading of history in Romans 9–11, Qur'an teaches that their rejection of Islam is part of God's plan: Allah desires that they be misled and suffer appropriate punishment (3:176–78, 5:41).

Several passages assert that Muhammad's coming was predicted in Jewish and Christian texts—e.g., Qur'an 7:157: "I will prescribe [mercy] for those who are godfearing and pay zakat and those who believe in Our Signs: those who follow the Messenger, the Unlettered Prophet, whom they find written down with them in the Torah and the Injil" (gospel, see also 61:6). By denying Muhammad's prophetic call, Jews and Christians reportedly violate their own pledge (3:81): "Remember when Allah made a covenant with the Prophets: 'Now that We have given you a share of the Book and Wisdom, and then a Messenger comes to you confirming what is with you, you must believe in him and help him.' He asked, 'Do you agree and undertake My commission on that condition?' They replied, 'We agree.'"

Yet Qur'an insists that no amount of human opposition will be able to thwart God's ongoing work for redemption: "They desire to extinguish Allah's Light with their mouths but Allah will perfect His Light, though the unbelievers hate it. It is He who sent His Messenger with guidance and the Deen [religion] of Truth to exalt it over every other deen, even though the idolaters hate it" (61:8–9).

As with Tanakh, Islamic scripture encompasses a period of military encounters, territorial acquisition, and political rule. While there are passages that promote peace negotiations and reconciliation with enemies (2:193, 5:13, 8:60–61), war is also canonized. On occasion, Qur'an calls for active battle against unbelievers: "When the sacred months are over, kill the idolaters wherever you find them, and seize and besiege them and lie in wait for them on every road" (9:5)—although the next verse allows them to request asylum to hear God's word, after which they are conveyed to a place of safety. People of the Book fare better: they are required to pay the *jizya*, an indemnity tax payable to the state authorities, in return for which they are allowed to live peaceably under Muslim rule and practice their religion (9:29).[12] The ninth sura is a late Medinan passage, which unfortunately means that many commentators and jurists believed that its "verse of the sword" abrogates earlier, more tolerant teachings.[13]

Nonetheless, the earlier passages establish a textual foundation for scholars seeking a tradition of nonviolence,[14] a positive theology of non-Muslim religions, and more fruitful relations with their adherents. This Meccan text speaks plainly of a pluralist peace: "Unto you your religion, and unto me my religion" (109:6 *SQ*). Muhammad is instructed to argue with People of the Book only in the kindest way, recognizing commonalities between the traditions: "We believe in what has been sent down to us and what was sent down to you. Our God and your God are one and we submit to Him" (29:46; cf. 2:136). Other passages note that many People of the Book are upright, pious, and ethical. Like Muslims, they "enjoin the right and forbid the wrong, and compete in doing good. They are among the righteous. You will not be denied the reward for any good thing you do. Allah knows the godfearing" (3:113–5).

This last passage gives the impression that faithful observance of other monotheistic traditions may, in fact, be salvific. It certainly applied to biblical figures such as Abraham: "We chose him in this world, and in the Next World he will be one of the righteous" (2:130). Other verses appear to extend the promise to Jews, Christians, and Sabians in Muhammad's time (5:69, 2:62).[15] Arguing that all who submit to Allah and do good may receive reward, an early Medinan sura specifically challenges those Jews or Christians who claim that only one faith can secure access to paradise (2:111–12). It also insists that there is no compulsion in religion (2:256), a protection of personal conscience that Abdulaziz Sachedina calls "the major argument for religious pluralism in the Qur'an."[16] Sura 5 implies that Jews, Christians, and Muslims should each follow what Allah sent down for them and then charges them all: "We have appointed a law and a practice for every one of you. Had Allah willed, He would have made you a single community, but He wanted to test you regarding what has come to you. So compete with each other in doing good. Every one of you will return to Allah and He will inform you regarding the things about which you differed" (5:48).

It is a pluralist notion with a dash of epistemological humility: live in faithfulness with the covenant you have received, for only God knows the ultimate Truth. The competition to do good raises the possibility that multiple religions are part of the divine plan for creation; if adherents are so anxious to prove their path is the best way, might they not compete in righteousness and thus improve the human condition?[17]

Islamic jurisprudence continued to distinguish between the status of idolaters and that of People of the Book, but it historically did not read these model examples of religious tolerance as decisive, or did not interpret them as generously as some scholars urge today. Nonetheless, while the dangerous association with conquest and othering remained, Qur'an shares the multivocal quality of Tanakh and New Testament that has allowed different understandings of election to emerge.

THE SHAPING OF EMPIRE AND OTHERNESS

It is not clear to what extent religion was the driving force of Islam's imperial ambitions. Various records suggest the conquerors were Arabs more than Muslims. According to Jonathan Berkey, "Umar seems to have regarded himself, first and foremost, as the leader of the Arabs, and their monotheistic creed as the religious component of their new political identity." One telling example is that he did not require Christian Arabs to pay the jizya, the head-tax theoretically imposed on all non-Muslims in the new empire.[18] Yet it is worth calling to mind Walter Wink's comment: "The gods are not a fictive masking of the power of the human state; *they are its actual spirituality*."[19] Islam forged a theology that justified conquest and shaped the emerging culture at the same time that the rapid growth of empire influenced the faith's early development. There are numerous religious themes that relate to conquest, including greater and lesser jihad, ethics of military engagement, the conceptual division of *dar el Islam* and *dar el harb* (abode of Islam and abode of war), and *dhimmi* status for People of the Book.[20]

Of these, dhimmitude seems to be most substantially linked to ideas of chosenness in Islam, but the others require at least brief attention, particularly in the current political climate that overemphasizes militant expressions of Islam. Jihad means struggle, not holy war; it designates striving to follow in the way of Allah. Islamic tradition recognizes many different kinds of jihad; while it includes military struggle, it can also connote struggle against persecution, against materialism, or for deeper commitment to God's will. A well-known hadith reports that Muhammad charged a group coming home from battle, "You have returned from the lesser struggle to the greater struggle," which is understood to mean that spiritual striving is more challenging or more religiously significant than conquest.[21] Although the chain of transmission is contested, the teaching still shapes the way most Muslims think about jihad; the distinction it makes actually facilitates self-critical faith. Some argue that jihad is by definition nonviolent. Nadia Yassine (b. 1958), a spokeswoman for a prominent Islamist movement in Morocco, maintained that the sin of *istikbar* (arrogance) is the driving force of Islamist violence. Muslims are required to struggle against this lust for power: "A true *mujahid* will never deploy violent instruments or engage in practices that themselves express the urge to dominate others."[22] Education, protest, and peaceful political activism are their tools for societal transformation.

Islam's instructions for the conduct of war require a capacity of self-restraint. Qur'an 2:190 authorizes the community to fight against those who fight against them, but without transgressing limits. Although contemporary extremists lead many people to presume otherwise, Islamic law forbids harm of noncombatants, mutilation, and other excesses of battle.[23] Today's Islamophobia industry contributes to the erroneous assumption that Muslims divide the world into the abode of Islam and the abode of war, a binary perspective that conjures images of global conquest. The medieval terminology merely sought to establish the rules that apply in each realm; there are also abodes of treaty and safety, and there is no requirement to conquer the world.

Yet the empire did view Islam as the natural religion of humanity. It also considered its military expansion a civilizing mission, much as European colonialism imagined centuries later. John Kelsay described dhimmitude as a theology of beneficent paternalism: the caliphate's protection was a means to save non-Muslims from the full extent of their errors, and to save the world from the spread of lesser religions.[24] Although dhimmi has a semantic range that includes mutual faithfulness, divine favor, and protection—and it established basic principles of religious freedom and civil rights for Peoples of the Book—the status also entailed a broad range of disabilities.[25] The Covenant of Umar (conventionally dated to the seventh century, although the earliest record is much later) identified the following restrictions, ostensibly agreed to by Christian inhabitants of conquered cities in Syria: they were not allowed to build new religious facilities, or to repair old ones in Muslim areas; they could not proselytize or hold public religious ceremonies; they could not display crosses or Christian books in Muslim thoroughfares; they could not dress like Muslims, adopt their naming customs, ride on saddles, bear weapons, build houses higher than a Muslim home, or strike a Muslim; and they were required to wear the *zunnar*, a belt identifying them as Christian.[26]

While these stipulations (along with the jizya) remained core elements in regulating dhimmi populations, enforcement varied. There are reports of a dramatic increase in taxation and oppressive measures under Umayyad caliph 'Abd al-Malik ibn Marwan (d. 705), but also more generous dhimmi rights in Yemen during the late Middle Ages.[27] The Ottomans were responsible both for a relatively pluralist millet system that allowed religious minorities a degree of self-rule, and also for the Armenian genocide that murdered over one million Christian inhabitants of the empire.[28] The last example again demonstrates how difficult it can be to untangle the web of political ambitions, religious ideology, cultural chauvinism, economic interests, and other factors that weigh heavily on the scales of history. The religious otherness of the mostly Christian Armenian population was neither irrelevant to the assault nor its singular cause. The young Turks who led the onslaught were not religious radicals—and, officially, "Islam" would have stood against the murder of dhimmi populations—but culturally it contributed to their demise.[29] Again, since this study cannot provide deep analysis of the manifold influences on historical events, we explore the way that religious discourse is deployed—especially imagery that evokes election—in various contexts.

In the ninth century, Abbasid leader Mutawakkil launched a campaign of persecution against Christians, whom he viewed as a political threat outside the Muslim world and a potential fifth column within. He sought to challenge their rising economic and social status by bringing back the injunctions of Umar and inaugurating a literary assault. In a polemic he commissioned, Christians were excoriated for hypocrisy, blind faith, irrational hatred of Jews, and utter lack of compassion. They were described as inwardly polluted because they did not practice circumcision or cleansing rituals, and because they ate swine. Low-born and impure of blood, they should gladly pay the jizya and be thankful that Muslim rulers tolerated them, for "God verily doomed them to abjectness and destitution."[30] Muslims stood as the rightly guided counterpoint.

Medieval voices built on the Qur'anic notion that other faiths distorted their revelations. Often designed for Muslim audiences to affirm Islam's superiority, the concept of *tahrif* is a "projected criterion by which the Other is measured as deficient in reference to self."[31] Ibn Hazm's (994–1064) study of religion reported that the Sabians were the oldest religion in the world, reigning high, until they introduced innovations into their received teaching and changed God's law. In an ongoing effort to restore true faith, Allah then sent "his friend Abraham." Yet the Jews also introduced innovations, and so it went until Muhammad. Ibn Hazm identified Qur'an as the single scripture that perfectly preserved divine instruction.[32] In a vituperative polemic against the Jews, he vehemently dismissed their own claim of chosenness: "There is no greater wonder than that they make themselves children of God. All who know them know that they are the dirtiest of nations in clothing, the most inane in appearance. They are the most wretched, abominable, perfect in wickedness. They are the greatest in deceit, most cowardly of spirit, strongest in despicableness, most deceitful of tongue, weakest of determination, and most frivolous of character. God forbid this foul election."[33]

Nonetheless, treatment of minority populations was likely substantially better under Muslim governments than in Christian Europe, at least until the seventeenth century.[34] With robust cultural exchange between resident Jewish, Christian, and Muslim populations during Islamic rule in Spain—*la convivencia* (living together)—some scholars view it as a model of tolerance. Yet it was also a period of substantial rivalry.[35] The success of non-Muslim minorities spurred more hostile voices to protest and violence, as in the case of Joseph ibn Nagrela, a Jewish vizier in Grenada. His appointment prompted a poetical rant by Abu Ishaq in 1066, who complained that Muslims must now obey "the vilest ape among these miscreants." Cited as a catalyst for the mob that stormed the royal palace, assassinated Ibn Nagrela, and massacred thousands of Jews in Grenada, he expressly incited violence:

> *Hasten to slaughter him as an offering, sacrifice him for he is a fat ram.*
> *And do not spare his people, for they have amassed every precious thing.*
> *Break loose their grip and take their money; you have a better right to*
>   *what they collect.*
> *Do not consider it a breach of faith to kill them—*
> *The breach of faith would be to let them carry on.*[36]

Muslim presumptions of election also made military defeats theologically perplexing. After the fall of Seville (1267), the poet al-Rundi's lament translated the loss in spiritual terms: "The tap of the white ablution fount weeps in despair" as their dwellings became inhabited by unbelief and their mosques converted into churches. As for the faithful, "Yesterday they were kings in their own homes, but today they are slaves in the land of the infidel!" Al-Rundi also used religious otherness to convey moral turpitude, as did the Crusader call to arms discussed in chapter 9; he portrayed opposing troops as defilers of women and murderers of innocent children. "The heart melts with sorrow at such signs, if there is any Islam or faith in that heart!"[37]

Mainstream medieval opinion was generally exclusive. Al-Ghazali and al-Shahrastani, giants of Asharite theology, declared that non-Muslim monotheists are not believers and the law of Islam abrogates all other laws.[38] In fact, all the legal schools agreed that previous religious dispensations are displaced by Islamic fiqh, and that living as a non-Muslim is a moral failure. "Non-Muslim religious practices may be protected under law, but non-Muslims live in error merely on sufferance, a toleration mercifully dictated by God."[39] In this view, the path to success and eternal life is the property of a single religious community. With an idiom well-suited to our contemporary sound-bite culture, the medieval scholar Ibn Qayyim al-Jawziyya (d. 1350) stated, "The ways to Hell are many, but the way to Heaven is one."[40]

To counter apparent assurances for non-Muslim monotheists given in 2:62, exclusivist commentators indicated that the verse includes only those who converted to Islam, or who lived before Muhammad's prophetic call.[41] Others applied the principle of *naskh* and claimed that the verse was abrogated. Al-Tabari, in his monumental *Jami al-bayan* II:155–56, collected a multitude of classical exegeses (*tafsir*) that endorsed such a cancellation. Ultimately, however, he rejected their conclusion because it seemed incompatible with justice and the divine promise.[42] Allah has a covenantal commitment to every human soul.

Prominent voices shared this more pluralist embrace, including the caliph Ali b. Abi Talib (d. 660) in his letter appointing a new governor of Egypt: "Infuse your heart with mercy for the people in your charge. . . . They are either your brother in religion or your equal in creation."[43] Ismaili missionary Jafar bin Mansur al-Yaman affirmed a place in heaven for Christians, Jews, Sabians, and "people of any other religion who believe in God and in an afterlife, who do good and obey God." His opinion echoed the more inclusive Qur'anic teachings and reflected a broader Ismaili viewpoint, at least among the ninth- to tenth-century Brethren of Purity, who recognized the relative truth of all religion.[44]

Mystical perspectives often emphasized a capacious theology. The great Andalusian Sufi Ibn Arabi described his deep understanding of a Qur'anic verse that affirmed Allah's revelations to diverse prophets (3:84) as the peak in his spiritual ascent. Cautioning against being bound by a particular creed, he insisted that Allah is greater than any single religion. He spoke of the "elect," not by their religious affiliation, but by their capacity to combine reason and imagination in proper balance, lifting the veils between themselves and God.[45] His poetry rejoiced,

My heart has become capable of every form:
it is a pasture for gazelles, and a convent for Christian monks,
And a temple for idols and the pilgrim's Ka'ba
and the tables of the Torah and the book of the Qur'an.
I follow the religion of Love:
whatever way Love's camels take, that is my religion and my faith.[46]

The Persian Sufi poet-theologian-jurist Jalal ad-Din Muhammad Rumi (1207–1273) similarly sang of divine unity that transcends boundaries. Claiming in one poem that he is neither Christian nor Jew nor Muslim nor Hindu nor Buddhist nor Sufi nor Zen, he saw the divine and human worlds as one, all existing only in God.[47] Since Sufism infuses most expressions of Islam, we find related affirmations beyond the parameters of mystical literature. For example: Abu'l Fadl (1551–1602), a court philosopher under the Mughal emperor Akbar, professed, "There are wise men to be found ready at hand in all religions. . . . Truth is the inhabitant of every place; and how could it be right to consider it as necessarily confined to one religion or creed?"[48]

Such illustrations should not suggest a teaching of equivalency. While Ibn Arabi did not consider the earlier traditions completely null, he compared them to the light of distant stars and Islam to the light of the sun: "When the sun appears, the lights of the stars are hidden, and their lights are included in the light of the sun."[49] Somewhat similar to Christian claims, Ibn Arabi believed that Muhammad's mission represented not the erasure of previous revelations but their restoration and fulfillment.

Two rather remarkable medieval literatures illustrate the self-critical potential within Islam's spirit of tolerance. In the flowering of the Islamic Renaissance during the ninth and tenth centuries, diverse religious spokespersons gathered together in *majalis* (councils), debating religious truth with freedom of expression and respect promised for all participants. In a Christian account of a majlis in the court of al-Ma'mun (echoed in Muslim sources), the caliph announced: "This *majlis* is fair; in it no one is going to be assailed. Speak your disclaimer; answer without fear. Here there is 'nothing but the best.' No one will threaten you with anything, nor should you be distressed personally with regard to anyone. This is the day on which the truth is to be made evident. With whomever there is any knowledge for the verification of his religion, let him speak."[50] A frequent refrain, "nothing but the best" was likely a reference to the Qur'anic teachings to engage religious dispute only in the best way (16:125, 29:46).

While respectful, most Muslims who took part saw the enterprise as *da'wa*, an invitation to embrace Islam as the true faith, and assurances of fair treatment in the literature did not always reflect reality.[51] Yet the perceived progressiveness of this approach can be appreciated by noting the reaction of a pious tenth-century Andalusian scholar named Abu Umar. Living far from Baghdad, outside the cosmopolitan center of Abbasid Islam, he could not abide the respectful treatment accorded to non-Muslims and their religious ideas: "At the first session I attended I saw a *majlis* which included every kind of group: *Sunni* Muslims and heretics, and all kinds of infidels: Majus [Zoroastrians], materialists, atheists, Jews and Christians. Each group had a leader who would speak on its doctrine and debate about it. Whenever a leader arrived, from whichever of the groups he was, the assembly rose up for him." The thing that angered him most was that they all agreed to argue based on reason, without reference to Qur'an or teachings of the Prophet Muhammad, since non-Muslims put no credence in them. When Abu Umar heard that, he determined never to return to the majlis.[52]

Medieval Muslim literature also includes a fledging scientific study of comparative religion. One of the most impressive works is a twelfth-century encyclopedia by Shahrastani, *The Book of Religions and Sects*. In the preface, he declared, "I impose upon myself the obligation of presenting the views of each sect as I find them in their works without favor or prejudice, without distinguishing which are correct and which are in error, which are true and which are false; though, indeed, for minds that understand the ways of rational thought, the light of truth and the stench of falsehood will not remain hidden."[53] His analysis revealed both an effort at dispassionate study and an inevitable tendenz amidst the dominance of Islamic civilization. The basic definition of religion (*deen*) that Shahrastani offered is submission and obedience—not coincidentally, the lexical meaning of *Islam*.[54] In his construction of self and other, there was one religion and these various groups were religious to the extent that they conformed to its shape.

UMMAH, PRIMORDIAL RELIGION, AND SHARIAH: FEATURES OF CHOSENNESS IN ISLAM

While ummah in Qur'an could refer to other groups (10:47, 28:23), and the Constitution of Medina described the signatories of various religions as a single ummah, the term came to signify the spiritual, trans-territorial community of Muslims: God's chosen ones. The ummah was endowed with ultimate political authority and entrusted with faithful transmission of divine teaching.[55] Let us recall how the sense of belonging to the ummah, elect or not, fulfills a positive social function. Like concepts of Jewish peoplehood or members of the church as the body of Christ, it communicates a transcendent unity of the entire Muslim population. As discussed in chapter 1, religion draws people together with a common identity, praxis, values, and narrative.

While the resulting bond can construct barriers between different lifestances, it builds bridges across other types of difference. Malcolm X's reflection following his pilgrimage to Mecca in 1965 offers a dramatic example. He not only moved closer to classical Sunni tradition but also relinquished his blanket sense of alienation from white people:

> Never have I witnessed such sincere hospitality and overwhelming spirit of true brotherhood as is practiced by people of all colors and races here in this ancient Holy Land, the home of Abraham, Muhammad and all the other Prophets of the Holy Scriptures. . . . There were tens of thousands of pilgrims, from all over the world. They were of all colors, from blue-eyed blondes to black-skinned Africans. But we were all participating in the same ritual, displaying a spirit of unity and brotherhood that my experiences in America had led me to believe never could exist between the white and non-white.

Traveling through the Muslim world, he felt "the white attitude was removed from their minds by the religion of Islam."[56] This intersectionality of otherness reminds us that religion is not the unique driver of any dangerous idea, and religion's capacity to build both bridges and walls illuminates the dialectical nature of human groupishness.

Explanations for how all of the other religions of the world fit into a particular tradition's system of belief, often framed as "theologies of religions," similarly bind together positive and negative potential. They impact thinking about who can be elect and how it comes to pass in God's plan: Is there one right path or many? How/why are you not like me? Because they address the relationship of those who are "in" with those who are "out," and their respective relationships with God, they can magnify problematic

aspects of difference. However, all three traditions have within their exegetical history both inclusive and exclusive interpretations of the other,
both benign and aggressive ways of dealing with the non-elect. Within Islam, one predominant theology of religions plays a central role in thinking
about chosenness: primordial religion. An ontology as well as a theology, it
forms the foundation both for supersession and for a concept of pluralism
built into the fabric of the universe.

In this view, there is one primordial religion that has existed from the
beginning of human life and is imprinted in human nature. It was revealed
by God at regular intervals through the teachings and lives of the prophets.
While Islam is seen to represent this primordial faith in its fullness—"a
return to the truth that stands above and beyond all historical contingen-
cies"[57]—previous scriptures and monotheistic traditions accordingly represent Allah's ongoing efforts to guide the peoples.[58] Humanity did not need
to wait for Muhammad; there were many who were "rightly guided" before
him, and the revealed scriptures are all valid to the extent that they preserve
the eternal teachings. The chosen people and the elect faith are those who
follow this religion of truth. According to a strongly authenticated hadith Muhammad was asked, "Which religion is the most beloved to God?"
He replied, "Primordial and generous faith (al-ḥanifiyya al-samḥa)."[59] It is
striking that he did not specify "Islam," although he surely understood his
own teaching to exemplify the standard. Abraham's faith did as well: "a
man of pure natural belief (ḥanif), one who submits [to God]" (3:67).

In fact, Islamic theology contends that every human being is born with
the capacity for true faith, with an innate disposition that enables one to
know Allah and to discern right from wrong (fitra). An essential prooftext
is provided in Qur'an 30:30: "Set your face firmly towards the religion as
a pure natural believer (ḥanif), Allah's natural pattern (fitra) on which He
made humanity. There is no changing Allah's creation. That is the true
religion, but most people do not know it." Viewed through this lens, divine
revelations and prophetic teaching appear as reminders so that we may re-
absorb what we know through fitra.[60] This concept of human anthropology
is radically different from the Christian concept of original sin, since the
"original" nature of human beings is pure. Theoretically, any one of us may
be elect, any one of us may have "success" in living out the fullness of divine
instruction. Heaven is our normative destination.

The theology of primordial religion and anthropology of innate faith provide additional strategies, rooted in tradition, for contemporary scholars to affirm the continuing sufficiency of non-Muslim faiths and to envisage election in nonsectarian terms. They revive readings that imagine Qur'anic reference to islam with a lower-case *i*. Looay Fatoohi, for example, interpreted it to mean every religion revealed to the prophets, and Tariq Ramadan understood it simply as submission to God.[61] Asghar Ali Engineer presented Islam as one particular expression of primordial religion; like the others, it establishes ethical action as its core.[62] Seyyed Hossein Nasr identified outer forms of different religions as necessary gateways to the shared depths of true faith. Each is valid and coherent in its own religious "universe."[63]

Many pluralist interpretations rely also on mystical precedents and perspective. Building on the teachings of Rumi, Mahmut Aydin stressed the idea that God is bigger than any single faith: "No one religious tradition can claim to see all of the Divine reality."[64] Reminiscent of Sufi hermeneutics (especially the work of Ibn Arabi), Reza Shah-Kazemi recognized the transcendent unity of all religions while still emphasizing the value of their particularity. He identified the diversity of lifestances as a sign of divine creativity, each essential to God's redemptive plan, and their distinct paths cannot be nullified or blended together.[65]

A tension embedded in this discourse is ambivalence about the Enlightenment project. While contemporary scholarship reflects a broad desire to grapple constructively with the religiously diverse contexts in which many Muslims live, theological pluralism (with secularism as its common companion) is frequently perceived as another imposition of the Western colonialist enterprise.[66] Thus, anchoring inclusive theology deeply in Islamic thought is a critical step in reimagining chosenness. Within the framework of primordial religion, the chosen *can* be all those who live in faithfulness with their own tradition—each endowed with meaning in the unfolding of creation, power to shape a distinctive response to the divine call, and the success of living in harmony with one's nature (fitra) in submission to the Most High. The natural pattern of a universe with an omnipotent deity and multiple religions, after all, was presented in Qur'an: "We have appointed a law and a practice for every one of you. Had Allah willed, He would have made you a single community, but He wanted to test you regarding what has come to you. So compete with each other in doing good" (5:48).

A third concept to discuss here is shariah. In significant measure, shariah parallels the rabbinic construction of halakhah: discerning and following divine instructions for daily living fulfills the charge of the elect. The root appears in Qur'an 45:18: "Then We placed you on the right road (*shari'atan*) of Our Command, so follow it." Etymologically, it refers to "the way" (as does halakhah) or "the way to the watering hole." Given the context of Arabian desert terrain, the latter evokes the word's eventual significance as a path of life-sustaining felicity or salvation.

Yet there is an important distinction between shariah and halakhah. As Mohammad Hashim Kamali pointed out, the verse was revealed early in Muhammad's career and cannot refer to later legal material when the Muslim community had political authority.[67] Comprising a moral religious system more than a code of law, shariah is distinguished from the Islamic science of jurisprudence (fiqh) that represents ongoing efforts to translate divine guidance into human contexts.[68] Shariah is thus more akin to the broad concept of Torah as divine instruction, and fiqh aligns with halakhah. Consequently, while Muslim adherents generally consider shariah to be eternal—not subject to human judgment or efforts at reform—its concretization into praxis is necessarily approximate, contingent, and contextual. As noted in part II, fiqh affirms multiple schools of legal thought that diverge on substantive matters of theology and praxis.[69]

Religious law (halakhah, canon law, fiqh) could fill its own section in this volume, since it has the power to endow every aspect of life with purpose and to push society to seek the collective good, but also to justify diverse forms of oppression in the name of God. Islam offers a way to circumscribe its ultimacy by distinguishing human legal constructs from Divine teaching. "The *Shari'ah* corresponds to a reality that transcends time and history," according to Seyyed Nasr. He described it as "the blueprint of the ideal human life. It is a transcendent law which is at the same time applied in human society, but never fully realized because of the imperfections of all that is human."[70] And yet, it provides the *muslim* with "the way" toward becoming the human creature Allah intended, on the path of the rightly guided. This is an important distinction in a world with various Muslim state and nonstate actors who claim to enact shariah and assert their control over God's truth. It is an important distinction in the climate of Islamophobia that has driven multiple localities in the United States to ban or attempt to ban shariah, misrepresenting it as a totalitarian body of law that threatens constitutional protections. (There are already adequate defenses against "foreign law" on the books; anti-shariah legislation instead threatens Muslims' free exercise of religion.) The distinction affirms that even if the way of God is one, it is necessarily mediated humanly by those who *seek to be* rightly guided, chosen, elect. They are only "on the path."

So when Qur'an speaks of "the best community brought forth unto mankind" (3:110 *SQ*), it is aspirational. Ibn Kathir said it praises those who are the best toward other people; Ibn Arabi declared, "'You are the best community' because you are the people of divine oneness, establishing justice which is God's shadow." He emphasized walking a path of moderation.[71] According to Ibn Qayyim (1292–1350), the spirit that guides the elect community must emulate shariah's values: "In its entirety it is justice, mercy, benefit, and wisdom. Every matter which abandons justice for tyranny, mercy for cruelty, benefit for corruption, and wisdom for foolishness is not a part of the *shariah* even if it was introduced therein by an interpretation" (*I'lam al-Muwaqqi'in* 3/11). Similar to Judaism's conviction that chosenness is linked to the embodiment of Torah's highest values, Islam binds its claims of election to a comparable obligation and purpose. It is a call to establish goodness and justice, not only in one's personal life, but in the social fabric as well.

CHAPTER 11

ENDURING CHALLENGES

Each tradition's teaching of chosenness contains an aspirational quality. It presents an invitation to examine one's attunement to divine purposes, with a humility that stands as the beginning of self-critical faith. Particular voices, historical and contemporary, have sought a sense of their essential role in God's unfolding plan without assuming that everyone else stood against it. They discerned a global perspective that did not require taking over the world. They found compelling teachings within the matrix of election—teachings that endowed their efforts with meaning, nurtured hope, sewed their community together, and shaped their culture. Yet the dangers of chosenness remain. Hateful expressions and oppressive applications are still cultivated in the soil of election.

One objective of this book is to demonstrate that the dangers are not all located among extremists. The drives that feed chosenness are so fundamental that even those who resist denigrating religious difference sometimes struggle in the inescapable co-formation of self and other. Groupishness and bias seem hard-wired into the human psyche. The desire to mold a community in particular ways is integral to religious instruction and it invites the exercise of power. Election also bursts the bounds of religion to find compelling expression in nationalism, with attendant politicization and racialization of religious difference.

This chapter explores contemporary expressions that demonstrate the continuing volatility of chosenness in the Abrahamic traditions and in American exceptionalism. Some of the examples come from the margins, but they are growing in power, numbers, and visibility. In these reactionary times, it becomes increasingly important to shine a light on such manifestations and on the voices that rise to contest them.

JUDAISM

The first chief rabbi of Israel, Rabbi Abraham Isaac Kook (1865–1935), cautioned that "the narrow-mindedness that leads one to see whatever is outside the bounds of one's own people . . . as ugly and defiled is a terrible darkness that causes general destruction to the entire edifice of spiritual good."[1] Making a place for Jewish particularity without bias against non-Jews, aspiring toward chosenness through a life of Torah and righteousness, he believed Judaism cultivated divine sensitivity toward the absolute good. Still, his perspective did not escape chauvinism: "It is a fundamental error for us to retreat from our distinctive excellence, to cease recognizing ourselves as chosen for a Divine vocation. We are not only different from other nations, differentiated and set apart by a distinctive historic experience that is unlike that of all other nations, but we indeed surpass the other nations. If we shall know our greatness then we shall know ourselves, but if we forget it then we shall forget our own identity."[2]

Many Jewish voices today, more rigorously committed to avoiding ideas of exceptionalism, still recognize how chosenness has been vital to the continuing existence of Jews and Judaism. Like Kook, they build on historical themes.[3] They may emphasize the humility that chosenness should inculcate, as well as a sense of undeservedness that traces back to the narratives of Genesis.[4] Or, as in the story of Babel, they see it unfolding within a celebration of mutually enriching, divinely ordained diversity. Similar to ancient midrashim, some see Jews as the choosing rather than the chosen people.[5] Or, like Rabbi Greenberg, who was quoted in chapter 8, they affirm that God calls many peoples, each in unique relationship. The prophet Amos (9:7), Saadiah Gaon, and Moses Maimonides said as much long ago.

There is certainly much more critical examination of chosenness in contemporary Jewish discourse than in previous eras. Jewish Emancipation, the late eighteenth- to early twentieth-century development in which Jews were awarded citizenship rights and legal disabilities were removed, contributed substantially to this growth. As Jews became increasingly integrated into society with a variety of religious others, the other became more familiar. A classic 1966 edition of *Commentary* magazine posed five questions to leading Jewish thinkers of the day. One of them wrestled with the meaning and validity of chosenness. Responses ranged from classical defenses to that of Rabbi Mordecai Kaplan (1881–1983), the founder of Reconstructionist Judaism, who was prepared to forfeit chosenness as a theological conviction. Kaplan believed that it promoted self-infatuation, and that the correlate concept of "mission" promoted religious imperialism. In its place, he suggested the idea of vocation—a call to establish truth and goodness for which Jews and others strive. He stripped traditional references to chosenness out of the Reconstructionist movement's liturgy. What began, he imagined, as a psychological defense against persecution ultimately bred prejudice among Jews and resentment among the nations.[6]

His fears were not unfounded. The previous chapters relate multiple examples of both concerns. An alarming expression of contemporary Jewish bias can be found in *Torat haMelech* (The King's Torah), a racist tract published in 2009 by two right-wing ultra-orthodox Israeli rabbis, Yitzhak Shapira and Yosef Elitzur. The text tries to build halakhic arguments for distinguishing the value of Jewish life over others, for denying housing and employment to Arabs and migrant workers, and for encouraging acts of revenge. They do not explicitly name chosenness as justification, but it is deeply embedded there.[7] While their opinions are extreme, they help fuel an increasingly powerful group of ideological settlers in the West Bank and a rising tide of racism in Israel. The Israel Religious Action Center (IRAC), a social justice organization aligned with the Reform Movement, urged the Attorney General to indict the authors for incitement to violence, but his office has proved itself hesitant to pick a fight with rabbis. So IRAC filed a petition in the Israel Supreme Court, forcing legal action. IRAC also challenged the book on religious grounds in their publication *Love the Stranger as Yourself? Racism in the Name of Halacha* (2011). Jewish leaders from across the religious spectrum vehemently condemned *Torat haMelech*, including one yeshivah student who wrote a book-length rebuttal with carefully constructed halakhic arguments.[8]

As indispensable as these critiques are, it is facile to assume that problematic versions of chosenness today always belong to those "other" Jews, such as ideological settlers on the West Bank, without seeing how they also float closer to home. Nancy Fuchs-Kreimer acknowledged that a sense of Jewish superiority can still appear in progressive Jewish subcultures: "I discovered this from listening to Christians condemn other Christians for their antisemitism. After renouncing the theology those 'others' believe, they would then reveal, in much subtler form, the same prejudices." Her encounter with religious others, "self-critically but lovingly engaged with the breadth of their traditions and communities," deepened her perspective on her own.[9]

The dangerous linkage of chosenness to conquest may be more contained on the extreme, but it remains salient. Even though rabbinic circumscription of conquest shaped an ethos in which most Jews understand chosenness in wholly different terms, their hermeneutic solution merely postponed the problems until the messianic era. (Messianism, of course, could stand as its own section in this volume, with the potential to inspire deep commitment to social justice and world repair, as well as violence and upheaval—often simultaneously.) The election of land and people are still linked. With the restoration of Jewish political autonomy after the founding of the modern State of Israel, the potential dangers have returned ahead of schedule.

Most nineteenth-century Zionist thinkers were secular in orientation and specifically rejected the notion of the Jewish homeland as a messianic fulfillment of election; they strove instead for "normalcy" as a national liberation movement in the age of nationalism.[10] They were driven by ongoing persecution of Jews, alongside abiding attachment to the land of Israel as the only national home Jews had ever known. A minority, however, saw God's hand in bringing about messianic redemption through the unwitting vehicle of secular Zionism. Ascribing to the latter opinion did not necessarily mean promoting military aggression. Prominent orthodox Zionists, including Rabbi Kook, insisted that human participation in the messianic drama must be conducted without initiating violence—even as they rejected the passive waiting modeled by rabbis of old and some of their non-Zionist peers.[11] They grappled with the serious challenges of a Judaism that again could wield political power and echoed the prophetic charge that chosenness entails a standard of ethical and spiritual excellence rather than entitlement.

Rabbi Kook's son (R. Zvi Yehudah Kook, 1891–1982), however, helped to transform and radicalize a branch of messianic religious Zionism. Stimulated by the global rise of fundamentalism as well as regional political developments, various ultranationalist orthodox groups took shape. Their numbers are relatively small, but their influence grows. As they endow the political state and its army with holiness, conquest becomes reinscribed within election. Rabbi Zvi Tau's (b. 1936) theology is emblematic: "From the perspective of faith we see the divine hand spread over us, and especially over our wars. It leads us to recognize the righteousness of our actions and our wars and their indispensability, not only for us but for all the nations! . . . The wars of Israel are essentially wars against war, for whoever rises up against Israel rises up against the light of God in the world, which is the supernal peace!"[12]

With Orwellian logic, Tau strips out any capacity for self-critical examination. The interests of the state become the interests of the world, authorized by God. Again, this reading of election prompted vociferous opposition, both secular and religious. Other orthodox thinkers, like Yeshayahu Leibowitz, warned against the idolatry of turning the state into an absolute that overrides moral judgment and worship of God.[13] Religious Zionist groups working for peace, such as *Oz veShalom-Netivot Shalom* and *Meimad*, insisted that chosenness requires rigorous ethical principles that restrict the use of violence and strive for a "purity of arms."[14]

Such a brief discussion cannot do justice to the diversity and complexity of Zionism, and there is no straight line from the ancient texts to the realities of Middle East politics. The ultranationalist voice is lifted up here simply to illustrate that the problems of chosenness are never cured; they are only treated. Rabbis of the classical era provided a way to decouple chosenness from conquest long ago, but hermeneutical movement does not travel in only one direction. Contemporary voices who argue passionately *against* interpretations that legitimate violence and discrimination cannot prevent others from promoting them. Neither can the longstanding precedent of more enlightened readings in biblical and rabbinic literature, or the rich development of a peace tradition, completely thwart the will to power.

Nor can we claim that progressive voices are the "true" expressions of the traditions while all the oppressive ones are "false." That would be a type of the reductionist analysis of religion that I contested at the start. But self-critique necessarily includes explicit opposition to dangerous interpretations and must continue to provide alternative understandings. Precisely because chosenness is so powerful a concept, and because it has been essential to Jewish survival, those who see its problems cannot respond by abandoning the concept altogether. As Todd Gitlin and Liel Leibowitz wrote: "It would be unwise to allow sole custody over this volatile idea to zealots of any persuasion. The idea of chosenness is too deeply ingrained in us to be overlooked, patronized, or definitively repealed. Whether or not we believe that the descendants of Abraham were singled out, in perpetuity, by God, and whether or not we find this to be an outlandish, if not offensive, notion—no matter what, we must grapple with it, for it is, behind our backs, grappling with us."[15]

ISLAM

Contemporary Islam also continues to exhibit diverse perceptions of religious others, ranging from polemical to pluralistic. These responses are not driven solely by religious influences, but also by intellectual, political, and social developments—from the epistemological revolution to the rise of individualism, from European colonialism to the collapse of the Ottoman Empire, from the birth of the State of Israel to the Arab Spring, from the terror campaign of Al Qaeda to the dramatic expansion of the interfaith movement after September 11, 2001.

Historically European antisemitic tropes have migrated into the Arab and global Muslim world, with new blood libels and copious printings of the notorious forgery *The Protocols of the Elders of Zion*.[16] Geopolitical and cultural conflicts are sometimes drawn in classical form, with the West cast as a reincarnation of the Crusaders and the rise of secularism decried as *jahiliyya* (the period of religious "ignorance" in pre-Islamic Arabia).[17] Although this analysis arose in Muslim-majority countries, it had certain appeal among immigrant Muslims communities in the West who were anxious about assimilation as well as international politics. Marcia Hermansen has expressed concern about the rise of "Identity" Islam among second-generation American Muslims, with "rigid rejection of 'the Other'" overtaking genuine spirituality and self-critical faith. She nonetheless acknowledged how a sense of Islam's preeminence could be compelling: "One can well imagine the problems of Muslim youth, often isolated by having distinctive names, physical appearance, and being associated with a stigmatized culture and religion. No wonder the concept that they were actually the superior ones, fending off the corrupt and evil society around them, rang pleasant."[18]

At the same time, there has also emerged an extensive collection of Muslim voices committed to constructive engagement with religious difference, building on historical foundations of tolerance, coexistence, and the recognition of common ground. Imam Feisal Abdul Rauf sought to invoke the vibrant crosscultural aspects of la convivencia in calling his proposed Muslim community center in Lower Manhattan "Cordoba House"—a project that was ironically torpedoed by anti-Muslim discrimination after 9/11. A Common Word, the 2009 outreach initiative to Christian communities, cited scriptural invitations for cooperation and called upon the shared values of loving God and neighbor. It was signed by hundreds of Muslim leaders and launched a range of academic, media, and public initiatives.[19]

Muslim writers who embrace the multifaith context regularly go back to the sources to recover a richer, thicker reading of the Other. They disavow prejudicial readings of tradition and assert the fundamental equality of all human beings. Jerusha Rhodes examined all the relevant Qur'anic verses and identified a range of dynamic, overlapping categories that yield a more complex reading of difference in Muslim tradition—*mu'min, muslim, mushrik, kafir, ahl al-kitab, munafiq, hanif*—commonly translated as "believer, submitter, associator, disbeliever, People of the Book, hypocrite and [non-denominational] monotheist." She concluded that all claims of chosenness based on membership in an essentialized "religion" are suspect, and emphasized that Qur'an is not primarily a verdict on difference. It is a guide.[20] As discussed in chapter 10, numerous scholars affirm the religious value or even the theological sufficiency of other faiths. Like Abdulaziz Sachedina, they accept "the dignity of all humans as equal in creation and as equally endowed with the knowledge of and the will to do the good."[21]

Theological pluralism is not uncontested, however. Tim Winter, for instance, took issue with Sachedina and others, arguing that they contorted the tradition in order to "harmonize the faith with the modern axiom of equality."[22] It is true that pluralist scholarship is more common in the West, where Muslims are a religious minority and equality is a fundamental cultural value. This cultural shaping of attitudes toward pluralism is also reflected in the general Muslim population, especially in the United States: Pew surveys reveal a majority of US Muslims believe that many religions can lead to eternal life, while the global median is 18 percent.[23] Although inclusive perspectives are not unanimous, they are authentic, indigenous, and profound readings of the tradition. The contemporary context merely amplifies Islam's multivocal history, sophisticated hermeneutics, and self-critical capacity.

An even more animated conversation ensues in relation to modern Islamism, including concerns regarding conquest. Islamism refers to "those ideologies and movements that strive to establish some kind of 'Islamic order'—a religious state, shari'a law, and moral codes in Muslim societies and communities."[24] The rhetoric of election is embedded in a number of ways. First, Islamism seeks to reclaim "true" Islam by relying on the foundational texts of Qur'an, sunna, and hadith. Actual relationship with the accumulated store of Islamic juridical and exegetical tradition is more complex than the oratory, revealing significant continuities as well as radical breaks; nonetheless, the desire to restore the absolute primacy of the early texts undergirds Islamists' claim to be the rightly guided ones. Second, they tend to view Islam as the "antidote to the moral bankruptcy inaugurated by Western cultural dominance from abroad, aided and abetted by corrupt Muslim rulers from within the *umma*."[25] Islam is regarded as the curative force that can usher in a just and ethical society. While establishing religious authority through the power of the state is a key feature of Islamist politics, different from calls for personal spiritual renewal and religious reform, there are diverse emphases and strategies.

The founder of the Egyptian Society of Muslim Brothers (later the transnational Muslim Brotherhood), Hasan al-Banna (1906–1949), is frequently described as the father of modern Islamism. He recounts a history in which Islam arose "under the shadow of God's banner, with the standard of the Qur'an fluttering at its head," rescuing the world from tyranny and injustice, leading the world to Allah and to peace. In the modern age, the West is crumbling, leaving all of humanity "tormented, wretched, worried, and confused, having been scorched by the fires of greed and materialism. They are in dire need of some sweet portion of the waters of True Islam to wash from them the filth of misery and lead them to happiness."[26] Even though the rhetoric is often universal, most Islamists concentrate their efforts on transforming Muslim-majority countries. Radicals who promote global jihad, like Osama bin Laden, represent a minority.

Many Islamists, however, presume that coercion and/or violence will be necessary to accomplish their goals. According to Sayyid Qutb (1906–1966), an Egyptian Sunni thinker who has influenced Islamist voices both radical and moderate, "Nothing of all this is achieved through verbal advocacy of Islam. The problem is that the people in power who have usurped God's authority on earth will not relinquish their power at the mere explanation and advocacy of the true faith."[27] In a pamphlet entitled *The Neglected Duty*, Muhammad Abd al-Salam Faraj (1954–1982, Egypt) cited the

Qur'anic admonition, "Those who do not govern by what God has revealed are unbelievers" (5:44), to support his conviction that insurrection against irreligious Muslims rulers is imperative.[28]

Other Islamist leaders challenge this militant approach to varying degrees. A prominent scholar among the Muslim ulama, Yusuf al-Qaradawi (b. 1926, Egypt/Qatar), compared it to the seventh-century Khariji rebels who attacked Muslim rulers when they judged their leadership insufficiently Islamic. The verdict of history is that their violent sectarianism was enormously destructive. Yet he has justified violence in other instances, specifically regarding suicide attacks against Israelis.[29] The Justice and Charity group in Morocco, on the other hand, renounces violence as a method of achieving political aims. A prominent leader, Nadia Yassine, characterized the original ummah as participatory, egalitarian, committed to freedom, expressive of Allah's mercy, and governed by a deliberative philosophy of power that places sovereignty within the community.[30] She emphasized that Islamic law has always adapted to context, so contemporary values necessarily inform their endeavors, and she acknowledged that efforts to legislate the rightly guided path are inherently imperfect. In her primary work, *Full Sails Ahead*, Yassine argued for the importance of ijtihad, ongoing reason and adaptation applied to reading the sacred sources of Islam. Quoting Michel Jobert, she wrote: "Revelation is thus not a moment in history. It is continued in our efforts to find 'the right path,' and to make our own progress intelligible. This effort is *ijtihad.* It is to be performed in uncertainty and humility."[31]

The degree of moderation is strongly associated with the political, religious, and cultural climates in which the thinkers and activists live.[32] Nonetheless, there are also Islamists in places like Iran who advocate greater separation of powers and narrowing the scope of shariah, expressing concern about oppressive tactics and religious standards becoming subservient to political goals. Mohsen Kadivar, for example, maintained that religious commandments must be "just, moral, reasonable and normal" to be part of God's eternal law; aspects of Islam that are not experienced that way in the present must be considered part of variable tradition and cannot wear the garb of absolute truth. In 2018 he was among fifteen prominent Iranians who called for a referendum on the theocratic state. Their statement reads, "The state has become the main obstacle to the progress and liberation of the Iranian nation by abusing and hiding behind religious concepts."[33]

The idea that one might fashion a society as God has asked, with a promise that it will yield justice and goodness, is compelling, but it is also fraught. While these thinkers labor to check Islamism's most coercive tendencies, many Muslims reject all efforts to embed Islam in state governance. "Renewalists" in Southeast Asia echoed concerns about the politicization of religion and sought stronger separation of religion and state; they advocated governance based on religious pluralism, civic freedoms, and constitutional protections, citing the Medina charter as precedent.[34] Bassam Tibi has opposed Islamism as dangerously bound up with religious conquest: "It is a great mistake to view Islamism as liberation theology characterized by an 'attempt to repair.' No, it is an agenda of cultural-totalitarian purification." He cautioned against differentiating much between those who embrace violence and those who condemn it, viewing their goal as identical—the supremacy of Islam in a theocentric universe and shariah-based social order. Yet Tibi acknowledged that Islamism in some form is popular within Muslim-majority countries.[35] It often appeals as grassroots resistance to ruling elites who impose Western socioeconomic models and do not represent public interests; Islamist organizations sometimes build support by offering basic social services that the state fails to provide.

The vibrancy of intellectual debate does not simply interrogate to what extent the religious notion of a chosen path might be implemented on a national level without conquest as its byproduct. It also presses a broad critical conversation about modern constructions of "Islam" both inside and outside Muslim communities.[36] As noted in chapter 7, the dominant (elect) culture defines itself over against others, presenting them as inferior. So the thousand-year-old discourse in "the West" that presents Islam as inherently violent, irrational, misogynistic, and antiscientific continues to be recycled. Driven by economic, cultural, and political motives, the imagery does not reflect the complex reality of Islam and Muslim history, including its substantial contributions to "Western" science, culture, and philosophy. Nor does the discourse acknowledge that secular humanism has been the reigning ideology of nations that pursue conquest and even genocide. Muslim leaders are regularly called upon to renounce the dangers of Islamism, but liberalism is not subjected to the same critique, even though it can also be accused of cultural totalitarianism and violence.[37]

Women's rights offer a case in point. American leaders who are not exactly advocates for feminism raged against oppression of Muslim women

in order to solidify support for war against "radical Islam." They did not
demonstrate comparable anguish about continuing patriarchy, misogyny,
discrimination, and violence against women in the US. They did not consult the women who lived in Afghanistan or Iraq. Instead they campaigned
against the veil using age-old tropes that had helped to justify colonial
domination of the Muslim world a century ago.[38] They trotted out native
informants like Ayaan Hirsi Ali to demonstrate that they are not bigoted
against Islam.[39] Western ideas of women's liberation, however, fail to recognize the possibility of agency within religious observance. And secular
values can be just as oppressive, increasingly evident as European states legislate what Muslim women cannot wear (niqab, hijab, etc.) in the name of
women's equality.[40] Even Muslim feminists who mirror liberalism's idea of
political and social equality, excavating indigenous resources for the cause,
are forced to struggle against the false dichotomy between secular freedom
and religious domination.[41]

CHRISTIANITY

Scholars have sometimes pointed to Christianity's negative images of Jews
and Muslims, along with its history of violence and discriminatory legislation, in looking for the roots of modern antisemitism and anti-Muslim
bias. Although these hatreds are often expressed in secular ways, many of
the old religious figures continue to be deployed and there are archetypes of
otherness (legalism, carnality, exoticism, etc.) that are difficult to dislodge.[42]
It cannot be a coincidence that Jews—Christianity's paradigmatic "other"
for centuries—are the targets of 59 percent of religiously motivated hate
crimes in the US, while they represent only 2 percent of the population.[43]
When white supremacists marched in Charlottesville in 2017, chanting
"Jews will not replace us," and when Robert Bowers murdered eleven Jews
at the Tree of Life Synagogue in Pittsburgh (2018), many Christians ago-
nized about how their faith contributes to the hate.

The precise role of religion is rarely clear. Christian relations with Muslims and Islam, for example, are complicated by a history of military conflict
and the current war on terror, the legacy of colonialism, economic agendas,
current events, the residual impact of historical polemics, and other factors.
Contemporary racial and political issues, however, are frequently filtered
through the lens of religious ideology and conflict, with special intensity
after the terrorist attacks on September 11, 2001, and the subsequent US

invasions in Afghanistan and Iraq. In this volatile context, religious responses of American Christians range broadly, reflecting the same contrast we have seen in contemporary Jewish and Muslim ideas about religious difference. While white evangelical Christians largely supported President Trump's anti-Muslim policies, mainline Christians of all races were out on the front lines protesting the "travel ban."[44] Christians who embrace the clash of civilizations paradigm often perpetuate the vilest of medieval anti-Muslim bigotries, and help fuel a media engine of fear about terrorism, shariah law and "civilizational jihad" to destroy America from within.[45] At the same time, other Christians reach out to build bridges of understanding and cooperation with Muslim communities, contesting the racialized image of the Muslim "other."[46]

Efforts to undo the legacy of hostility are not new. The World Council of Churches, in its first assembly in 1948, denounced antisemitism as a sin against God that is irreconcilable with Christian faith. Denominational statements repudiating the teaching of contempt and denouncing anti-Judaism/antisemitism abound, including the "Relationship Between the United Church of Christ and the Jewish Community" (1987), the Episcopal Church's "Guidelines for Christian–Jewish Relations" (1988), and "Declaration of the Evangelical Lutheran Church to the Jewish Community" (1994). Official religious bodies also issued statements seeking to heal Muslim–Christian relations, with urgent declarations against Islamophobia in the last decade.

Christian scholars have developed (and critiqued and revised multiple times) a tripartite theological framework for thinking about other religions—exclusivist, inclusivist, and pluralist—that tends to focus on a central Christian question: can non-Christians be saved?[47] While there are lifestances with different questions or no need to explain religious diversity, the categories can be useful in Christian theology. Pluralist perspectives draw on a variety of Christian conceptions, including the multiplicity of a triune God, the manifold ways in which the Holy Spirit works in the world, an emphasis on the multiple perspectives within the New Testament and early Christianity, faith in God's continuing power of creative transformation, and celebration of God incarnate in the riotous diversity of creation.[48] They tend to be less invested in questions of election than exclusivist and inclusivist attitudes, which can vary among and within denominations but tend to hew closely to historical dogmatic positions.

Many Christians continue to affirm Christianity as the one true path, however, even if they do not use the language of election to salvation. Recognizing the associated issues of othering, they often pursue civic pluralism to engage constructively with religious diversity while maintaining their theological differentiation.[49] Vatican II's *Nostra aetate* (1965), the most famous Catholic statement of interfaith fraternity, is an interesting example that tries to walk this middle road. The Catholic Church believes its own path is the fullest expression of God's redeeming grace. Yet it affirms the Jewish covenant with the assertion in Romans 11:29 that God does not revoke divine promises, and expresses regard for Muslims by delineating ways in which Islam approximates Christian teaching:

> They adore the one God, living and subsisting in Himself; merciful and all-powerful, the Creator of heaven and earth, who has spoken to men; they take pains to submit wholeheartedly to even His inscrutable decrees, just as Abraham, with whom the faith of Islam takes pleasure in linking itself, submitted to God. Though they do not acknowledge Jesus as God, they revere Him as a prophet. They also honor Mary, His virgin Mother; at times they even call on her with devotion. In addition, they await the day of judgment when God will render their deserts to all those who have been raised up from the dead. Finally, they value the moral life and worship God especially through prayer, almsgiving and fasting.[50]

By grounding the work of reconciliation deeply in the soil of Christian values, the proclamation cannot avoid the mutual construction of self and other. It also continues to privilege theistic traditions. The goal is clearly respectful coexistence, but the tendency to interpret religious difference in our own categories also perpetuates more subtle forms of othering.

With serious commitment to ongoing self-critique, confessional Christian scholars call out the problems within such constructions. Caryn Riswold cautioned how Christian privilege also distorts academic study and teaching of religion; it is a fundamentally Christian construct that defines categories, norms and curricula.[51] Mary Boys challenged misleading claims that reveal residual disdain for Jews and Judaism: 1) the God of the Old Testament is a God of wrath, while the God of the New Testament is a God of love; 2) Jews rejected Jesus because they could not recognize the profound truth of a suffering savior; 3) the self-righteous and hypocritical

Pharisees reveal the legalistic nature of Judaism; 4) Jews were unfaithful to their covenant, so it was replaced by the covenant of Christ. She wrote, "Supersessionism is still deeply ingrained in the church because it is carried in a 'story line'—what I will call the 'conventional account of Christian origins'—presented in countless Christian education classes, sermons, and theological works."[52] Christian leaders who recognize such dangers are working diligently to tell a better story.

Analogous to these efforts, Letty Russell and others have struggled with the ways in which the doctrine of election is historically bound up with colonialism and can still perpetuate imperial practices, using difference as a means to oppress people.[53] A little historical background is helpful: even after Christianity began to be uncoupled from state power, colonialism—with religious mission at its side—sustained the links between spiritual, cultural, and political domination. Christianity was almost inseparable from European life and thought, so its presumption of religious superiority was built into the imposition of Western culture on colonial states.[54] Physical aggression was frequently justified as protecting missionaries even when there were clear political objectives, and Christian education was the "civilizing" tool used to destabilize native cultures like those in the United States.[55] Rev. Josiah Strong's *Our Country: Its Possible Future and Present Crisis* was a bestseller in the late nineteenth century. Warning against what he viewed as perils threatening America's destiny (immigration, Catholicism, secular education, Mormonism, intemperance, socialism, urban decadence, materialism), Strong argued that the nation must be "God's right arm" in battle against the world's ignorance and sin. He claimed that the "Western races," especially those living in the US, "must take the lead in the final conflicts of Christianity for possession of the world. Ours is the elect nation for the age to come. We are the chosen people. We cannot afford to wait. The plans of God will not wait."[56]

While there has been profound spiritual reckoning with the religious role in colonialist oppression,[57] recent decades have also revealed the momentum of Christian "dominion" ideologies in America. They unabashedly promote the doctrine that the US is a Christian nation and they should rule over nonbelievers as God's elect.[58] This form of fundamentalist Christian nationalism is vigorously opposed in many quarters, but it stands in uncanny relationship to American exceptionalism. Religious communities are not the only groups to see themselves as chosen. Nations do as well.

ELECTION AND NATIONALISM

Without mention of Christianity, national chosenness still justifies conquest and cultural imperialism. In 1900, Senator Albert Jeremiah Beveridge stumped across America to advocate for the annexation of the Philippines, and his arguments were incorporated into the Republican platform. Advancing the cause, he declaimed on the Senate floor that God "has marked the American people as His chosen nation to finally lead in the regeneration of the world. This is the divine mission of America, and it holds for us all the profit, all the glory, all the happiness possible to man. We are trustees of the world's progress, guardians of its righteous peace."[59] Less bombastically, Woodrow Wilson stated that America is "chosen, and prominently chosen, to show the way to the nations of the world how they shall walk in the paths of liberty."[60] Presidents are generally still expected to affirm a unique, divinely ordained destiny for the United States. Although it is called American exceptionalism, the thinking is not all that exceptional. Literature of the European colonial powers was rife with similar claims, as was literature from the Third Reich. One of Dostoyevsky's characters in *The Possessed* proclaims that Russians are "the only god-bearing people on earth, destined to regenerate and save the world."[61]

There is allure in imagining one's national history as the fundamental story of the universe. Modern nationalism is particularly deft in drawing on longstanding cultural resources, especially religious ones, that shape and strengthen the "sacred communion" of the nation. Anthony Smith identified four elements, several of which are redolent of chosenness, that magnify nationalism's power to frame group identity and ideals: (1) a myth of ethnic election; (2) attachment to particular terrains; (3) yearning to recover a golden age of communal heroism and creativity; and (4) belief in the regenerative power of sacrifice to ensure their glorious destiny. He did not argue causality: religion is not the reason for nationalism or its destructive excesses. Smith stated simply that the traditions provide some of the most salient structures for developing the imagined community of a nation, and he highlighted powerful parallels: "The nation state replaces the deity, history assumes the role of divine providence, the leader becomes the prophet, his writings and speeches form the sacred texts, the national movement becomes the new church, and its celebratory and commemorative rites take the place of religious ceremonies."[62] It is easy to see how election of nation *or* faith fulfills the fundamental human needs discussed in chapter 1: the will to meaning, pleasure and power, the building blocks of a society, the framework for cultural values. There is a transcendent purpose, a compelling claim on our ultimate concern, institutions that can mediate between thought and action, and an abiding community that transcends our own finitude. Yet national chosenness also comes with a dark side, just as it does in religious forms.

Conor Cruise O'Brien called this holy nationalism "chosen people with tenure," believing it to be more sinister because it is less likely to imagine forfeiting its status for moral failing.[63] It is possible, however, that the most important parallel between "chosen" nations and "chosen" religious communities is that they share a dialectical tension in regard to their vocation. Their claims can justify bellicosity, conceit, and self-absorption, but they can also catalyze ethical aspiration, humility, and self-critique. En route to Washington in 1861, Abraham Lincoln told the New Jersey Senate that he was honored to serve as "an humble instrument in the hands of the Almighty, and of this, his almost chosen people" in his efforts to preserve the Union, the Constitution, and American liberties.[64] The single word, *almost*, bore the weight of a nation in crisis about its very character. Franklin Delano Roosevelt spoke of a frontier that remained unconquered; he was not referring to Manifest Destiny or foreign acquisitions but rather "the nation-wide frontier of insecurity, of human want and fear. This is the frontier—the America—we have set ourselves to reclaim."[65]

Langston Hughes's famous poem "Let America Be America Again" reckons with the fact that the idea of America was largely defined by and reserved for white Christians. Yet he invoked faith in the promise of a place, like Eden, that has never existed yet shapes the very vision of what the nation seeks to become:

O, let America be America again—
The land that never has been yet—
And yet must be—the land where every man is free.
The land that's mine—the poor man's, Indian's, Negro's, ME—
Who made America,
Whose sweat and blood, whose faith and pain,
Whose hand at the foundry, whose plow in the rain,
Must bring back our mighty dream again. . . .
O, yes,

I say it plain,
America never was America to me,
And yet I swear this oath—
America will be![66]

We see how secular and religious ideas of election can serve both as a catalyst of violence and oppression and as impetus to self-critique and improvement. They can inspire and justify domination or restrict the natural human drive to establish power over others. Neither conquest nor chosenness is likely to be uprooted from the human catalog of concepts; they can only be interpreted and channeled. Even though moderates' investment in election may grant "legitimacy" to a dangerous religious idea and inadvertently hone its usefulness as a weapon, its power can be wielded for good. As Todd Gitlin and Liel Leibovitz remarked, "We began writing this book wishing to put out the fires of chosenness, but completed it thinking that—however dangerous they are if allowed to rage out of control—they are here to stay and just might light a way forward."[67]

PART IV

GOOD AND DANGEROUS

CHAPTER 12

RELIGION IN THE PUBLIC SQUARE?

The Case of Criminal Justice

RELIGION IN THE PUBLIC SQUARE

The subjects in this volume repeatedly converge with religious expression in the public sphere. Political leaders periodically invoke scripture to support their ethics and policy positions. American exceptionalism permeates political speech. Anti-Muslim bias, embedded in media and public campaigns, reveals the ongoing exercise of religious othering. Violent conflicts are often molded around religious identity, even though they are generally embedded in competition for power and resources. Certainly, the dangers illuminated in this volume have maximal impact in the ways that religious ideas shape social realities. Given these intersections, the tools of self-critical faith have the potential to improve religion in the public square. Nuanced conceptions of scriptural truth can chasten the moral certainty used to excuse hateful religious speech and discriminatory policies. If chosenness, in its secular and religious forms, includes the commitment to make space for difference, to identify with the suffering of humanity, and to affirm every person's innate capacity for moral reasoning—taught as real possibilities within the Abrahamic traditions—then it can help the body politic better support its diverse members.

Since harmful versions of these ideas never disappear, however, it might be better to keep religious influence at bay. Perhaps public theology is just a bad idea. I was raised in the tradition of John Rawls, believing that we should utilize "public reason" rather than religious beliefs in arguing a policy position. The rules that regulate our common life should be based on arguments to which we all have equal access, framed so that diverse people might reasonably be expected to agree.[1] As a religious minority, I am grateful for the continuing disestablishment of Protestantism, concerned that legally privileged religious voices impinge on the liberty of others. Yet I am also appreciative that religious perspectives have been brought to bear on issues of social justice, from abolition to civil rights, and were instrumental in changing the system in critical ways. While most white people did not support civil rights agitation during the 1950s and early 1960s, and many of those with strong religious identity lived in the segregationist South, Dr. King's spiritual rhetoric helped catalyze the transformation of our public conscience.

For much of my life, progressives seemed to cede the public religious voice to illiberal perspectives, to people who were making religious ideas ever more dangerous. It was not for lack of religious conviction, but rather for liberal commitment to pluralism and Rawlsian public reason. It gave the erroneous impressions that political liberalism was hostile to religion, that religious voices were being pushed out of public debate, and that "religious" increasingly meant "conservative." Urging progressives to reclaim public religious discourse and "tap into the moral underpinnings of the nation," President Obama (then a senator) declared, "When we discuss religion only in the negative sense of where or how it should not be practiced, rather than in the positive sense of what it tells us about our obligations toward one another . . . others will fill the vacuum, those with the most insular views of faith, or those who cynically use religion to justify partisan ends." He went on to assert in Rawlsian style, however, that democracy requires religiously motivated individuals to translate their convictions into universal values, "accessible to people of all faiths, including those with no faith at all."[2]

I am sympathetic to both dimensions of his argument. It is unwise to relinquish the public voice of religion to people who use it to deny individuals access to public services, reject climate science, legislate bias, and limit our responsibilities to support the disadvantaged. Yet the separation of religion and state serves a vital role in preserving American democracy, and also creates broad space for spirituality in all its polymorphous beauty to flourish. Roger Williams, James Madison, and Alexis de Tocqueville all understood that keeping religion out of state affairs—and government control out of religion—fosters the vitality of religious life.[3] It still allows people to vote for religious reasons, and officials to act for religious reasons. It is not true that "religious citizens are forced to split off vital components of their personalities," as Stephen Carter argued.[4] Wilfred McClay's complaint that religious expression "has been pushed to the margins, to a sort of cultural red-light district, along with other unfortunate frailties and vices to which we are liable" is disingenuous.[5] The controversy is how we talk about, enshrine, and embody religious values in our collective public life.

Ultimately, I advocate a "conversation" model in public discourse rather than one of strict separation—a conversation in which religious ideas are critically engaged. Danièle Hervieu-Léger's understanding of secularism is important here: it is *not* a process of eradication of religion from the public square or from society in general, but "one of re-composition of the religious within a broader distribution of beliefs in a society within which no institution can lay claim to a monopoly of meaning."[6] Individuals and communities are encouraged to share their religious perspectives on public policy, but without expectation that they operate as a trump card. They may claim to speak *from* a tradition, but not to speak exclusively *for* it, since it is evident that people interpret the same spiritual inheritance in diverse ways. They may present teachings that shape their values as people of faith, but they function in public space as ideas rather than religious truths. In the "conversation," such teachings provide inspiration, not authority; motivation, not warrant.[7] Protected but not privileged speech, religious discourse can also be challenged when put forward in public discussion, as we collectively examine every side of critical issues in our body politic and try to discern the path forward. Presenting a religious reason for one's public policy position should not stifle debate.

John Rawls asked, "How is it possible that there may exist over time a stable and just society of free and equal citizens profoundly divided by reasonable though incompatible religious, philosophical and moral doctrines?"[8] My answer is: with substantive and civil conversation that seeks to have all our sources of value interrogate and augment one another. This should not be surprising, since I have gone to great lengths to collect a multiplicity of religious voices, highlighting their provisional nature and self-critical capacities. By identifying the dangers of religious ideas, I mean to improve them, not to disqualify them.

Nonetheless, I remain wary about how religion exerts its influence in the public square. People use religion for partisan advantage and politics for sectarian gains. Given the ongoing privilege that Christianity bears in the US context, the potential for abuse is clear. Its power has been deployed to erode women's reproductive rights, discredit the teaching of science, and demonize Muslims. Recent government actions appear to define religious freedom as the freedom to discriminate, as when the Supreme Court authorized a baker to withhold services because he does not approve of same-sex marriage, and when Health and Human Services regulations allowed health care providers to deny treatment based on religious convictions.[9] Even religious values I would support, such as nonviolence, seem fraught if given sway over political decisions.

Thus I am attracted to Robert Audi's notion of theo-ethical equilibrium: "Where religious considerations appropriately bear on matters of public morality or of political choice, religious people have a prima facie obligation . . . to seek an equilibrium between those considerations and relevant secular standards of ethics and political responsibility."[10] It is not a matter of translation, à la Rawls. It requires balancing what their religion teaches with a plural understanding of the broader public good. It requires them to stand both inside and outside their lifestance to examine its impact. It requires self-critical faith and reclaiming the complexities of their traditions. This balancing act both defends against powerful religious voices legislating morality for everyone, and helps to construct a common civic virtue. But the incorporation of secular ethics and reasoning exists alongside religious discourse, not instead of it. It invites us to explore diverse religious teachings to discover if there is something we might learn. Sometimes the dangers of religious ideas are good—challenging the status quo and providing a lens to see the world a little differently. Airing in the public square can potentially advance self-critical faith and public policy at the same time.

As a test case, this chapter investigates yet another dangerous religious idea, reward and punishment. It has the familiar mix of destructive and constructive powers we saw in previous sections. Like the other concepts, it is deeply embedded in human nature even as religious expressions give it special resonance. Rather than provide an extensive historical review to highlight the dangers as in previous sections, however, this more condensed discussion emphasizes what religion might contribute to thinking about criminal justice in the United States. It draws from scripture and later tradition in Judaism, Christianity, and Islam in search of establishing equilibrium—a dynamic working balance between interdependent parts—with secular and religious conceptions of justice.

THE DANGERS OF REWARD AND PUNISHMENT

Religious ideas about justice generally begin on the divine plane. Faith in a God who cares about justice is fundamental in theistic traditions; the concept of reward and punishment as one means to effect it is deeply embedded in their scriptures and theologies. Although the concept was not born there, its articulation in sacred text lends an ultimacy that magnifies its significance. Torah's portrayal of God as the one true judge promises abundant produce, peace, and procreation to an obedient community, as well as horrific suffering if the people stray significantly from the prescribed path (Lev. 26, Deut. 27–28, Exod. 23). Israel is instructed to create a parallel human system of justice, punishing measure for measure; its classic formulation is expressed in the law of talion: eye for eye, tooth for tooth, etc. (Exod. 21, Lev. 24, Deut. 19). In New Testament, individuals are punished by God either immediately, as with the deaths of Ananias and Sapphira when they withhold part of the sale price of property from the apostles (Acts 5), or more frequently in the eschatological future. Matthew 25, for instance, promises the kingdom of God to those who provide support for people in need, and age-long punishment (historically interpreted as everlasting) to those who do not. Qur'an attaches eternal consequences to divine judgment: well-watered gardens for those who obey Allah and eternal fire for those who do not, timelessly and forever (4:13–14).

The idea of reward and punishment may at times motivate goodness or deter wrongdoing, provide a sense of agency and enable people to discern meaning in suffering, or contribute to the construction of a just political order. Even if one rejects the underlying theology, the effort to ground history in a moral framework can be compelling. Consider President Lincoln's moving second inaugural address, when he lamented of the Civil War: "If God wills that it continue until all the wealth piled by the bondsman's two hundred and fifty years of unrequited toil shall be sunk, and until every drop of blood drawn with the lash shall be paid by another drawn with the sword . . . , *the judgments of the Lord are true and righteous altogether*" (Ps. 19:10, italics added).

Since most Americans today probably do not believe that God thrust the war upon the nation as retribution for the sin of slavery, it is strange that this speech so captures the imagination. Is it simply the elegant rhetoric? Do we embrace it as the poetic justice sometimes revealed in historical rhythms of the universe? I believe that Lincoln's address is persuasive because it explains us to ourselves; reward and punishment is fundamental to how we learn. The Civil War helped reorganize Americans' moral and political understanding of slavery.[11] It catalyzed a slow, painful process of reeducating our sensibilities—still being worked out in public monuments and voting rights and policing and affirmative action and a host of other issues.

Yet the concept of reward and punishment is fraught with theological and historical problems. It often serves less as a theology than as a self-serving worldview, a truism brilliantly captured by the nursery rhyme: *Little Jack Horner sat in the corner eating his Christmas pie. He stuck in his thumb, pulled out a plum and said, "What a good boy am I!"* Although we rarely stop to reflect on its meaning, it reveals a common and problematic presumption of religious causality: Jack proclaims that some force has rewarded him for his goodness. Since he is sitting in the corner rather than at the table, it seems just as likely that he landed there because he was misbehaving, but that does not enter into his calculus. When people imagine they can discern God's judgment in good fortune and disaster, it invites responses like Jack's—interpreting events to align with their own biases. Such perils were on display in the profane pointing of fingers after 9/11, Hurricane Katrina, and the earthquake in Haiti. Religious figures blamed the victims for these disasters, or insisted that efforts by gays, feminists, and others to claim equal rights had lifted God's veil of protection from the United States.[12] Their blasphemy epitomized everything that is wrong with religion in the public square.

Danger is also evident when people who are diagnosed with terminal illness, women who are abused by their husbands, or friends and neighbors suddenly struck by tragedy presume they have done something wrong, and that God authorizes the wounds inflicted upon them. While the theology that drives their conclusions may help them find meaning in their experience and to identify a course of action, it ultimately perpetuates the potential for cruelty or suffering to be divinely justified. Not all experiences of hardship come as payment due. Even the reward side of the equation has problems. The danger of self-satisfaction in material or social success is exacerbated when it is interpreted as a sign of divine favor, and it creates an excuse to judge others who are not similarly "blessed." Prosperity gospel in the United States has proven itself to be prone to such abuse.[13]

Religious discourse has at times rationalized social and economic inequalities as somehow deserved, making it far too easy to do far too little about poverty and discrimination. Russell Conwell's *Acres of Diamonds*, for example, asserted that we should not give charity because God made people poor for a reason: "I sympathize with the poor, but the number of poor to be sympathized with are very small. To sympathize with a man whom God has punished for a reason, thus to help him when God would still continue a just punishment, is to do wrong."[14] Conwell made so much money from publication of this tract and related speeches that he founded Temple University with the proceeds.

The concept of reward and punishment, however, is not exclusively or primarily religious. Driving along the highway once, I saw a billboard: *"Don't make Me come down there"—God.* I laughed so hard I almost had to pull off the road. Even though I do not believe in a God who works that way, it evoked the familiar parental threat, part of our basic training in right and wrong. In his work on education, John Locke wrote, "Good and evil, reward and punishment, are the only motives to a rational creature; these are the spur and reins whereby all mankind are set on work, and guided."[15] Hopefully he overstated the case, but we are hardwired to think this way. We love to see "bad guys" get what we think they deserve, an appetite whetted far more by Hollywood than holy texts as contemporary films continually feed our craving for punishment. Evolutionary biologists explain how ideas of reward and punishment are embedded in our DNA, how their ancient tribal forms ensured survival of the group. Sociologists declare that retributive justice is integral to how we developed human community and will always be a fundamental part of our law codes.

Shifting our critique from theology to jurisprudence, it is evident that a system built almost entirely on retributive justice remains deeply problematic. The law and order drive of the 1970s marked the end of a century of penal reform that had focused on the rights and reformability of offenders.[16] Today, America's racially imbalanced retributive justice system has created a massive prison–industrial complex with the highest incarceration and recidivism rates in the world.[17] The economic and social legacy of a nation that claims 5 percent of the global population but 25 percent of the world's prisoners is deeply compromised. In *The New Jim Crow*, Michelle Alexander made a compelling case that our criminal justice system serves as a "stunningly comprehensive and well-disguised system of racialized social control" designed to continue disenfranchising African Americans.[18] It is a specific and scandalous iteration of Michel Foucault's insight that reward and punishment works to perpetuate dominant forces of social, economic, and political power, inside and outside the criminal justice system.[19]

Several authors have theorized that the United States' penchant for punishment grows all too naturally from Christian teaching of a brutal God, a theology of sin that deems all of humanity unworthy save for divine grace, and an emphasis on personal salvation rather than communal redemption.[20] According to this perspective, Christian influence renders criminals deserving of suffering, human character incapable of reform, and the justice system blind to social ills. Given how intrinsic reward and punishment is to human psyche and society, however, it seems unlikely that the US penal code is a direct result of scriptural teaching or theology. As with other dangerous religious ideas, the religious aspect provides spiritual support for social, political, and legislative agendas. People quote "an eye for an eye" (even though most consider it barbaric in its literal sense—except, incongruously, the life for life part) because it justifies the human thirst for vengeance. They quote it, even if they do not thump the Bible very often or know it very well, because the scriptural reference seems to ground our instincts in a moral framework. Yet the idea of reward and punishment is not all that religious traditions have to say about justice, human or divine; its place in religious discourse has been magnified by its prominence in contemporary culture. A thicker reading of the scriptures and religious teachings yields a far more supple, sophisticated conception of justice that has potential implications for public theology, political discourse, and the criminal justice system.

RESTORING THE FULLNESS OF RELIGIOUS TEACHING ON JUSTICE

Four of the most prominent approaches to justice today—retributive, restorative, distributive, and procedural—are all addressed creatively and substantively in scriptural texts and later tradition.

- *Retributive justice* focuses on punishment as a response to violation. The offender violated the law and must pay. It bestows "satisfaction" on the aggrieved party and is assigned a deterrent effect. It can also incapacitate perpetrators so that they cannot do it again.
- *Restorative justice* emphasizes repairing damage, restitution, taking responsibility, rehabilitation, and restoring relationships. It is also committed to satisfaction, but differs from retributive justice in its strategies for righting the balance.[21]

- *Procedural justice* aims for equality in the processes of decision making, including but not limited to the adjudication of sin or crime.
- *Distributive justice* sets as its goal the equitable distribution of resources to all members of society, even if the means for doing so contradict some aspects of equal treatment under the law.

Political discourse in the United States tends to treat these as pairs of binary choices. People support either retributive or restorative methods of justice. They measure fairness by either procedural or distributive means. Our religious sources do not. They expect that *all* these forms of justice are required in dynamic relationship.

A quick peek in a dictionary reveals the inadequacy of basic conceptions about justice. Merriam-Webster's primary definition is "the maintenance or administration of what is just, especially by the impartial adjustment of conflicting claims or the assignment of merited rewards or punishments." Its simplified definition for English-language learners is even starker: "the process or result of using laws to fairly judge and punish crimes and criminals."[22] Contrary to this narrow focus, Judaism, Christianity, and Islam recognize that criminal justice unfolds within systems of economic and other forms of justice, that the state cannot fully represent the whole of the project, and that the social weal depends on restoration as well as punishment. Excavating the robust religious synthesis of approaches to justice, we can clarify our ethical commitments and reexamine whether our current policies achieve them.

Fundamentals of procedural justice are established through Torah instructions, including equal justice, direct justice, proportional response, and fairness in adjudication. Citizen and stranger, rich and poor, all are to be treated equally (Exod. 23). Yet distributive justice is also legislated: portions of one's field and a tithe are set aside for the poor; there are special protections for the widow, orphan, and stranger (Exod. 22, Lev. 19, Deut. 24, 26); debts are released in the sabbatical year (Deut. 15); and a redistribution of wealth is commanded in the jubilee so that society does not allow the growth of a perpetual underclass (Lev. 25).[23]

Reflections on justice also appear in narrative, including the story of Sodom and Gomorrah in Genesis 18–19. At first, it appears to be a tale of God's retribution, destroying the cities for their sinfulness. Warned of the impending disaster, however, Abraham challenges the God of justice to do justly, and the equation shifts from one of collective punishment to one in which a whole city might be spared because of a righteous few. The fact that this agreement is reached in a call for "justice" rather than mercy is remarkable. Lot's wife and daughters pay steep prices for the social violence that envelops them (as women frequently do) and destruction does ultimately befall the cities, but the introduction to the narrative contains an important message for human constructions of justice. God feels obliged to consult Abraham: "for I have singled him out, that he may instruct his children and his household after him to keep the way of the Lord by doing righteousness and judgment" (Gen. 18:19). Jewish interpretation discerned two distinct and equally essential approaches to justice in the final phrase, distributive and retributive. A law-governed society is a place of *mishpat* (judgment); societies need the rule of law to survive. But law cannot alone create a good society. It must have *tzedakah* (righteousness), a Hebrew root that has become so linked to the redistribution of resources that can make for justice, it often gets translated as "charity."[24] This word pair—*tzedakah umishpat*—is Hebrew Bible's expression for social justice.[25] If there is no equitable distribution of resources, if people are driven to steal by abject poverty or lack of opportunity, the law cannot effect justice.

There is "an eye for an eye," but there is also restorative justice. Theft, robbery, and fraud, for instance, require return of the stolen object, an additional payment to the victim, and a process of atonement and forgiveness (Lev. 5:20–26).[26] The teaching of reproof (Lev. 19:17) is understood to require that we address the one who has wronged us, hold that person accountable, and repair the breach.[27] Covenant withstands violation and develops mechanisms for reestablishing right relationship. Pervasive in Hebrew Bible, it is the organizing principle of the polity and becomes the foundation of justice with its mutual obligations and profoundly restorative dimensions. Covenantal bonds are not mere contracts, but dynamic relationships that embody *ḥesed* (a kindness greater than one has a "right" to claim) and set shalom as their goal.[28]

Rabbinic tradition expanded on these restorative foundations: it insisted on the importance of repentance and the reformability of human character, it identified reconciliation between individuals as central to legal redress, and it affirmed the ultimate goal of repairing the community.[29] As mentioned in chapter 2, the Mishnah translated "eye for an eye" into a system of restorative justice: One is liable to compensate the injured party for pain, for time lost from work, for medical expenses, for any permanent loss in earning potential, and for emotional suffering (m. B. Qam. 8:1). This rabbinic text, redacted in the second century but evidently recounting law that was already in force in the Jewish community, was then buttressed by the Talmud, which justified the principle through creative and engaging exegesis. It reimagined the biblical teaching of *lex talionis* by applying procedural requirements. Since there must be equal justice, for instance, the case of a one-eyed attacker presents a problem. Physical retaliation would make the assailant blind, but the original victim would still be able to see. That is not equal justice! It is also possible that the assailant might die as a result of the operation, resulting in "life and eye for eye," a clear violation of proportional response. Taking the argument to the point of absurdity to demonstrate that retributive justice cannot fulfill the underlying values of Torah, the Talmud inquired: Can it be equal justice if a small man kills a large one? Is the "smaller" penalty sufficient when he forfeits his life? (b. B. Qam. 83b–84a).[30] Still, rabbinic interpretation grasped how scripture's diverse modalities of justice are inextricably linked. The sages expressed an abiding commitment to the value of reward and punishment and the ideal of measure for measure.[31] They were unwilling to give up the idea of a God committed to justice or to deny our need to make moral sense of human experience.

Rabbinic tradition also deliberated on the ethics of distributive justice. In t. Bava Metzi'a 11:33–37 (Lieberman), for instance, the sages discussed the case of a wellspring that flows through a city. The majority asserted that residents of that city have first claim on the water, even if those downstream suffer as a result. People who live downstream, however, have priority over the animals of the city, and over household tasks such as laundry. Rabbi Yosi maintained in each instance that the needs of the city take precedence. Later layers of rabbinic literature relate the story of a student who struggled mightily to understand what logic or scriptural support could justify these conclusions. In the Babylonian Talmud, the student's incredulity stemmed from Rabbi Yosi's claim that city residents could do their laundry before providing essential drinking water to others (b. Ned. 81a). In the Jerusalem Talmud, however, the student found an ethical conundrum simply in the determination that the lives of the city's residents take precedence over those who are outside (y. Shev. 8:5). Given the American context in which property rights are so deeply ingrained in our culture that the ethics of water policies are barely debated, this open-ended deliberation is striking. With the dialectical reasoning so central to Talmudic thought, Oral Torah advances Tanakh's multiperspectival vision of justice.

Parables in the New Testament also productively complicate our thinking about justice. In Matthew 20:1–16, the kingdom of heaven is compared to a landowner who pays his day-laborers the same amount, no matter what time of day they were hired. When the workers who were hired first complained that they should be paid more, the landowner replies, "Friend, I am doing you no wrong; did you not agree with me for the usual daily wage? . . . Are you envious because I am generous?" Recognizing the human tendency to resist distributive justice as unfair, the text suggests a higher order of justice where everyone receives what they need. The story of the prodigal son (Luke 15:11–32) has a different reason for "unfair" allocation of favor. The father is so overjoyed to have his lost son return to him that he gives him fine clothes and celebrates with a great feast. The tale recognizes the pain of the son who remained at home, faithfully serving his father while his brother squandered a share of the family wealth in faraway lands. But it insists on the goal of restoration, of reintegrating the wayward child into the family and community. While these passages are frequently interpreted as kingdom parables, teaching about God's eschatological justice that is overflowing with grace, the human casting illuminates interpersonal and social justice as well. The US Conference of Catholic Bishops, for instance, invoked the prodigal son in a letter on criminal justice to commend a more forgiving jurisprudence.[32] The centrality of repentance in all three traditions keeps open a door that incarceration tends to shut.

There is another parable in Luke (10:25–37) that potentially illuminates restorative justice: the tale of the Good Samaritan. It is enshrined, at least in name, in American law. Good Samaritan regulations address what obligation we have to help a stranger in trouble, at what risk, and what protections we have if we try but something goes wrong. The parable, on the other hand, can be read as a victim-centered narrative that revolves around the value or lack thereof that attaches to the unnamed man who is assaulted by robbers. He is the first character and the only one who interacts with every other. In a book on restorative justice, Christopher Marshall demonstrated how such a reading aligns with the contemporary argument that the experience of the victim should not be effaced by the standing of the state in criminal proceedings.[33] He also noted that the parable does not focus on the crime, but rather on people's response to it.

Marshall's broader analysis reflects a problem common to Christian exegesis of the passage, presuming that the Kohen (priest) and the Levite pass by without helping in order to preserve their ritual purity. The original Jewish audience of the parable would have known that these ostensible communal leaders had a legal obligation to save a life or tend to an unclaimed corpse regardless of purity concerns, and the listeners would recognize the story pattern: if there is a Kohen and a Levite, then the third character should be an Israelite. They would expect to learn that the Israelite did the right thing. Status does not make one holy; your actions do. By making the final figure a Samaritan instead, Jesus addresses the true crux of the tale: "Who is my neighbor?" (Luke 10:29) in the command to "love your neighbor as yourself" (Lev. 19:18).[34] Since the Samaritans were often antagonists of the Jews in the Persian and Roman periods,[35] Jesus challenges his listeners to accept that goodness may be found among those whom we expect intend us harm. This conviction has implications for the modern criminal justice system. It challenges our propensity to dehumanize people who break the law, seeing them only as criminals deserving of punishment. At the end of the passage Jesus instructs his interlocutor, "Go and do likewise" (10:37), pressing us all to expand our circle of concern. That concern surely includes the incarcerated, since many figures in Hebrew Bible and New Testament were arrested due to unjust systems, Joseph, Samson, Jeremiah, Daniel, John the Baptist, Peter, James, John, Silas, Paul, and Jesus included.

Efforts to humanize transgressors also appeared in teachings of the Church Fathers. Athanasius (296–373) spoke theologically of sin as sickness; Augustine applied the principle in a murder case to argue against the death penalty. He wrote to the judge, Marcellinus: "Fulfill, Christian judge, the duty of an affectionate father; let your indignation against their crimes be tempered by consideration of humanity; be not provoked by the atrocity of their sinful deeds to gratify the passion of revenge, but rather be moved by the wounds which these deeds have inflicted on their own souls to exercise a desire to heal them."[36]

Lactantius (240–c. 320) undertook a systemic analysis of what justice requires, editing his *Divine Institutes* to address Constantine after the emperor's conversion. Seeking to imbue the source of law in the empire with religious values, Lactantius wrote not only about personal Christian virtue (e.g., almsgiving, hospitality, care for the most vulnerable [book VI]), but also about foundational principles of social equity due to all people, created in the image of God (book V). It was "a manifesto for reform of the empire under the law of God," an objective full of both danger and promise.[37]

The Church Fathers also built on New Testament teachings of distributive justice, where concern for the poor is manifest. When the church started to acquire political power, they moved from a focus on personal charity and storing up treasure in heaven[38] to include broader notions of economic justice. Basil of Caesarea (330–79), for example, founded Basileias—a new city with a hospital, a residence for travelers and the poor, and treatment for lepers. He established training programs for able-bodied people living in poverty and businesses to give them work, extending these services to immigrants as well. "Basil repeatedly made the rhetorical point that wealth should come off the walls and up from the floors and out of the treasuries of rich men's houses, in order to find its way back into philanthropic and productive circulation."[39]

Qur'an and Muslim tradition also add compelling dimensions to thinking about justice. The Arabic term for justice, *adl*, draws from the root "to set something in its rightful place"—an image that conjures the mix of approaches we have been discussing. There is definitely a commitment to distributive justice, with the reallocation of resources through *zakat* established as one of the five pillars (2:277, 9:60), and enacted through fiqh.[40] Texts also record efforts to ameliorate harsh juridical penalties, making the requirements for conviction quite stringent and expanding procedural exceptions. Muhammad reportedly ordered Muslim judges to ward off hudud punishments by probing ambiguities.[41] The example of Umar cited in chapter 5, suspending hudud penalties for theft in a year of drought because scarcity drove people to steal, recognized exigency as one such ambiguity. There are also records of leniency in cases when the offenders confessed and repented, demonstrating a commitment to restorative justice.[42]

Several facets of Muslim juridical practice prompt particularly fruitful questions about criminal justice in the West. One is the involvement of the victims and their families in decision-making. Secular criminal law generally appoints the state in their stead, presuming that personal connection can only cloud the proceedings, but there are increasing challenges to this assumption. Susan Hascall wrote, "The restorative justice movement criticizes the lack of direct involvement by the community and the victims in sentencing and the modes of punishment utilized by criminal justice systems. More direct involvement by the stakeholders is thought to advance one of the goals of this movement, which is to humanize both the victims and the perpetrators of the crime."[43]

Long development of Islamic jurisprudence throughout the Middle Ages provides an extensive written record of theory and practice, facilitating reflection on this issue. In Islamic law, victims and their families in most criminal cases can choose the default retributive punishment (*kasas*), or elect compensation, conciliation, or pardon. The alternative paths are considered preferable to retaliation, each option ranked higher than the one before. Inclusion of family members is designed to make people more accountable as they explain their positions to one another.[44]

These mechanisms and the idea of victim's choice trace back to Qur'an: e.g., "The repayment of a bad action is one equivalent to it. But if someone pardons and puts things right, his reward is with Allah" (42:40). It presents a concept of measure for measure, but the goal is to put things right, something that can often be best accomplished through restorative justice. The sura continues: "If someone is steadfast and forgives, that is the most resolute course to follow" (42:44). The possibility of compensation also addresses retributive and restorative justice together as a pair: "Retribution is prescribed for you in the matter of the slain: freeman for freeman, slave for slave, female for female. But for one who receives any pardon from his brother, let it be observed honorably, and let the restitution (*diya*) be made to him with goodness. This is an alleviation from your Lord, and a mercy" (2:178).

Another useful facet of religious thinking about justice is its emphasis on mediation. The Medina Charter (622 CE) that Muhammad negotiated among the warring tribes in Yathrib was a real-world model, establishing constitutional processes for reconciliation.[45] Various informal mediation customs emerged in the subcultures of the Muslim world,[46] and medieval Jewish practice similarly encouraged conciliation. Maimonides wrote, "Every court that constantly effects mediation is to be praised, and it is of such a court that the verse says: 'Render a judgment of peace in your gates' (Zech 8:16). Which judgment contains peace? Surely it is mediation."[47]

Conciliation (*sulh*) is mentioned thirteen times in Qur'an in small- and large-scale conflicts. When "two parties among the believers fall to fighting," for example, the community is instructed to "make peace between them with justice and act equitably; truly God loves the just" (49:9).[48] Subsequent discourse addressed how judges should encourage but not impose mediation, what cases might not be appropriate to refer, the appointment of an adjudicator (with a preference for one who knows both parties rather than an outside "objective" observer), types of actions and payments an offender might agree to provide, etc. According to Mutaz Qafisheh, "Given this general guidance, coupled with myriad conciliation cases undertaken through the history, Islamic jurisprudence has thoroughly elaborated on the question of conciliation between offenders and victims to settle criminal cases, for the purpose of restoring peace and love."[49]

Feminist critiques warn that pursuit of forgiveness and reconciliation has at times been at women's expense, used to sustain injustice and abuse.[50] Across religious traditions and within secular society, prioritizing peace can certainly perpetuate existing power relationships and social realities. While reckoning with this concern, Islam's approach emphasizes something our professionalized system often forgets: crime is at its core a violation of one person by another. Like contemporary thinking about restorative justice, it does not eliminate the role of the state or the involvement of credentialed experts, but it offers a counterweight.[51]

Spiritual communities contribute in ways that go beyond public discourse and analysis. Experiments in restorative justice processes, like peace circles, are frequently adapted from indigenous models. The Mennonite Central Committee was involved in establishing the Victim–Offender Reconciliation Project in the 1970s. It was an effort to reclaim humanity within the mechanisms of justice, and to emphasize outcomes over procedures.[52] Today, religiously grounded reentry programs like Healing Communities USA and the Inner-City Muslim Action Network's Green ReEntry project lead the field to help recently incarcerated individuals rebuild their lives on the outside. Such efforts reveal religion's deep commitment to repentance, to faith in the mutability of human behavior or character, and to the importance of community in human flourishing, all as integral to the establishment of justice.

SELF-CRITICAL FAITH IN THE PUBLIC SQUARE

Expanded beyond "an eye for an eye," it is evident that religious ideas and praxis can be a "good and dangerous" influence in thinking about justice.

It is true in the various connotations of the phrase. "Good and . . ." serves as a colloquial modifier meaning "very." Some religious ideas about justice are very perilous. Theocratic systems in the world today demonstrate that restoring the normative authority of ancient texts does not necessarily advance the cause of justice; often these governments distill religion's harshest values, twisted to sustain various forms of social and economic power. Good *and* dangerous also suggests it can be both at the same time, an argument that has been central to this volume. Religious ideas about justice, like the issues discussed in previous sections, have positive and negative power. Lastly, *good* and dangerous can connote that they are dangerous in a good way, poking at assumptions, subverting oppressive structures, and provoking new ways of thinking about justice. Religion in the public square is still fraught, and religious ideas must be critically engaged. Without presuming to take the moral high ground, however, religious voices can offer their insight and experience in equilibrium with other sources of knowledge and value. They interrogate each other in pursuit of social repair.

Consequently, it is a valuable exercise to recover the broad range of religious teachings on justice in this age of mass incarceration, police violence, dehumanization, expanding wealth disparity, and other social inequities. The traditions do not furnish us with a ready-made set of policies. Instead, they point in a particular direction, one that in some ways is more holistic and humane than our modern system.[53] The multifaceted, integrated approach to justice in Judaism, Christianity, and Islam presents fertile soil for cultivating anew our own moral and political understandings.

It goes beyond recognition that retributive, restorative, procedural, and distributive justice are interdependent foundations rather than partisan divides. The complex relationship of personal, penal, and social justice in religious teachings prompts a deeper dive into the sea of intersectional justice issues. Connections between economic and criminal justice, for example, are rampant. It is not simply that economic opportunity and provision for everyone's basic needs are part of a justice "system." It is not simply that poverty and lack of opportunity can foster criminal behavior—although distributive injustice *is* central to the problem. Consider the depiction of justice as a blindfolded goddess holding a balance: it emphasizes equality in procedures rather than equity in circumstances—and even so, she is not as impartial as we might hope. Poor people and people of color consistently fare worse. By ignoring social, economic, racial, and political differences, inequities are multiplied.[54] The incarceration life cycle is a prime example; from bail to parole, the system disadvantages people of limited means.

Money is bound up with criminal justice in other ways as well. Agencies funded by civil forfeiture and the increasingly privatized prison–industrial complex, with an economic stake in locking people up, are driving unjust policies. Even the growing consensus regarding certain measures of criminal justice reform has an economic motivation: governments are reckoning with the enormous financial burden of housing over two million people in county jails and state and federal prisons: $80 billion a year that is surely needed elsewhere. Criminal *justice* cannot be achieved without attention to economic and social justice.

The religious traditions also contribute their capacities for self-critique, including explicit warnings about the ways people judge one another. Qur'an often speaks of Allah as the one who will judge between peoples (2:113, 7:87; see chapter 5), and deferring judgment (*irja*) became a principle within Islamic law. In wisdom literature within Tanakh, presumably orthodox ideas about reward and punishment are problematized, especially in the book of Job. It announces at the outset that Job is "blameless and upright," yet he suffers tremendously. As his troubles multiply, his friends come to sit with him in the dust for a long time before they even speak, and then they begin rather gently when engaging Job to explore the meaning of his experience. Eventually, however, they blame the victim in increasingly vociferous tones, inventing all sorts of wickedness he must have committed to fit the measure of his pain. They come to care more about justifying God than showing compassion for the afflicted and, in the text, God condemns them for it.

Paul's epistles also wrestle with the human propensity to judge each another harshly. His theology conveys clear expectations of divine reward and punishment, but he assails those who would arrogate unto themselves the powers of God's judgment (Rom. 2), suggesting he would have chastised those religious leaders who assigned guilt for recent natural disasters. Other texts (e.g., 1 Thess. 2:14–16) demonstrate that this constraint was sometimes observed in the breach, but presentations of Jesus have him repeatedly demur from the role of judge. In John 8, he reportedly tries to ignore the "teachers of the law" who bring forward an adulteress to test whether he will affirm Torah's prescribed punishment. When they press the issue, he eventually responds that the one without sin should cast the first stone—and she is spared. Bryan Stevenson, in *Just Mercy*, said we should go a step further and become "stone-catchers," shielding the marginalized from societal condemnation.[55]

Judaism, Christianity, and Islam—shaped over centuries and revealing diverse contexts, perspectives, and agendas—present contradictions and dialectical tensions that serve as catalysts for critical self-reflection. Simply recognizing the absurd reduction of religious teaching to "an eye for an eye" forces a reckoning with our human instinct for vengeance and the way it shapes our criminal justice system. It presses for a realignment of priorities and expansion of the public imagination when it comes to justice. Critically engaged public theology, then, is not only a defense against those who would arrogate the power of religious ideas to do harm. For all the hazards of religion in the public square, there is a good and dangerous role to play.

CHAPTER 13

THE SPACE-IN-BETWEEN

Previous chapters have demonstrated that the manifest dangers of religious ideas are not limited to extremist violence. Concepts at the heart of faith contribute to a catalogue of human woes. The same convictions that inspire compassion, commitment, and inclusivity can justify brutality, apathy, and intolerance. So at some point in the "Dangerous Religious Ideas" course, I find myself saying to students, "If you never wake up in the middle of the night with a deep dread, thinking that the world might be a better place without religion, you are not paying close enough attention." But the fire that is religion is elemental—it cannot be "disappeared"—and it has to power to do wondrous things as well. Vivekananda was right.

The particular themes addressed in this volume represent only a few examples of the ways that religion is deeply embedded in human nature and society. Scripture supports the will to meaning in its fundamental structure, whether it is received as divine instruction or as human efforts to discern a path through the universe. Its power is palpable in the course of human history, whether it is invoked as a container of eternal truths with binding authority or a fount of inspiration with an inexhaustible store of teachings to be discovered. Scripture supports the construction of community in its crafting of a sacred story, and in shared rituals for recitation and re-experience, triggering emotions that strengthen bonds and catalyze collective action. It transmits values that can both shape and challenge cultural norms. Through narrative, command, and reflection, the texts transmit critical information for individuals to sort the infinite data set of existence, and they provide a model of community with rules for its mutual flourishing.

Even spiritual traditions without a written canon that is considered sacred frequently have stories and sayings that fulfill many of these functions.

Concepts of chosenness and election, salvation and supersession, reward and punishment present a similar array of foundational human needs and capacities. It suggests why these cultural memes have been so successful in copying themselves and adapting through the generations. The Enlightenment led many people to believe that religion would fall by the wayside of human history, replaced by reason as our lodestar. But religion has proven to be resilient, repeatedly reforming and re-forming itself, including a continuing negotiation with reason that has been going on since antiquity. This gift for adaptation prompts certain critics to issue dire warnings about religion as an infection. Richard Dawkins, for example, described "faith as one of the world's great evils, comparable to the smallpox virus but harder to eradicate."[1]

It is tempting to tweak the metaphor and argue that religion is instead more like bacteria: important for healthy human functioning with astounding curative powers (think penicillin), even though it can also run amok. But I am grateful for the critique. We need to be far more rigorous in investigating the cellular structure of our religious ideas. Although there are plenty of humanist voices that engage religion more constructively than Dawkins, I require my "Dangerous Religious Ideas" students to read his book or one of the other "new atheists." Sikivu Hutchinson and Hector Avalos are generally more nuanced than the usual collection of white men—e.g., Dawkins, Sam Harris, Christopher Hitchens—but they all create comparable struggles for my students, who are aghast that the arguments do not generally distinguish between liberal and fundamentalist expressions of religion. As David Hollinger catalogued this objection, "Can these writers not distinguish between Methodists and morons?"[2]

Apparently not. The entirety of religion is considered, at best, superstitious nonsense. More trenchantly, progressive religious voices are characterized as some of the many heads sustaining a murderous Hydra that spits venom into the human psyche and body politic, multiplying repression and inequity. I instruct my students not to deny or disprove the critique, but rather to utilize its strongest arguments to improve the religious project. I ask them to take seriously the accusation that our ideal of religious tolerance leads toward uncritical protection of rotten ideas and that moderates perpetuating even refined notions of scripture, election, or religion itself also enable those who wield them as weapons. And I tell them to dig out the dangers lurking in their own closets, because they are there. As discussed in the introduction to this book, the purest states of metals and ideas are not found in nature; they are always mixed with other substances. What makes religion a powerful force for good is to a large extent that which makes it potentially dangerous as well.

The detailed thematic treatments in parts II and III illustrate the traditions' multivocality and dynamism and reveal their capacity for incisive self-critique. The discussions are not designed as an exercise in apologetics, however. They do not simply argue that scripture can be holy without being hateful, or that election can be imagined in ways that do not denigrate or damn vast swaths of humanity. Each section begins by elucidating the particular threats entrenched within a foundational religious concept because all religious ideas are potentially dangerous and we cannot refine our ideas unless we see that. As with fire, it requires vigilance to prevent accidental harm and deliberate abuse. The deep roots of self-critical faith in Judaism, Christianity, and Islam present both a gift and an obligation.

Our own religious teaching should consistently be processed through the crucible of rigorous self-examination. We need to recognize how our texts, teachings, and practices have implications for others, in themselves and as echoes of historical interpretations. Examples abound: Are tithing expectations economically just? Do teachings of forgiveness put a dangerous burden on abused partners? How does our fundamental conception of religion continue to disadvantage indigenous traditions so they do not enjoy the same protections?

We should also be willing to subject other people's religious ideas to the same kind of critical scrutiny. The First Amendment protects people from *government* establishment and *government* interference in the free exercise of religion.[3] It does not require that we smile politely as people deploy their faiths in ways we consider harmful. Undermining science, marginalizing women and LGBTQ+ individuals, justifying legal discrimination—these interpretations cannot take shelter in freedom of religion or our commitment to tolerance. Instead, we must call out the peril and fight harder to establish meanings we see as liberative. "You will know them by their fruits" (Matt. 7:16, from a passage with a contested history of its own), by the real impact they have in the world. Critical reflection does not guarantee, of course, that the resulting perspective upholds an objective standard.

Rather, it represents a subjective voice in the ongoing construction of religious meaning. But the power of religion is too great merely to hope it is channeled to do good.

The idea of managing religious diversity primarily through silence may seem logical, but it promotes religious ignorance and ignorance ultimately breeds suspicion. Civil debates in public theology advance deeper understanding of texts, beliefs, and praxis. Alongside interreligious engagement of all sorts, they can develop literacy in and appreciation for diverse lifestances, and cultivate fruitful relationships between people who orient around religion differently. They reveal shared struggles across traditions, and help to clarify commitments as we work together for the common good. They illuminate the broad intrafaith diversity that exists, with the most important arguments unfolding, not between secularists and believers nor between different traditions battling for dominance but between adherents of the same faith contesting for the soul of their religion.

Encouraging debate about religious ideas certainly carries dangers of its own, but to ask tough questions is not to belittle. It is not an invitation to demonstrate religious bigotry or reengage in medieval battles between claimants of the "true faith." Pointing out the critical distinction between *condemn* and *contemn*, Cathleen Kaveny urged a public discourse that is not afraid to express strong disapproval, without characterizing opponents as despicable.[4]

It can be perplexing to determine how to respond when we encounter a dangerous religious idea in real time. Diana Eck offered a strategy that recognizes the diverse registers of our "voice." Commenting on a prayer guide published by Southern Baptists that described Hindus as lost in total darkness, she wrote:

> As a scholar of Hinduism, I must say you have seriously misrepresented the Hindu tradition . . . and I would be happy to speak with you about where I think your portrayal is misleading. As an American and fellow citizen, however, I will defend your right to believe and practice Christianity as you do, to believe the worst about our Hindu neighbors, to believe they are all going to hell, and to say so, both privately and publicly. But as a Christian, let me challenge you here, for I believe that your views of our neighbors are not well grounded in the Gospel of Christ, as I understand it.[5]

She did not disparage the Southern Baptists, but she challenged them, asserting her scholarly expertise and moral conviction. She did not claim to speak for all of Christianity, but she staked her ground. Careful deployment of our multiple voices can help navigate the difficult terrain, affirming freedom of religion without silently tolerating intolerance. Vigorous religious argument has been a vital part of the intellectual and political history of the West for centuries, and it continues to play a role in academic and theological discussions. As religion is increasingly inserted into the public square, however, it seems necessary to broaden this tradition.

Why does the history of interpretation matter in this work? As a scholar of scriptural exegesis, I appreciate the historical conversation for its own sake, delighting in recovering voices from the past and exploring ways they may still shine a light on our present. More importantly, the dynamism and multiplicity of interpretations expand the space between dismissing religious ideas as hopelessly problematic or embracing them uncritically. Peter Ochs spoke of giving religious texts "both the benefit of the doubt and the benefit of doubt." With the former, he attached value to scriptural meaning as transmitted by believing communities. With the latter, he sifted this inheritance through application of philosophical, historical, and textual/ rhetorical criticism.[6] Collectively, the interpretations mediate between past and present. Gadamer explained that the distance between us and a text from centuries ago "is not a yawning abyss, but is filled with the continuity of custom and tradition, in the light of which everything handed down presents itself to us."[7] We are inescapably effected by sacred text and the ways it has been understood; our religious ideas of today are shaped by our spiritual genealogy. In reconstructing parts of this family tree, we acquire an essential tool in the work of critique, inwardly and outwardly directed. In exploring the "surplus of meaning"[8] embedded in scripture and tradition, expanding our understanding of the past, we also open new possibilities for the future.

People do not easily let go of expectations, however. Faulkner's insight that "the past is never dead. It's not even past" is particularly true when it comes to religion. In many synagogues, there is a Hebrew phrase carved above the ark that translates, "Know before Whom you stand." One of the professors in my rabbinical school, working to reimagine the synagogue for the twenty-first century, used to joke that people often behave as if it says, "But we've always done it this way." He was urging congregations to design a different future, to swim in the stream of tradition but carve out new directions that renegotiate its boundaries. This, too, expands the space between discarding religion as irrelevant and resisting necessary change.

The space-in-between investigates the irreducible interconnectedness of religious ideas with the story of humanity, contending with those secularists who are still hoping for the Enlightenment to finish the job and do away with religion. The space-in-between acknowledges how the powers of religious ideas for good and ill are bound together, reckoning unafraid with dangers at the heart of faith. It excavates ones we might not readily see, challenging the facile notion sometimes held in progressive quarters that the necessary work of refinement is already complete. The space-in-between embraces ambiguity and confronts those who want to wield scripture's authority as their own. It refutes people who assume a text or a theological concept must inevitably mean what they imagine it means. Religious ideas have never "always" meant anything; they have been fluid, multiple, and contested.

The space-in-between highlights the traditions' long history of self-critique, disputing those who assert that their beliefs cannot be questioned. Change is not heresy and criticism is not blasphemy. The seeds for penetrating and ongoing assessment of religious ideas were planted long ago, integral to the blossoming of faith. This is the litmus that properly distinguishes contemporary camps, not religious identity or degree of orthodoxy but the willingness to grapple substantively with the potential harm their ideas may inflict. Dislodging assumptions about meaning and constructing a conduit for critical inquiry, the history of interpretation resists the binary reductionism of the digital age that allows people to decide that religion is all good or all bad. Traditionally rooted and radically engaged, the collection of religious voices certainly substantiates the dangers of religious ideas. Yet it also initiates a complementary discourse that brings religious wisdom and insight to enhance public discussion in pursuit of the common good.

ACKNOWLEDGMENTS

Reading work in progress, to help clarify and correct the ideas contained within, is one of the most generous things that academic colleagues do for one another. They also provide detailed replies to email questions that come from out of the blue. I am grateful for the thoughtful comments and challenging insights contributed by numerous scholars, even as the remaining faults are my own. Thank you to Younus Mirza, Burton Visotzky, David Cunningham, Umar AbdAllah, Scott Alexander, Reza Aslan, Deeana Klepper, Dalia Marx, Ingrid Mattson, Kevin Minister, John Pawlikowski, Laurel Schneider, Elsie Stern, Seung Ai Yang, and Jared Beverly. I am also indebted to the Lilly Foundation for awarding a Faculty Fellowship to support the research and writing of this book. The book would not be here without Amy Caldwell's enthusiasm for the project and the amazing staff at Beacon Press. And I would not be able to accomplish much at all without the patience, faith, and love of my soul mate, Mark Rosenberg.

NOTES

INTRODUCTION

1. Vivekananda, "The Ideal of Universal Religion," *The Complete Works of Swami Vivekananda* (Kolkata: Advaita Ashrama, 1971), 2:375–76.

2. The number is shrinking, but still represents a substantial percentage of Americans. See Gregory A. Smith, "A Growing Share of Americans Say It's Not Necessary to Believe in God to Be Moral," Pew Research Center, October 16, 2017, http://www.pewresearch.org/fact-tank/2017/10/16/a-growing-share-of-americans-say-its-not-necessary-to-believe-in-god-to-be-moral.

3. William T. Cavanaugh, *The Myth of Religious Violence: Secular Ideology and the Roots of Modern Conflict* (Oxford, UK: Oxford University Press, 2009), doi:10.1093/acprof:oso/9780195385045.001.0001.

4. See Reza Aslan, "Sam Harris and 'New Atheists' Aren't New, Aren't Even Atheists," *Salon*, November 21, 2014, https://www.salon.com/2014/11/21/reza_aslan_sam_harris_and_new_atheists_arent_new_arent_even_atheists.

5. Sigmund Freud, *The Future of an Illusion*, ed. Todd Dufresne, trans. Gregory Richter (Peterborough, ON: Broadview Press, 2012), 103.

6. Keith Ward, *Is Religion Dangerous?* (Grand Rapids, MI: Eerdmans, 2007), 42–55. His work is primarily a defense of religion.

7. Martin E. Marty, foreword to *The Destructive Power of Religion: Violence in Judaism, Christianity, and Islam*, ed. J. Harold Ellens (Westport, CT: Praeger, 2004), 1:xi.

8. Susan Brooks Thistlethwaite, ed., *Interfaith Just Peacemaking* (New York: Palgrave Macmillan, 2012), 3.

9. See Carol Bakhos, *The Family of Abraham: Jewish, Christian and Muslim Interpretations* (Cambridge, MA: Harvard University Press, 2014); Aaron W. Hughes, *Abrahamic Religions: On the Uses and Abuses of History* (Oxford, UK: Oxford University Press, 2012), doi:10.1093/acprof:oso/9780199934645.001.0001.

10. Georgia Warnke, *Gadamer: Hermeneutics, Tradition and Reason* (Stanford, CA: Stanford University Press, 1987), 39.

11. Critique emerged in the context of jurisprudence to repair ruptures in the ideal operation of the polis. See Wendy Brown, introduction to *Is Critique Secular? Blasphemy, Injury, and Free Speech*, ed. Talal Asad et al. (Berkeley: University of California Townsend Center for the Humanities, 2009), 9, https://escholarship.org/uc/item/84q9c6ft.

12. *Babylonian Talmud Yoma* 69b. Compelling analyses can be found in Daniel Boyarin, *Carnal Israel: Reading Sex in Talmud Culture* (Berkeley: University of California

Press, 1993), 61–76; Ishay Rosen-Zvi, "Refuting the *Yetzer:* The Evil Inclination and the Limits of Rabbinic Discourse," *Journal of Jewish Thought and Philosophy* 17:2 (2009): 117–41, doi:10.1163/105369909X12506863090396.

13. See Danièle Hervieu-Léger, "'What Scripture Tells Me': Spontaneity and Regulation within the Catholic Charismatic Renewal," in *Lived Religion in America: Toward a History of Practice,* ed. David Hall (Princeton, NJ: Princeton University Press, 1997), 27. Talal Asad, *Formations of the Secular: Christianity, Islam, Modernity* (Stanford, CA: Stanford University Press, 2003), helpfully unsettles the fixity of "secular."

CHAPTER 1: WHAT ARE DANGEROUS RELIGIOUS IDEAS?

1. For "cultures of violence," see Mark Juergensmeyer, *Terror in the Mind of God: The Global Rise of Religious Violence* (Oakland: University of California Press, 2003), 10–15. Cavanaugh contests the focus on religion as a unique impetus for violence, *The Myth of Religious Violence.*

2. See Meerten B. ter Borg and Jan Willem van Henten, *Powers: Religion as a Social and Spiritual Force* (New York: Fordham University Press, 2010), doi:10.5422 /fso/9780823231560.001.0001.

3. See Lloyd Steffen, *The Demonic Turn: The Power of Religion to Inspire or Restrain Violence* (Cleveland: Pilgrim Press, 2003); Hector Avalos, *Fighting Words: The Origins of Religious Violence* (Amherst, NY: Prometheus Books, 2005); Charles Kimball, *When Religion Becomes Evil* (San Francisco: HarperOne, 2002).

4. Rutilius, *A Voyage Home to Gaul,* c. 413. The citation can be found in Peter Schäfer, *Judeophobia: Attitudes Toward the Jews in the Ancient World* (Cambridge, MA: Harvard University Press, 1997), 87–88; Seneca, "Belief and Prayer," as cited in Augustine, *The City of God* 6:11, trans. Marcus Dods (New York: Random House, 1993), 203.

5. See Émile Durkheim, *The Elementary Forms of Religious Life,* trans. Karen E. Fields (New York: Free Press, 1995); Mircea Eliade, *The Sacred and the Profane: The Nature of Religion,* trans. Willard R. Trask (San Diego: Harcourt Brace Jovanovich, 1987).

6. Wilfred Cantwell Smith, *The Meaning and End of Religion* (Minneapolis: Fortress Press, 1991), 8.

7. Tomoko Masuzawa, *The Invention of World Religions: or, How European Universalism Was Preserved in the Language of Pluralism* (Chicago: University of Chicago Press, 2005); Richard King, *Orientalism and Religion: Postcolonial Theory, India, and "The Mystic East"* (London: Routledge, 1999).

8. See Daniel Pals, *Eight Theories of Religion* (Oxford, UK: Oxford University Press, 2006), 294. He argued that no theoretical approach can today claim dominance, leading many scholars in the field to adopt a similarly ad hoc methodology.

9. Alfred Adler, *The Practice and Theory of Individual Psychology* (London: Routledge, 1999). Gilles Deleuze nuances Nietzsche's power analysis in *Nietzsche and Philosophy,* trans. Hugh Tomlinson (New York: Columbia University Press, 2006).

10. Viktor E. Frankl, *Man's Search for Meaning* (Boston: Beacon Press, 2006), 66. Scholars of psychology positively disposed toward religion include Carl Jung, Gordon Allport, Abraham Maslow, Michael McCullough, Kenneth Pargament, and Carl Thoresen.

11. Durkheim, *The Elementary Forms of Religious Life,* 421.

12. Georges Khodr, "Violence and the Gospel," *CrossCurrents* 37:4 (1987–88), 405.

13. René Girard, *Violence and the Sacred*, trans. Patrick Gregory (Baltimore: Johns Hopkins University Press, 1979).

14. Walter Wink, "The Myth of Redemptive Violence," in *The Destructive Power of Religion: Violence in Judaism, Christianity, and Islam*, ed. J. Harold Ellens (Westport, CT: Praeger, 2004), 3:278, 269.

15. Søren Kierkegaard, *Fear and Trembling* (Cambridge, UK: Cambridge University Press, 2006); Reinhold Niebuhr, *Moral Man and Immoral Society: A Study in Ethics and Politics* (Whitefish, MT: Kessinger Publishing, 2010); Regina M. Schwartz, *The Curse of Cain: The Violent Legacy of Monotheism* (Chicago: University of Chicago Press, 1997); Juergensmeyer, *Terror in the Mind of God*.

16. Robert Bellah described key aspects of human development "as the acquisition of a series of capacities, all of which have contributed to the formation of religion." *Religion in Human Evolution: From the Paleolithic to the Axial Age* (Cambridge, MA: Belknap Press, 2011), 44.

17. Pascal Boyer, *Religion Explained: The Evolutionary Origins of Religious Thought* (New York: Basic Books, 2001), 34, 50, 120–122.

18. Luther H. Martin, "Religion and Cognition," in *The Routledge Companion to the Study of Religion*, ed. John Hinnells (London: Routledge, 2005), 476. David Sloan Wilson, *Darwin's Cathedral: Evolution, Religion, and the Nature of Society* (Chicago: University of Chicago Press, 2002) challenges this consensus.

19. See Boyer, *Religion Explained*, 137–67; Ralph D. Mecklenburger, *Our Religious Brains: What Cognitive Science Reveals about Belief* (Woodstock, VT: Jewish Lights, 2012), 1–36.

20. See Frans de Waal, *Primates and Philosophers: How Morality Evolved* (Princeton, NJ: Princeton University Press, 2006), 14.

21. "Universal" does not mean that everyone everywhere embraces the value; rather it does not appear to be culturally bound. See Marc Hauser, *Moral Minds: How Nature Designed Our Universal Sense of Right and Wrong* (New York: Ecco, 2006).

22. Wilson argued that nonrational features of religion should "be studied respectfully as potential adaptations in their own right rather than as idiot relatives of rational thought" in *Darwin's Cathedral*, 122–23.

23. See Andrew Newberg, Eugene D'Aquili, and Vince Rause, *Why God Won't Go Away: Brain Science and the Biology of Belief* (New York: Ballantine Books, 2001), 1–10.

24. See Andrew Newberg, *Principles of Neurotheology* (London: Routledge, 2010), 84, 91.

25. Malcolm A. Jeeves and Warren S. Brown, *Neuroscience, Psychology and Religion: Illusions, Delusions, and Realities about Human Nature* (West Conshohocken, PA: Templeton, 2009), 134–35. See Bellah, *Religion in Human Evolution*, xii–xiv.

26. Meister Eckhart, *Mystische Schriften*, as cited in Evelyn Underhill, *Mysticism: A Study in the Nature and Development of Spiritual Consciousness* (Mineola, NY: Dover, 2002), 305, n. 3.

27. Newberg, D'Aquili, and Rause, *Why God Won't Go Away*, 37.

28. Ignacio Castuera, "A Social History of Christian Thought on Abortion: Ambiguity vs. Certainty in Moral Debate," *American Journal of Economics and Sociology* 76:1 (2017): 121–227, doi:10.1111/ajes.12174.

29. It can be operative in Shi'a cultures as well, but with somewhat different requirements.

30. Clifford Geertz, "Thick Description: Toward an Interpretive Theory of Culture," *The Interpretation of Cultures: Selected Essays* (New York: Basic Books, 1973), 17.

31. Geertz, *Islam Observed: Religious Development in Morocco and Indonesia* (Chicago: University of Chicago Press, 1971).

32. Charles Selengut, *Sacred Fury: Understanding Religious Violence*, 3rd ed. (Lanham, MD: Rowman and Littlefield, 2017), 193.

33. Avalos, *Fighting Words*, 68.

34. Vivekananda, "The Ideal of Universal Religion," 396.

CHAPTER 2: SCRIPTURE AS A DANGEROUS RELIGIOUS IDEA

1. Wilfred Cantwell Smith, *What is Scripture? A Comparative Approach* (Minneapolis: Fortress Press, 2005), x, 14–15.

2. William Shakespeare, *The Merchant of Venice*, I:3.

3. See James Watts, "The Three Dimensions of Scripture," *Postscripts: The Journal of Sacred Texts and Contemporary Worlds* 2:2–3 (2006): 135–69; Benjamin Sommer, *Revelation and Authority: Sinai in Jewish Scripture and Tradition* (New Haven, CT: Yale University Press, 2015), 11–26.

4. See R. S. Sugirtharajah, *The Bible and the Third World: Precolonial, Colonial and Postcolonial Encounters* (Cambridge, UK: Cambridge University Press, 2001), 45–72, doi:10.1017/CBO9780511612619.

5. Scriptures are multivocal, and some interpretations are debatable. Nonetheless, problematic verses on the identified concerns include the following:

    a. Slavery: Exod. 21:1–27, Lev. 25:39–55, Deut. 15:12–18, Eph. 6:5–9, 1 Tim. 6:1–3, Philemon, Qur'an 4:24, 24:32–33, 30:28

    b. Homosexuality: Lev. 18:22, 20:13, Rom. 1:26–27, 1 Cor. 6:9–10, Qur'an 7:80–81, 26:165–66

    c. Punishment: Gen. 6, 18:16–19:28, Lev. 24:15–22, Matt. 25:41–46, 10:11–15, Acts 5:1–10, Heb. 10:26–30, Qur'an 5:33–40; 14:48–51; 32:20–22

    d. Women: Gen. 3:16, Exod. 21:7, Num. 5, 1 Cor. 14:33–35, Eph. 5:22–24, 1 Tim. 2:11–15, Qur'an 4:11, 34; 24:31

    e. Religious others: Num. 31:9–18, Deut. 7:1–6, 18:9–14, Matt. 23, John 8:31–47, Acts 7:51–53, 1 Cor. 6:9–10, Qur'an 5:72–86, 9:1–17, 81:1–14

6. Reuven Firestone, "Islamophobia and Anti-Semitism: History and Possibility," *Arches Quarterly* 4:7 (2010): 10.

7. Benedict de Spinoza, *A Theologico-Political Treatise, and A Political Treatise* (New York: Cosimo Classics, 2007), 182.

8. Gregory of Nyssa condemned slavery in the fourth century ("Fourth Homily on Ecclesiastes"). See Trevor Dennis, "Man Beyond Price: Gregory of Nyssa and Slavery," in *Heaven and Earth: Essex Essays in Theology and Ethics*, ed. Andrew Linzey and Peter J. Wexler (Worthing, UK: Churchman, 1986), 129.

9. Amina Wadud, *Qur'an and Woman: Rereading the Sacred Text from a Woman's Perspective* (Oxford, UK: Oxford University Press, 1999), xiii. Sura 90 and other passages exhort individuals to free slaves as an act of piety.

10. Albert Bledsoe, *An Essay on Liberty and Slavery* (Philadelphia: J. B. Lippincott, 1856), 223. See Granville Sharp, *The Just Limitation of Slavery* (London: B. White, E. & C. Dilly, 1776); Willard Swartley, *Slavery, Sabbath, War and Women* (Scottdale, PA:

Herald Press, 1983); Hector Avalos, *Slavery, Abolitionism and the Ethics of Biblical Scholarship* (Sheffield, UK: Sheffield Phoenix Press, 2011).

11. Ingrid Mattson, *The Story of the Qur'an: Its History and Place in Muslim Life* (Malden, MA: Wiley-Blackwell, 2007), 184.

12. Paul Achtemeier, *Inspiration and Authority: Nature and Function of Christian Scripture* (Grand Rapids, MI: Baker Academic, 1998), 145.

13. Cited in Nasr, *The Study Quran*, 515. See chap. 10 for further discussion of *taḥrif* (corruption).

14. The meaning of evangelical claims regarding inerrancy is contested. Compare, for example, the "Chicago Statement on Biblical Inerrancy," 1978, http://www.bible-researcher.com/chicago1.html, to that of Fuller Theological Seminary ("What We Believe and Teach," 2019, http://fuller.edu/About/Mission-and-Values/What-We-Believe-and-Teach).

15. Robert A. J. Gagnon, *The Bible and Homosexual Practice: Texts and Hermeneutics* (Nashville: Abingdon Press, 2001), 31.

16. See Kierkegaard, *Fear and Trembling*, 83–95 (reflecting on Hebrew Bible's "Binding of Isaac" in Gen. 21).

17. Khaled Abou El Fadl, *Speaking in God's Name: Islamic Law, Authority and Women* (London: Oneworld, 2001), 93. See also Stephen Fowl, "Texts Don't Have Ideologies," *Biblical Interpretation* 3:1 (1995): 15–34, doi:10.1163/156851595X00023.

18. See, e.g., Elisabeth Schüssler Fiorenza, *In Memory of Her: A Feminist Theological Reconstruction of Christian Origins* (New York: Crossroad, 1983); Tikva Frymer-Kensky, *Reading the Women of the Bible* (New York: Schocken Books, 2002); Wadud, *Qur'an and Woman*.

19. Philo, *Allegorical Commentary*, "The Worse Attacks the Better" (*Quod deterius potiori insidiari soleat*), 125; quoted in Maren Niehoff, *Jewish Exegesis and Homeric Scholarship in Alexandria* (Cambridge, UK: Cambridge University Press, 2011), 173. See also Christian Hayes, *What's Divine about Divine Law?* (Princeton, NJ: Princeton University Press, 2015), 1–3.

20. See, e.g., Maimonides, *Guide for the Perplexed* 3:31; Ibn Tufayl, *Hayy ibn Yaqzan*; Ibn Rushd, *The Incoherence of the Incoherence*; Thomas Aquinas, *Summa Theologica* I–II.90.1.

21. A locus classicus for this claim is found in b. Hagiga 3a-b. See Shmuel Safrai, "Oral Tora," in *The Literature of the Sages*, vol. 3 of *The Literature of the Jewish People in the Period of the Second Temple and the Talmud* (Leiden: Brill, 1987), 35–88, doi:10.1163/9789004275133_003.

22. See Francis Sullivan, *Magisterium: Teaching Authority in the Catholic Church* (Eugene, OR: Wipf and Stock, 2002).

23. Augustine, "Against the Epistle of Manichaeus Called Fundamental" 4:5, trans. Richard Stothert, in *Nicene and Post-Nicene Fathers of the Christian Church*, ed. Philip Schaff (London: T&T Clark, 1887), 4:135.

24. See Jonathan Brown, *Hadith: Muhammad's Legacy in the Medieval and Modern World* (London: Oneworld, 2009). There are modern scripturalist movements in Islam (e.g., Wahhabism), but they generally ascribe authority to the sunna.

25. *Code of Canon Law* 4, http://www.vatican.va/archive/ENG1104/__P3V.HTM. See also James A. Coriden, *An Introduction to Canon Law* (New York: Paulist Press, 2004), 147–48.

26. Narrated by al-Tirmidhi, 3895; Ibn Maajah, 1977; classified as *saheeh* (sound, authoritative) by al-Albaani in *Saheeh al-Tirmidhi*. See also Nasr, ed., *The Study Quran* (New York: HarperOne, 2015), 206–8.

27. Walter Wink, *The Bible in Human Transformation: Towards a New Paradigm for Biblical Study* (Minneapolis: Fortress Press, 1973).

28. David Nirenberg, *Anti-Judaism: The Western Tradition* (New York: W. W. Norton, 2014), 337. James L. Kugel discusses the goals of early historical criticism in *How to Read the Bible: A Guide to Scripture, Then and Now* (New York: Free Press, 2007), 686.

29. Elisabeth Schüssler Fiorenza, "Unmasking Ideologies in Biblical Interpretation," in *History of Biblical Interpretation: A Reader*, ed. William Yarchin (Peabody, MA: Hendrickson, 2004), 391–92.

30. S. Parvez Manzoor, "Method against Truth: Orientalism and Qur'anic Studies," *Muslim World Book Review* 7 (1987): 33. Hava Lazarus-Yafeh theorized that text-critical tools developed within medieval Islam led to modern historical-critical study of scripture; see *Intertwined Worlds: Medieval Islam and Bible Criticism* (Princeton, NJ: Princeton University Press, 1992), 130.

31. See Rahel Fishbach, "Politics of Scripture: Discussions of the Historical-Critical Approach to Qur'an" (PhD diss., Georgetown University, 2017).

CHAPTER 3: JUDAISM—THE CANONIZATION OF CONTROVERSY

1. For theories about the rise of the interpreter in the Second Temple period, see James Kugel, *Traditions of the Bible* (Cambridge, MA: Harvard University Press, 1999), 2–11.

2. See William Yarchin, ed., introduction to *History of Biblical Interpretation: A Reader* (Peabody, MA: Hendrickson, 2004), xvi; David Stern, *Midrash and Theory: Ancient Jewish Exegesis and Contemporary Literary Studies* (Evanston, IL: Northwestern University Press, 1998), 31.

3. George Steiner, *Real Presences* (Chicago: University of Chicago Press, 1991), 40.

4. Catholic exegesis similarly formalized four senses (Quadriga), as captured by this medieval Latin ditty: *Littera gesta docet, Quid credas allegoria, Moralis quid agas, Quo tendas anagogia.* ("The literal sense teaches the facts, the allegorical what you should believe, the moral what you should do, the anagogical where you are headed.")

5. The interpretation is based in part on Ps. 62:12: "One thing God has spoken; two things have I heard." A medieval text (Numbers Rabbah 13.15) speaks about the *seventy* faces or facets of Torah.

6. See Steven Fraade, "Rabbinic Polysemy and Pluralism Revisited: Between Praxis and Thematization," *AJS Review* 31:1 (2007): 1–40, doi:10.1017/S0364009407000219.

7. Stern, *Midrash and Theory*, 23, 33; see also Michael Walzer, Menachem Lorberbaum, and Noam J. Zohar, eds., *The Jewish Political Tradition* (New Haven, CT: Yale University Press, 2000), 1:307–20.

8. Decisions could be overturned by sages with superior numbers or wisdom. One sage argued that recording minority opinions precludes someone from later presenting them as alternative traditions of equal weight. Cf. t. Ed. 1:4.

9. Hillel and Shammai were prominent sages at the turn of the Common Era, often portrayed in disagreement. The tradition attributed to each a "school," a disciple circle that transmitted and expanded upon their teachings.

10. Tannaitic texts give the impression that rabbinic Judaism was normative for the community, but it was several centuries before it became the predominant form of Judaism that survived destruction of the Temple and exile.

11. See Fraade, "Rabbinic Polysemy." Like him, I sidestep to what degree the texts are literary constructions versus representations of actual rabbinic culture.

12. Scholars have invested tremendous energy exploring textual evidence, timing, context, and influences in the thematization of multivocality. I affirm Fraade's conclusion it was *"progressive* rather than sudden and *dialectical* rather than linear" ("Rabbinic Polysemy," 39). See also Azzan Yadin, *Scripture as Logos* (Philadelphia: University of Pennsylvania Press, 2004), 70–76; Jeffrey L. Rubenstein, *The Culture of the Babylonian Talmud* (Baltimore: Johns Hopkins University Press, 2003); Richard Hidary, "Classical Rhetorical Arrangement and Reasoning in the Talmud," *AJS Review* 34:1 (2010): 33–64, doi:10.1017/S0364009410000279; Daniel Boyarin, *Border Lines: The Partition of Judaeo-Christianity* (Philadelphia: University of Pennsylvania Press, 2004).

13. It is an expansion of m. Avot 2:8.

14. Rubenstein, "The Thematization of Dialectics in Bavli Aggada," *Journal of Jewish Studies* 54:1 (2003): 72, doi:10.18647/2457/JJS-2003.

15. Saadia's minimization of disagreement also served to defend rabbinic discourse against Karaite critique.

16. See Hanina Ben-Menahem, "Controversy and Dialogue in the Jewish Tradition: An Interpretive Essay," in *Controversy and Dialogue in the Jewish Tradition: A Reader*, ed. Ben-Menahem, Neil S. Hecht, and Shai Wosner (London: Routledge, 2005), 24–25; David Weiss Halivni, *Midrash, Mishnah and Gemara: The Jewish Predilection for Justified Law* (Cambridge, MA: Harvard University Press, 1986), 108–11. Other motives include encouraging high caliber intellectual leadership by honing critical thought and diminishing gaps between contradictory arguments by exploring them all.

17. The phrase is interpreted this way only once in Talmud, but is invoked frequently after the expulsion from Spain in 1492 brought diverse Jewish communities together. See Ben-Menahem, "Controversy and Dialogue," 19–29.

18. A portrait emerges through scattered texts. In m. Rosh Hash. 2:8–9, they disagree about the calendar, and Rabban Gamaliel commands Rabbi Joshua to appear before him dressed for business on a day that the latter considered a holy day. After Joshua yields, they reconcile and Gamaliel admits he is lesser in knowledge (but not authority).

19. Moshe Halbertal, *People of the Book: Canon, Meaning, and Authority* (Cambridge, MA: Harvard University Press, 1997), 46.

20. *Peirushei Ha'agadot L'Rabbi Azriel* on b. Hag. 3b; see Ben-Menahem et al., *Controversy and Dialogue*, 165–66. R. Moshe Chaim Luzzatto's work on ethics, *Derekh Eitz Chaim* (eighteenth century), imagined that every soul among the 600,000 who stood at Sinai received a part of Torah, and sparks that radiate from Torah study illumine in 600,000 ways. Gershom Scholem recounted Reb Mendel of Rymanov's interpretation that all the Israelites collectively heard on Sinai was the first letter of the first word of the Ten Commandments—*aleph*, a silent letter: "To hear the *aleph* is to hear next to nothing; it is the preparation for all audible language, but in itself conveys no determinate, specific meaning" (*On the Kabbalah and Its Symbolism*, trans. Ralph Manheim [New York: Schocken Books, 1965], 29–30).

21. See Halbertal, *People of the Book*, 63–72.

22. Cited in Ben-Menahem et al., *Controversy and Dialogue*, 161.

23. A parallel in y. Mo'ed Qatan 3:1 (81c-d) does not have God's response. The complex narrative has been treated in numerous places; see Boyarin, *Border Lines*, 152–201; Jeffrey Rubenstein, *Talmudic Stories: Narrative Art, Composition, and Culture* (Baltimore: Johns Hopkins University Press, 1999), 34–63.

24. See Halbertal, *People of the Book*, 54–63. Karaite critique challenged Oral Torah in part because it canonized controversy; see David Kraemer, *The Mind of the Talmud: An Intellectual History of the Bavli* (Oxford, UK: Oxford University Press, 1990), 106.

25. See Stephen D. Benin, "The Search for Truth in Sacred Scripture: Jews, Christians, and the Authority to Interpret," in *With Reverence for the Word: Medieval Scriptural Exegesis in Judaism, Christianity and Islam*, ed. Jane Dammen McAuliffe, Barry D. Walfish, and Joseph W. Goering (Oxford, UK: Oxford University Press, 2010), 16–17, doi:10.1093/acprof:oso/9780195137279.003.0002.

26. Kraemer, *Mind of the Talmud*, 146. See b. Pesah. 21b and b. Hul. 114b, which compare the roles of reason and revelation.

27. See Saul Berman, "*Lifnim Mishurat Hadin*," *Journal of Jewish Studies* 26:1–2 (1975): 86–104, doi: 10.18647/740/JJS-1975; 28:2 (1977): 181–93, doi: 10.18647/827/JJS-1977. For discussion of God's occasional disregard of truth, see Hayes, *What's Divine about Divine Law?*, 171–245.

28. Christine Hayes, "Legal Truth, Right Answers and Best Answers: Dworkin and the Rabbis," *Diné Israel* 25 (2008): 86. Cf. Richard Hidary, "Right Answers Revisited: Monism and Pluralism in the Talmud," *Diné Israel* 26–27 (2009–10): 229–55.

29. William Kolbrener, "'Chiseled from All Sides': Hermeneutics and Dispute in Rabbinic Tradition," *AJS Review* 28:2 (2004): 277.

30. See Shlomo Pines, "The Limitations of Human Knowledge According to Al-Farabi, ibn Bajja, and Maimonides," in *Studies in Medieval Jewish History and Literature*, ed. Isadore Twersky (Cambridge, MA: Harvard University Press, 1979), 1:82–109.

31. Cited in Halbertal, *People of the Book*, 79.

32. Deut. Rab. 3:13 speculates that Ezra wrote dots above problematic passages (preserved in Masoretic tradition).

33. Amos Funkenstein, *Perceptions of Jewish History* (Berkeley: University of California Press, 1993), 88.

34. See Ben-Menahem et al., *Controversy and Dialogue*, 126–29.

35. Stephen D. Benin, *The Footprints of God: Divine Accommodation in Jewish and Christian Thought* (Albany, NY: SUNY Press, 1993), 143–69.

36. Ahad Ha'am, "Perurim" (Crumbs), 1892, as cited in Yaacov Shavit and Mordechai Eran, *The Hebrew Bible Reborn: From Holy Scripture to the Book of Books*, trans. Chaya Naor (Berlin: Walter de Gruyter, 2007), 521–22.

37. Funkenstein, *Perceptions of Jewish History*, 10–17. See also Yosef Hayim Yerushalmi, *Zakhor: Jewish History and Jewish Memory* (Seattle: University of Washington Press, 1983), 18–22.

38. R. Eliyahu haCohen, *Shevet Musar* 22, as cited in Yehudah Levi's discussion of ḥidush in *Torah Study: A Survey of Classic Sources on Timely Issues* (Jerusalem: Feldheim, 1990), 202.

CHAPTER 4: CHRISTIANITY—THE HUMAN EQUATION

1. Harry Gamble, *The New Testament Canon: Its Making and Meaning* (Eugene, OR: Wipf and Stock, 2002), 76.

2. On tolerance in the early church, see Henry Chadwick, *East and West: The Making of a Rift in the Church* (Oxford, UK: Oxford University Press, 2003), 4. Irenaeus (130–202) allowed diversity in practice, seeing an underlying unanimity in faith. Firmilian (third century), bishop of Cappadocian Caesarea, declined to impose a single liturgical form (Eusebius, *Ecclesiastical History* 5.13). The fifth-century church historian Socrates affirmed Novatianist communities in Phrygia who granted autonomy to individual churches and embraced plural practices (*Church History* 5.20–21).

3. Robert W. Wall, "Ecumenicity and Ecclesiology: The Promise of the Multiple Letter Canon of the New Testament," in *The New Testament as Canon: A Reader in Canonical Criticism*, ed. Wall and Eugene E. Lemcio (Sheffield, UK: Sheffield Academic, 1992), 184–85. See also Rowan A. Greer, "The Christian Bible and its Interpretation," in *Early Biblical Interpretation*, ed. Wayne A. Meeks (Philadelphia: Westminster Press, 1986), 155–63.

4. John Reumann, *Variety and Unity in New Testament Thought* (Oxford, UK: Oxford University Press, 1991), 4–10.

5. The obvious differences, especially between John and Synoptic Gospels, inspired the *Diatessaron* (literally "through the four"), a synthesis of the four narratives that was popular in Syriac Christianity, until Theodoret destroyed all the known copies in 423.

6. See Elaine Pagels, *The Gnostic Gospels* (New York: Vintage Press, 1989).

7. Harry Gamble theorized that Marcionism, Gnosticism, Montanism, and other strains of Christian belief eventually declared heretical likely influenced the creation of the canon in the first place (*New Testament Canon*, 57, 88).

8. Charles Freeman, *A New History of Early Christianity* (New Haven, CT: Yale University Press, 2009); Gamble, *New Testament Canon*.

9. Freeman, *A New History*, 249, 253. An epistula (381 CE) declared that only men who affirmed the Nicene Creed could be bishops, classifying others as demented heretics and requiring them to forfeit churches and give up tax exemptions. Open protest met with expulsion; obedience was rewarded with privilege and patronage.

10. See Ross Shepard Kraemer and Mary Rose D'Angelo, *Women and Christian Origins* (Oxford, UK: Oxford University Press, 1999).

11. Saint Augustine, *Confessions*, trans. R. S. Pine-Coffin (London: Penguin, 1961), 335–36. For a comprehensive anthology of Jewish and Christian interpretations of Genesis 1:28, see Jeremy Cohen, *"Be Fertile and Increase, Fill the Earth and Master It": The Ancient and Medieval Career of a Biblical Text* (Ithaca, NY: Cornell University Press, 1992).

12. See Beryl Smalley, *The Study of the Bible in the Middle Ages* (Oxford, UK: Basil Blackwell, 1952); Yarchin, *History of Biblical Interpretation*; Magne Sæbø, ed., *Hebrew Bible/Old Testament: The History of Its Interpretation*, 3 vols. (Göttingen: Vanderhoeck and Ruprecht, 2000–2015).

13. Thomas Oden, series introduction to *Ancient Christian Commentary on Scripture* (Downers Grove, IL: InterVarsity Press, 2001), 1:xix.

14. See Donald K. McKim, ed., *Dictionary of Major Biblical Interpreters* (Downers Grove, IL: IVP Academic, 2007), 964–65; Karlfried Froehlich, *Biblical Interpretation in the Early Church* (Philadelphia: Fortress Press, 1980), 14–15.

15. Eusebius, *Ecclesiastical History* 3.32.7–8; Tertullian, *De praescriptione haereticorum* 29. See also Walter Bauer, *Orthodoxy and Heresy in Earliest Christianity* (Philadelphia: Fortress Press, 1979).

16. Christian Smith, *The Bible Made Impossible: Why Biblicism Is Not a Truly Evangelical Reading of Scripture* (Grand Rapids, MI: Brazos Press, 2012), viii, 151. See also Elisabeth Schüssler Fiorenza, *Power of the Word: Scripture and the Rhetoric of Empire* (Minneapolis: Augsburg Fortress, 2007), 264.

17. Gordon Fee, "Hermeneutics and the Gender Debate," in *Discovering Biblical Equality: Complementarity Without Hierarchy*, ed. Ronald Pierce and Rebecca Merrill Groothius (Downers Grove, IL: InterVarsity Press, 2005), 370.

18. Ellen F. Davis, "The Soil That Is Scripture," in *Engaging Biblical Authority: Perspectives on the Bible as Scripture*, ed. William P. Brown (Louisville, KY: Westminster John Knox, 2007), 36–37.

19. Lieven Boeve, "The Particularity of Religious Truth Claims: How to Deal with It in a So-Called Postmodern Context," in *Truth: Interdisciplinary Dialogues in a Pluralist Age*, ed. Christine Helmer and Kristin De Troyer (Leuven: Peeters, 2003), 183.

20. See Anselm of Canterbury, *De veritate* 2 and his preface; also Aquinas, *De veritate* Q1.A1–3; Marjorie Hewitt Suchocki, "To Tell the Truth," in *Truth*, ed. Helmer and De Troyer, 219–23.

21. See Alasdair MacIntyre, *Whose Justice? Whose Rationality?* (Notre Dame, IN: University of Notre Dame Press, 1988), 174.

22. Yarchin, *History of Biblical Interpretation*, 196–97.

23. Boeve, "The Particularity of Religious Truth Claims," 185–86.

24. Søren Kierkegaard, *Concluding Unscientific Postscript to "Philosophical Fragments,"* trans. Howard and Edna Hong (Princeton, NJ: Princeton University Press, 1992), 1:203.

25. Alister McGrath, *Reformation Thought: An Introduction*, 4th ed. (Malden, MA: Wiley-Blackwell, 2012), 93.

26. Cited in Kugel, *How to Read the Bible*, 26–27.

27. Bruce Vawter, "The Bible in the Roman Catholic Church," in *Scripture in the Jewish and Christian Traditions*, ed. Frederick Greenspahn (Nashville: Abingdon Press, 1982), 122.

28. Yarchin, *History of Biblical Interpretation*, xii.

29. Acts 17:23 speaks of the "unknown God," perhaps the earliest Christian apophatic statement.

30. Pseudo-Dionysius, *The Mystical Theology*. For examples of medieval mysticism, see Meister Eckhart (1260–1328), *The Cloud of Unknowing* and St. John of the Cross's *Dark Night of the Soul*.

31. Peter Casarella, *Cusanus: The Legacy of Learned Ignorance* (Washington, DC: Catholic University of America Press, 2006).

32. James L. Heft, "Learned Ignorance," in *Learned Ignorance: Intellectual Humility among Jews, Christians and Muslims*, ed. James L. Heft, Reuven Firestone, and Omid Safi (Oxford, UK: Oxford University Press, 2011), 4, doi:10.1093/acprof:osobl /9780199769308.003.0001.

33. Abelard, *Sic et Non* [Yes and No], introduction. The book collected conflicting teachings from scripture and the early Church Fathers on 158 controversial religious issues and let the contradictions stand.

34. Jerome spoke three times of *scriptoris errorem* (Ep. 77:5; Ep. 57:7; *In Mich.* 5:2), see Stephen R. Holmes, "Evangelical Doctrines of Scripture in Transatlantic Perspective," *Evangelical Quarterly* 81:1 (2009), 41:16. For a review of Origen and his doubts

about the historicity of select details, see Richard Hanson, *Allegory and Event: A Study of the Sources and Significance of Origin's Interpretation of Scripture* (Louisville, KY: Westminster John Knox, 2002), 259–88.

35. James Madison, *The Federalist Papers* 37.

36. See Origen, *On First Principles*. Irenaeus affirmed that the "apostles are found granting certain precepts in consideration of human infirmity" but—perhaps concerned about gnostic critique—simultaneously insisted that Christianity embodies eternal truth, without accommodation. See Benin, *Footprints of God*, 6–9.

37. Bertrande de Margerie, "Saint John Chrysostom, Doctor of Biblical 'Condescension,'" in *An Introduction to the History of Exegesis*, trans. Leonard Maluf (Petersham, MA: St. Bede's Publications, 1993), 1:189–212.

38. Benin, *Footprints of God*, 112. See, e.g., Augustine, *The City of God* 10.14.

39. Benin, *Footprints of God*, 181.

40. Vawter, "The Bible in the Roman Catholic Church," 125. See also Nicholas Lash, *Change in Focus: A Study of Doctrinal Change and Continuity* (London: Sheed and Ward, 1973).

41. Daniel Madigan, "Saving *Dominus Iesus*," in *Learned Ignorance*, ed. Heft, Firestone, and Safi, 266.

CHAPTER 5: ISLAM—THE RULE OF DOUBT IN FAITH

1. Abu Amaar Yasir Qadhi, *An Introduction to the Sciences of the Qur'an* (Birmingham, UK: Al-Hidaayah Publishing, 1999), 172–83; Muhammad Mustafa Al-Azami, *The History of the Qur'anic Text: From Revelation to Compilation* (Leicester: UK Islamic Academy, 2002), 153. Most academics view *harf* as a textual variant since there are differences in wording, while Muslim tradition considers it a dialect because "variant" suggests uncertainty in transmission.

2. See 3:7, 43:4, 85:21–22; also Kecia Ali and Oliver Leaman, *Islam: The Key Concepts* (London: Routledge, 2007), 102–3. Another interpretation portrays the Preserved Tablet as a repository with Allah's plan for all creation.

3. Alternatively, one can read an emphasis on "your" religion, indicating its particular design for Muhammad's community. See Fethullah Gulen, "*Lawhun Mahfuz* (The Supreme Preserved Tablet) and What Lies Before," February 10, 2015, https://fgulen.com/en/fethullah-gulens-works/sufism/key-concepts-in-the-practice-of-sufism-4/47576-lawhun-mahfuz-the-supreme-preserved-tablet-and-what-lies-before.

4. Reza Shah-Kazemi, *The Spirit of Tolerance in Islam* (London: I. B. Tauris, 2012), 88–89.

5. Asma Afsaruddin, "Finding Common Ground: 'Mutual Knowing,' Moderation, and the Fostering of Religious Pluralism," in *Learned Ignorance*, ed. Heft, Firestone, and Safi, 71. Qur'an 9:106 often served as a prooftext for *irja*.

6. Toby Mayer, "Traditions of Esoteric and Sapiential Quranic Commentary," in *The Study Quran*, ed. Nasr, 1660–61. One hadith instructs, "The Qur'an is malleable, capable of many types of interpretation. Interpret it, therefore, according to the best possible type" (Mahmoud Ayoub, *The Qur'an and Its Interpreters* [Albany: State University of New York Press, 1984], 1:23).

7. Cited in Charles Kurzman, "Liberal Islam and its Islamic Context," in *Liberal Islam: A Sourcebook*, ed. Charles Kurzman (Oxford, UK: Oxford University Press, 1998), 16.

8. See Nasr, introduction to *The Study Quran*, xlv; Hussein Abdul-Raof, *Schools of Qur'anic Exegesis* (London: Routledge, 2013); Saeed Abdullah, *Reading the Qur'an in the Twenty-First Century: A Contextualist Approach* (London: Routledge, 2013), 17.

9. Ibn Arabi, *The Meccan Revelations* II.119.21, as translated in Reza Shah-Kazemi, "Beyond Polemics and Pluralism: The Universal Message of the Qur'an," in *Between Heaven and Hell: Islam, Salvation, and the Fate of Others*, ed. Mohammad Hassan Khalil (Oxford, UK: Oxford University Press, 2013), 93.

10. Qadhi, *Introduction to the Sciences of the Qur'an*, 207–31.

11. Ahmad Muhammad al-Tayyib, "The Quran as Source of Islamic Law," in *The Study Quran*, ed. Nasr, 1717. See also Muhammad Hashim Kamali, *Principles of Islamic Jurisprudence* (Cambridge, UK: Islamic Texts Society, 2005), 109–56; Yaser Ellethy, *Islam, Context, Pluralism and Democracy: Classical and Modern Interpretations* (London: Routledge, 2014).

12. Cited in Brown, *Hadith*, 195.

13. Kurzman, "Liberal Islam and Its Islamic Context," 5. See Ahmed El Shamsy, "The Social Construction of Orthodoxy," in *The Cambridge Companion to Classical Islamic Theology*, ed. Tim Winter (Cambridge, UK: Cambridge University Press, 2008), 111–12, doi:10.1017/CCOL9780521780582.006.

14. Brown, *Misquoting Muhammad: The Challenge and Choices of Interpreting the Prophet's Legacy* (London: Oneworld, 2014), 16.

15. See Muhammad Iqbal, "The Principle of Movement in the Structure of Islam," in *Liberal Islam*, ed. Kurzman, 263; Intisar A. Rabb, *Doubt in Islamic Law: A History of Legal Maxims, Interpretation, and Islamic Criminal Law* (Cambridge, UK: Cambridge University Press, 2017), 204, doi:10.1017/CBO9781139953054; Brown, *Misquoting Muhammad*, 35. Geography had an impact: Hanifa (d. 767), for example, lived in Iraq. Being far from Medina, he could not rely on the Prophet's direct legacy, so he emphasized reliable hadiths and made more space for independent legal reasoning.

16. Brown, *Misquoting Muhammad*, 50. *Fiqh* (jurisprudence) comes from the Arabic root for "understanding."

17. Iqbal, "The Principle of Movement," 261; Brown, *Misquoting Muhammad*, 38.

18. Brown, *Misquoting Muhammad*, 189–98. Individuals seeking to expand women's role within Islam today can point to Umm Waraqa (a female Companion of the Prophet), the female Hanbali scholar Fatima bint Abbas (d. 1315), and the practice of al-Tabari. Contemporary feminists like Amina Wadud first privileged Qur'an over tradition; later efforts (Intisar Rabb, Kecia Ali) often focused more on reclaiming the multiplicity within historical tradition.

19. Cited in Brown, *Misquoting Muhammad*, 50. See Abu Amina Elias, "Shari'ah, Fiqh, and Islamic Law Explained," April 13, 2013, https://abuaminaelias.com/sharia -fiqh-islamic-law.

20. El Shamsy, "Social Construction of Orthodoxy," 107.

21. See Mohamed Arkoun, "Rethinking Islam Today," in *Liberal Islam*, ed. Kurzman, 213–14; also Sherman Jackson, "Taqlīd, Legal Scaffolding and the Scope of Legal Injunctions in Post-Formative Theory," *Islamic Law and Society* 3:2 (1996): 165–92, doi:10.1163/1568519962599104.

22. Qur'an repeatedly instructs followers to establish justice, or enjoin right and forbid wrong (7:29, 3:104, 110, 114; 7:157; 9:71, 112; 22:41; 31:17). Scholars exercised powers of exclusion, disqualifying teachers' opinions, banning books, prohibiting individuals

from leading prayer, and convicting people of disbelief—a crime that could carry a death sentence. The state had power to appoint judges, carry out judgments, ban airing of certain ideas, etc. (El Shamsy, "Social Construction of Orthodoxy," 108–15).

23. Toby Mayer, "Esoteric and Sapiential Quranic Commentary," 1659. Some nineteenth- and twentieth-century reform movements that privileged Qur'an over sunna pursued progressive possibilities, while others utilized freedom from the constraints of tradition to produce exclusive, reactionary exegesis.

24. Cited in Ebrahim Moosa, "Arabic and Islamic Hermeneutics," in *The Routledge Companion to Hermeneutics*, ed. Jeff Malpas and Hans Helmuth-Gander (London: Routledge, 2015), 714. Omid Safi lamented the modern tendency to brand each other as infidels; see "Introduction: The Times They are a-Changin'—A Muslim Quest for Justice, Gender Equality, and Pluralism," in *Progressive Muslims: Justice, Gender, and Pluralism*, ed. Omid Safi (London: Oneworld, 2003), 13. Sulayman al-Wahhab (brother of Wahhabi Islam's "founder") cited fifty-two traditions that identified it as sinful (Khaled Abou El Fadl, "The Ugly Modern and the Modern Ugly: Reclaiming the Beautiful in Islam," in *Progressive Muslims*, ed. Safi, 52).

25. Brown, *Misquoting Muhammad*, 116.

26. El Fadl, "The Ugly Modern," 33–77; El Shamsy, "Social Construction of Orthodoxy," 114. Ahmad S. Dallal in *Islam Without Europe: Traditions of Reform in Eighteenth-Century Islamic Thought* (Chapel Hill: University of North Carolina Press, 2018) argued that Muslim communities around the world were developing rich, plural intellectual traditions before the impact of European colonialism.

27. Arkoun, "Rethinking Islam Today," 209. See other chapters in Kurzman, ed., *Liberal Islam* as well as Safi, ed., *Progressive Muslims*, 15–20, 33–77; Brown, *Misquoting Muhammad*, 120.

28. Abdelhamid I. Sabra quoting *Aporias Against Ptolemy* in "Ibn al-Haytham," *Harvard Magazine* (September–October 2003), http://harvardmagazine.com/2003/09/ibn-al-haytham-html.

29. Arkoun, "Rethinking Islam Today," 220. See also Asharite author Abu Mansur al-Baghdadi's (d. 1037) chapter, "What Is Known by Reason and What Is Known Only through Law," in his *Principles of Religion (Usul al-Din)*.

30. Andrey Smirnov, "Truth and Islamic Thought," in *A Companion to World Philosophies*, ed. Eliot Deutsch and Ron Bontekoe (Malden, MA: Blackwell, 1997), 444.

31. See Arthur Buehler, *Sufi Heirs of the Prophet: The Indian Naqshbandiyya and the Rise of the Mediating Sufi Shaykh* (Columbia: University of South Carolina Press, 2008).

32. Abdulaziz Sachedina, *Islam and the Challenge of Human Rights* (Oxford, UK: Oxford University Press, 2014), 61, doi:10.1093/acprof:oso/9780195388428.001.0001.

33. Al-Tayyib, "The Quran as Source of Islamic Law," 1698–1703.

34. Brown, *Hadith*, 25.

35. Iqbal, "The Principle of Movement," 268. Mohammad Akram Khan (1868–1968) and other modern reformers insisted that the gates of ijtihad remained open at all times. Al-Jahiz (d. 868) contended that later generations inherited more edificatory admonition, giving them an advantage in self-critical assessment. See Ebrahim Moosa, "The Debts and Burdens of Critical Islam," in *Progressive Muslims*, ed. Safi, 113.

36. Brown, *Hadith*, 173. Authorities like Fakhr al-Din al-Razi (1149–1209) believed hadiths could not lead to certainty, only to presumption.

37. Rabb, *Doubt in Islamic Law*, 16, 28, 211, 185–221.

38. El Fadl, "The Ugly Modern," 48–49.

39. See Aron Zysow, *The Economy of Certainty: An Introduction to the Typology of Islamic Legal Theory* (Atlanta: Lockwood Press, 2013).

40. Nurcholish Madjid, "The Necessity of Renewing Islamic Thought *and* Reinvigorating Religious Understanding," in *Liberal Islam*, ed. Kurzman, 290–91.

41. A fourth reference to strong drink describes it as a sign of Allah's generous provision (16:67). See Nasr, *The Study Quran*, 211–212, 1703.

42. Ellethy, *Islam, Context, Pluralism and Democracy*, 49.

43. Brown, *Misquoting Muhammad*, 223.

44. The number of verses believed to be abrogated varies widely among Sunni scholars (5–214). Shi'a authorities apply *naskh* less frequently, Ahmadis reject the concept, and Mutazilites were disinclined to invoke it during the classical period. See Qur'an 2:106, 16:101, 13:39, 17:86; also Qadhi, *An Introduction to the Sciences of the Qur'an*, 232–56.

45. See Majid Khadduri, *War and Peace in the Law of Islam* (Clark, NJ: Lawbook Exchange, 2006), 45–47, 51–73.

46. See Looay Fatoohi, *Abrogation in the Qur'an and Islamic Law* (London: Routledge, 2012). One charting of the chronology of revelations is available at "Revelation Order," *Tanzil*, http://tanzil.net/docs/revelation_order, although there is not unanimity.

47. Brown, *Misquoting Muhammad*, 97–102.

48. See Andrew Rippin, "Occasions of Revelation," in *Encyclopaedia of the Qurān*, ed. Jane Dammen McAuliffe (Leiden: Brill, 2001–2006), doi:10.1163/1875-3922_q3_EQSIM_00305.

49. Wadud, *Qur'an and Woman*, 4.

50. Abdullah, *Reading the Qur'an in the Twenty-First Century*, 26–37. Hudud crimes include adultery, false accusation of adultery, theft, and highway robbery. Some authorities include apostasy and drinking alcohol, but they are not clearly specified with their punishments in the Qur'an. See Matthew Lippman et al., *Islamic Criminal Law and Procedure* (New York: Praeger, 1988), 39–41.

51. Farhang Rajaee, "Islam and Modernity: The Reconstruction of an Alternative Shi'ite Islamic Worldview in Iran," in *Fundamentalisms and Society: Reclaiming the Sciences, the Family, and Education*, ed. Martin Marty and R. Scott Appleby (Chicago: University of Chicago Press, 1993), 116.

52. Moosa, "Arabic and Islamic Hermeneutics," 707.

53. Moosa, "The Debts and Burdens of Critical Islam," 112.

54. Ellethy, *Islam, Context, Pluralism and Democracy*, 46.

CHAPTER 6: SCRIPTURE IN THE CONTEMPORARY CONTEXT

1. Schüssler Fiorenza, *Power of the Word*, 264. See David Clines, *Interested Parties: The Ideology of Writers and Readers of the Hebrew Bible* (Sheffield, UK: Sheffield Phoenix Press, 2009), 11.

2. Yehuda Amichai, *HaZman [Time]: Poems* (New York: Schocken Books, 1977), 29.

3. Gamble, *New Testament Canon*, 92.

4. Paul F. Knitter, introduction to *The Myth of Religious Superiority: A Multifaith Exploration* (Maryknoll, NY: Orbis Books, 2005), xi. More theologically conservative voices echo this principle; see Menachem Kellner, "Overcoming Chosenness," in *Covenant and*

Chosenness in Judaism and Mormonism, ed. Raphael Jospe, Truman Madsen, and Seth Ward (Madison, NJ: Farleigh Dickinson University Press, 2001), 160; Joseph O'Leary, *Religious Pluralism and Christian Truth* (Eugene, OR: Wipf and Stock, 2016), 4.

5. Marjorie Hewitt Suchocki, *Divinity and Diversity: A Christian Affirmation of Religious Pluralism* (Nashville: Abingdon Press, 2003). John Dewey challenged modernism's emphasis on unchanging and theoretical rather than dynamic and experiential knowledge (*The Quest for Certainty: A Study of the Relation of Knowledge and Action*, The Gifford Lectures [New York: Paragon, 1979], 1929); see also Donna Haraway's influential article, "Situated Knowledges: The Science Question in Feminism and the Privilege of Partial Perspective," *Feminist Studies* 14:3 (Fall 1988): 575–99, doi:10.2307/3178066.

6. Schüssler Fiorenza, *In Memory of Her*, 15–16.

7. Alicia Suskin Ostriker, *Feminist Revision and the Bible: The Unwritten Volume* (Malden, MA: Blackwell, 1993), 122. She believed "the notion of religious tolerance was invented [eighteenth century] to keep the Christian sects from killing each other."

8. Wayne A. Meeks, *Origins of Christian Morality: The First Two Centuries* (New Haven, CT: Yale University Press, 1993), 216.

9. See, e.g., Arthur F. McGovern, *Liberation Theology and Its Critics: Toward an Assessment* (Maryknoll, NY: Orbis Books, 1989; repr., Eugene, OR: Wipf and Stock, 2009), 30–46.

10. Jane Dammen McAuliffe, "The Tasks and Traditions of Interpretation," in *The Cambridge Companion to the Qurān*, (Cambridge, UK: Cambridge University Press, 2006), 202–3, doi:10.1017/CCOL0521831601.010.

11. Brown, *Misquoting Muhammad*, 162. It is comparable to the view of Nachmanides, discussed in chap. 3, that Jewish scholars *constitute* the tradition with their interpretations.

12. See N. T. Wright, *Scripture and the Authority of God: How to Read the Bible for Today* (New York: HarperOne, 2011), 5–6; Joseph Runzo, "Pluralism and Relativism," in *The Oxford Handbook of Religious Diversity*, ed. Chad Meister (Oxford, UK: Oxford University Press, 2011), 61–76, doi:10.1093/oxfordhb/9780195340136.003.0005.

13. Smith, *The Bible Made Impossible*, 3–26, 149–153. See also Peter Enns, *The Sin of Certainty: Why God Desires Our Trust More Than Our "Correct" Beliefs* (New York: HarperCollins, 2017), 16–19.

14. Janet Jakobsen utilized queer theory, with its decentering of normativity, for a critical lens on pluralism ("Ethics After Pluralism," in *After Pluralism: Reimagining Religious Engagement*, ed. Courtney Bender and Pamela Klassen [New York: Columbia University Press, 2010], 31–58).

15. Paul Ricoeur, foreword to *Tolerance Between Intolerance and the Intolerable* (Providence, RI: Berghahn Books, 1996), 1.

16. John D. Inazu, *Confident Pluralism: Surviving and Thriving Through Deep Difference* (Chicago: University of Chicago Press, 2016), 83–92.

17. See Lewis Feuer, *Spinoza and the Rise of Liberalism* (Boston: Beacon Press, 1966), 119.

18. Proclamation 5018 (Feb. 3, 1983), *Public Papers of the Presidents of the United States: Ronald Reagan 1983*, 179.

19. See Nina Totenberg, "Supreme Court Appears Ready to Let Cross Stand but Struggles with Church-State Test," National Public Radio, February 27, 2019, https://

www.npr.org/2019/02/27/697708856/supreme-court-to-decide-fate-of-world-war-i
-memorial-cross-on-public-land; "Religious Displays on Government Property," Legal
Information Institute, https://www.law.cornell.edu/constitution-conan/amendment
-1/religious-displays-on-government-property.

20. Kent Faulk, "Roy Moore Timeline: Ten Commandments to Gay Marriage
Stance," Al.com, May 7, 2016, modified January 13, 2019, www.al.com/news/birmingham
/index.ssf/2016/05/roy_moore_timeline_ten_command.html.

21. Formal swearing-in is collective, without scripture; see Jan Crawford-Greenburg,
"Quran to Be Used for Ellison's Swearing-In," December 1, 2006, https://abcnews.go
.com/Politics/story?id=2694106&page=1. For discussion of the Islamophobia industry,
see Nathan Lean, *The Islamophobia Industry: How the Right Manufactures Hatred of
Muslims*, 2nd ed. (London: Pluto Press, 2017).

22. Barton Swaim, "The Pitfalls of Politicians Citing Verses," *Washington Post*,
December 2, 2015, https://www.washingtonpost.com/news/the-fix/wp/2015/12/02/if
-a-2016-candidate-is-citing-a-bible-verse-theres-a-good-chance-its-not-quite-right.

23. Julie Zauzmer and Keith McMillan, "Sessions Cites Bible Passage Used to Defend Slavery in Defense of Separating Immigrant Families," *Washington Post*, June 15,
2018, https://www.washingtonpost.com/news/acts-of-faith/wp/2018/06/14/jeff-sessions
-points-to-the-bible-in-defense-of-separating-immigrant-families.

24. Lincoln Mullen, "The Fight to Define Romans 13," *Atlantic*, June 15, 2018,
https://www.theatlantic.com/ideas/archive/2018/06/romans-13/562916.

25. Ahad Ha'am, "Perurim" [Crumbs], 1892, as cited in Shavit and Eran, *Hebrew
Bible Reborn*, 521–22.

26. Meeks, *The Origins of Christian Morality*, 217.

CHAPTER 7: A MATRIX OF DANGEROUS RELIGIOUS IDEAS

1. See Shaye Cohen's discussion of Hellenism and the shifting nature of religious
identity in *The Beginnings of Jewishness: Boundaries, Varieties, Uncertainties* (Berkeley:
University of California Press, 2001), 104–5, 136.

2. Jeremy Cott, "The Biblical Problem of Election," *Journal of Ecumenical Studies*
21:2 (1984): 204.

3. Avalos, *Fighting Words*; see also Schwartz, *The Curse of Cain*.

4. Tim Winter, "The Last Trump Card: Islam and the Supersession of Other
Faiths," *Studies in Interreligious Dialogue* 9:2 (1992): 145–46. The Qu'ranic inscription
inside the Dome of the Rock addresses Christian theological claims, denying the
divinity of Jesus and triune nature of God (4:171).

5. De Mendieta, *Historia eclesiástica Indiana*, as cited in John Leddy Phelan, *The
Millennial Kingdom of the Franciscans in the New World: A Study of the Writings of
Gerónimo de Mendieta (1525–1604)* (Berkeley: University of California Press, 1970), 13.

6. John Cotton, *Gods Promise to His Plantation* (London: William Jones, 1630),
http://digitalcommons.unl.edu/cgi/viewcontent.cgi?article=1022&context=etas.

7. Musa W. Dube, *Postcolonial Feminist Interpretation of the Bible* (St. Louis: Chalice Press, 2012), 17–19.

8. Jonathan Z. Smith, *Relating Religion: Essays in the Study of Religion* (Chicago:
University of Chicago Press, 2004), 246. See Rachel S. Mikva, "The Change a Difference Makes," in *Hearing Vocation Differently: Meaning, Purpose, and Identity in the*

Multi-Faith Academy, ed. David S. Cunningham (Oxford, UK: Oxford University Press, 2019), 26–27.

9. Henri Tajfel and John Turner, "An Integrative Theory of Intergroup Conflict," in *The Social Psychology of Intergroup Relations*, ed. William G. Austin and Stephen Worchel (Monterey, CA: Brooks/Cole, 1979), 33–47. See David Berreby, *Us and Them: Understanding Your Tribal Mind* (New York: Little, Brown, 2005).

10. Jean-Jacques Rousseau, *On the Social Contract, with Geneva Manuscript and Political Economy*, ed. Roger Masters, trans. Judith Masters (New York: Bedford/St. Martin's, 1978), 131–32.

11. William Scott Green, "Otherness Within: Towards a Theory of Difference in Rabbinic Judaism," in *"To See Ourselves as Others See Us": Christians, Jews, "Others" in Late Antiquity*, ed. Jacob Neusner and Ernest S. Frerichs (Chico, CA: Scholars Press, 1985), 50–51. See Edward Said, *Orientalism* (New York: Vintage Books, 1979), 332. For the role of identity formation in early Jewish–Christian relationships, see Boyarin, *Border Lines*; Leonard V. Rutgers, *Making Myths: Jews in Early Christian Identity Formation* (Leuven, Belgium: Peeters, 2009); Adiel Schremer, *Brothers Estranged: Heresy, Christianity, and Jewish Identity in Late Antiquity* (Oxford, UK: Oxford University Press, 2010).

12. Zygmunt Bauman, *Modernity and Ambivalence* (Cambridge, UK: Polity Press, 1993), 14.

13. Smith, *Relating Religion*, 245.

14. Alar Kilp, "Religion in the Construction of the Cultural 'Self' and 'Other,'" *ENDC Proceedings* 14 (2012): 197, https://www.ksk.edu.ee/wp-content/uploads/2012/12/KVUOA_Toimetised_14_9_alar_kilp.pdf.

15. See Heinrich Bullinger, *The Decades of Heinrich Bullinger* and William Gouge, *God's Three Arrowes*, cited in Roland H. Bainton, *Christian Attitudes Toward War and Peace: A Historical Survey and Critical Re-evaluation* (Eugene, OR: Wipf and Stock, 1960), 165–72; Elimelekh Horowitz, "*Midoro shel Moshe ad doro shel Mashiah: hayehudim mul 'Amalek' v'gilgulav* [From the Generation of Moses to the Generation of the Messiah: The Jews Confront 'Amalek' and His Incarnations]," *Zion* 64:4 (1999): 429; Robert Eisen, *The Peace and Violence of Judaism: From the Bible to Modern Zionism* (Oxford, UK: Oxford University Press, 2001), 152.

16. Farid Esack, "The Portrayal of Jews and the Possibilities for Their Salvation in the Qur'an," in *Between Heaven and Hell*, ed. Khalil, 230.

CHAPTER 8: CHOSENNESS IN JUDAISM

1. See Hebrews 11:4; Philo, *The Sacrifices of Cain and Abel* 52; Ephraem, *Commentary on Genesis* 3.2.1; Gen Rab. 22:5.

2. See Joel Kaminsky, *Yet I Loved Jacob: Reclaiming the Biblical Concept of Election* (Eugene, OR: Wipf and Stock, 2007), 23–27.

3. R. Kendall Soulen argued that God's work as Consummator of creation is bound up with this "economy of mutual blessing" exemplified in the election of Israel, *The God of Israel and Christian Theology* (Minneapolis: Fortress Press, 1996), 111–12. Contemporary critique sees Joseph's management of the food crisis as problematic: the process dispossesses landowners in Egypt and may kindle the fires of tyranny that ultimately engulf the Israelites.

4. See Avivah Gottlieb Zornberg, *Genesis: The Beginning of Desire* (Philadelphia: Jewish Publication Society, 1996), 72–96.

5. Abraham is described as a friend of God in Isaiah 41:8 and 2 Chronicles 20:7 (also James 2:23). See Bernhard W. Anderson, "Abraham, the Friend of God," *Interpretation* 42:4 (1988): 353–66, doi:10.1177/002096438804200403. The promise of kingship abiding in David's house is similarly viewed as a covenant of friendship, linked to chosenness (see Ps. 89:4, 2 Sam. 7:8–16).

6. Jon D. Levenson, *The Universal Horizon of Biblical Particularism* (New York: American Jewish Committee, 1985), 147. See Genesis 6:16–9:17 for the biblical narrative of Noah; cf. Qur'an 11:25–49, 23:23–30, and sura 71.

7. The priestly authors underscore the notion of holiness (*kedushah*), sanctification established through distinctive praxis: "You shall be holy to Me, for I YHWH am holy, and I have set you apart from the peoples to be Mine" (Lev. 20:26).

8. Seock-Tae Sohn, *The Divine Election of Israel* (Eugene, OR: Wipf and Stock, 2001), explored these images in detail.

9. *Berit olam* (eternal covenant) appears a dozen times in Tanakh; see Steven Mason, *"Eternal Covenant" in the Pentateuch* (London: T&T Clark, 2008). Tanakh also records, however, *feelings* of abandonment during times of suffering, e.g., Isa. 33:7–8, Jer. 7:29–34, Pss. 13, 44.

10. Levenson, *Universal Horizon*, 160. For discussion of race in antiquity, see Cain Hope Felder, *Stony the Road We Trod: African American Biblical Interpretation* (Minneapolis: Fortress Press, 1991), 127–45.

11. Rabbinic tradition imagined that Abraham and Sarah gather followers from the surrounding populations (Gen. Rab. 39:14). Formal conversion is a postbiblical development, but non-Israelites join the community in various ways.

12. Ammonites and Moabites are not similarly welcomed, likely due to enduring conflict. Jeffrey Tigay noted that Deuteronomy "expects foreigners to visit and trade with Israel, and permits most (including escaped slaves) to settle in Israel, marry Israelites, and eventually to join the popular Assembly" (*The JPS Torah Commentary: Deuteronomy* [Philadelphia: Jewish Publication Society, 1996], xvi).

13. Ezra twists a phrase from Isaiah 6:13, who sees a returning remnant as the seed that can regrow the decimated nation. Nehemiah 13 also resists exogamy, but on pragmatic grounds.

14. Cott, "Biblical Problem of Election," 205–7. Instructions such as "You shall not oppress a stranger, for you know the heart of the stranger, having yourselves been strangers in the land of Egypt" (Exod. 23:9) and "Love the stranger as yourself" (Lev. 19:34) are repeated over thirty times in Tanakh.

15. Haman also offers to pay a large sum of money if the king agrees to order the Jews' destruction.

16. See Millard C. Lind, *Yahweh Is a Warrior: The Theology of Warfare in Ancient Israel* (Scottdale, PA: Herald Press, 2001); Susan Niditch, *War in the Hebrew Bible: A Study in the Ethics of Violence* (Oxford, UK: Oxford University Press, 1993), 143–49.

17. Only a few Canaanite cities appear to have been destroyed around the time of the Israelite conquest; see William Dever, *Recent Archaeological Discoveries and Biblical Research* (Seattle: University of Washington Press, 1993), 56–61. Exodus 23 and 34 command exiling the Canaanites instead. Passages in Joshua, Judges, and Kings indicate

that they remained in the land, and abiding temptation to participate in Canaanite cultic worship is evident throughout Tanakh.

18. Child sacrifice and sorcery are identified as some of their abhorrent practices (Deut. 12:31, 18:9–12).

19. Kaminsky, *Yet I Loved Jacob*, 107–36.

20. Robert Eisen, *The Peace and Violence of Judaism*, 15–64.

21. Jeffrey Tigay identified Celts, Gauls, Teutons, and Romans among those who proscribed enemy populations (*JPS Torah Commentary: Deuteronomy*, 538); see also "The Moabite Stone" in *Ancient Near Eastern Texts Relating to the Old Testament*, 3rd ed., ed. James Pritchard (Princeton, NJ: Princeton University Press, 1969), 320.

22. Eisen, *The Peace and Violence of Judaism*, 81–88. See Robert Goldenberg, "The Destruction of the Temple: Its Meanings and Consequences," in Volume 4 of *The Cambridge History of Judaism*, ed. Steven Katz (Cambridge, UK: Cambridge University Press, 2006), 191–205; David Kraemer, *Responses to Suffering in Classical Rabbinic Literature* (Oxford, UK: Oxford University Press, 1995), 51–221; Reuven Kimelman, "Nonviolence in the Talmud," *Judaism* 17:3 (1968): 316–33; Aviezer Ravitzky, *History and Faith: Studies in Jewish Philosophy* (Amsterdam: J. C. Gieben, 1996), 22–45.

23. See Moshe Greenberg, *HaSegulah vehaKoach* [*Particularity and Power*] (Kibbutz Hameuhad, 1986), 20.

24. Reuven Firestone, *Holy War in Judaism: The Fall and Rise of a Controversial Idea* (Oxford, UK: Oxford University Press, 2012), 77–89. The categorization is first recorded in m. Sotah 8:7; it is further developed in the Talmuds and later halakhic literature.

25. Attitudes about destruction of the Amalekites are less clear. Many medieval rabbinic authorities placed restrictions on the command or treated it as moot, but others saw it as an abiding mitzvah. See Avi Sagi, "The Punishment of Amalek in Jewish Tradition: Coping with the Moral Problem," *Harvard Theological Review* 87:3 (1994): 323–45, doi:10.1017/S0017816000030753.

26. See Rachel S. Mikva, "Brer Rabbit and the Destruction of the Temple in Jerusalem," *Comparative Literature Studies* 53:1 (2016): 6–12.

27. Cf. Gen. Rab. 83:5. See Burton Visotzky, "Anti-Christian Polemic in Leviticus Rabbah," *Proceedings of the American Academy for Jewish Research* 56 (1990): 88–100; Adam Gregerman, *Building on the Ruins of the Temple* (Tübingen: Mohr Siebeck, 2016).

28. See William Scott Green, "What's in a Name? The Problematic of Rabbinic 'Biography,'" in *Approaches to Ancient Judaism I* (Chico, CA: Scholars Press, 1978), 77–96; Jacob Neusner, "From History to Hermeneutics: The Talmud as a Historical Source," *Review of Rabbinic Judaism* 11:2 (2008): 200–27.

29. For discussion of non-Jews in rabbinic literature, see Gary Porton, *Goyim: Gentiles and Israelites in Mishnah-Tosefta* (Atlanta: Scholars Press, 1988); Sacha Stern, *Jewish Identity in Early Rabbinic Writings* (Leiden: Brill, 1997); Richard Kalmin, "Christians and Heretics in Rabbinic Literature of Late Antiquity," *Harvard Theological Review* 87:2 (1994): 155–69, doi:10.1017/S0017816000032764; Christine Hayes, "The 'Other' in Rabbinic Literature," in *The Cambridge Companion to the Talmud and Rabbinic Literature*, ed. Charlotte Elisheva Fonrobert and Martin S. Jaffee (Cambridge, UK: Cambridge University Press, 2007), 243–69.

30. The descendants of Noah received seven commandments: establish laws and prohibit blasphemy, idolatry, adultery, bloodshed, theft, and consuming the blood of

a living animal (b. Sanh. 56a). See David Novak, *The Image of the Non-Jew in Judaism: The Idea of Noahide Law* (Oxford, UK: Littmann Library of Jewish Civilization, 2011).

31. Ruth Langer, "The Censorship of Aleinu in Ashkenaz and its Aftermath," in *The Experience of Jewish Liturgy*, ed. Debra Reed Blank (Leiden: Brill, 2011), 147–66, doi:10.1163/9789004208032_010; *Cursing the Christians? A History of Birkat haMinim* (Oxford, UK: Oxford University Press, 2011). Justin Martyr's complaint that Jewish liturgy cursed Christians (*Dialogue with Trypho* 16:4; cf. 47:4, 96:2) is no longer presumed to describe this late text. His comments may have been designed to produce alienation rather than reflect it (Boyarin, *Border Lines*, 67–74).

32. Shlomo Eidelberg, *The Jews and the Crusaders: The Hebrew Chronicles of the First and Second Crusades* (Hoboken, NJ: KTAV, 1996), 26, 99. The quote is from an anonymous Mainz chronicle.

33. T. Carmi, *The Penguin Book of Hebrew Verse* (London: Penguin Books, 1981), 372 (an anonymous dirge for the Mainz martyrs).

34. Shalom Spiegel, *The Last Trial*, trans. Judah Goldin (Woodstock, VT: Jewish Lights, 1993), 135–37.

35. Eidelberg, *The Jews and the Crusaders*, 65. Christians also wrote Crusader chronicles with martyrological themes linked to election. See Jeremy Cohen, *Sanctifying the Name of God: Jewish Martyrs and Jewish Memories of the First Crusade* (Philadelphia: University of Pennsylvania Press, 2004), 29.

36. See Michael Meerson and Peter Schäfer, eds., *Toledot Yeshu* (Tübingen: Mohr Siebeck, 2014); Hillel Newman, "The Death of Jesus in the *Toledot Yeshu* Literature," *Journal of Theological Studies* 50:1 (1999): 59–63, doi:10.1093/jts/50.1.59. The earliest extant manuscript is from the eleventh century. Non-Jews used the texts to indict Judaism; see Martin Lockshin, "Translation as Polemic," in *Minḥah le-Naḥum: Biblical and Other Studies Presented to Nahum M. Sarna in Honour of His 70th Birthday*, ed. Marc Brettler and Michael Fishbane (Sheffield, UK: JSOT Press, 1993), 226–92. Christian sources also portrayed Jesus as a magician; see Morton Smith, *Jesus the Magician* (San Francisco: Hampton Roads, 2014).

37. David Biale, "Counter-History and Jewish Polemic against Christianity: The *Sefer toldot yeshu* and the *Sefer zerubavel*," *Jewish Social Studies* 6 (1999): 130–45.

38. Joseph Kimchi, *Sefer haBrit* [Book of the Covenant], trans. Frank Talmadge (Toronto: Mediaeval Institute of Pontifical Studies, 1972), 65.

39. Mark Cohen, *Under Crescent and Cross: The Jews in the Middle Ages* (Princeton, NJ: Princeton University Press, 2008), 160. See also Prosper Murciano, "*Keshet uMagen*: A Critical Edition" (PhD diss., New York University, 1975); Daniel J. Lasker, *Jewish Philosophical Polemics against Christianity in the Middle Ages* (Oxford, UK: Littman Library, 2007).

40. HaLevi, *Kuzari, Book One* 27.1, 103.1, 115.3. See Robert Eisen, *Gersonides on Providence, Covenant, and the Chosen People* (Albany, NY: SUNY Press, 1995), 172–78.

41. Saadia Gaon, *Emunot veDeot*, Article 2. See *The Book of Beliefs and Opinions*, trans. Samuel Rosenblatt (New Haven, CT: Yale University Press, 1958), 125–26.

42. See his Talmud commentary, *Beit haBekhira*, on b. B. Qam. 37b, 113a–b, b. B. Metz. 59a, b. Avod. Zar. 26a, and b. Hor. 11a for a range of his rulings and reasoning; also Moshe Halbertal, "'Ones Possessed of Religion': Religious Tolerance in the Teachings of the Me'iri," *Edah* 1:1 (2000): 1–24. Isaac Arama (1420–94) similarly suggested that righteous Jews and non-Jews are spiritually identical (*Akedat Yitzhak* 20).

43. Maimonides wrote to Ovadiah the proselyte: You are just like any native-born Jew . . . for Abraham is your spiritual father, and our inheritance is yours as well, since there is no racial distinction in our faith" (*Responsa* II: 293). See Menahem Kellner, *Maimonides on Judaism and the Jewish People* (Albany, NY: SUNY Press, 1991), 92–94.

44. Maimonides, *Mishnah Torah, Melachim* 11.4. Parts of this passage were sometimes eliminated by Christian censors. Jacob Emden (1697–1796, Germany) also wrote that "the Nazarene" did much good by leading Gentiles to embrace Torah and move away from idolatry (*Seder Olam Rabbah v'Zuta*).

45. Unbelieving Arab contemporaries similarly accused Muhammad of being a madman (*majnun*). See Mark Cohen, *Under Crescent and Cross*, 154.

46. Maimonides, *Epistle to Yemen*, trans. Boaz Cohen, reprinted in *A Maimonides Reader*, ed. Isadore Twersky (Springfield, NJ: Behrman House, 1972), 439. See also Menachem Kellner, "Chosenness, Not Chauvinism," in *A People Apart*, ed. David Frank (Albany, NY: SUNY Press, 1993), 51–75; Ibn Kammuna, *Examination of the Three Faiths: A Thirteenth-Century Essay in Comparative Study of Religion*, trans. Moshe Perlman (Berkeley: University of California Press, 1971). The Jewish author had to flee Baghdad after an imam attacked it for its criticisms of Islam and riots broke out; he was condemned to death in absentia.

47. Brueggemann, *Reverberations of Faith: A Theological Handbook of Old Testament Themes* (Louisville, KY: Westminster John Knox, 2002), 63.

48. Jonathan Sacks, *Dignity of Difference: How to Avoid the Clash of Civilizations* (London: Continuum, 2007), 45–66.

49. Immanuel Kant, *Religion within the Boundaries of Mere Reason and Other Writings*, trans. Allen Wood and George di Giovanni (Cambridge, UK: Cambridge University Press, 1998), 130, doi:10.1017/CBO9780511809637.007.

50. See Daniel Dubuisson, *The Western Construction of Religion* (Baltimore: Johns Hopkins University Press, 2003), 147–50; Anders Runesson, "Particularistic Judaism and Universal Christianity? Some Critical Remarks on Terminology and Theology," *Studia Theologica* 54:1 (2000): 58, doi:10.1080/003933800750041520.

51. Sacks, *Dignity of Difference*, 50–52.

52. Mendelssohn, *Jerusalem: or On Religious Power and Judaism*, trans. Allan Arkush (Lebanon, NH: Brandeis University Press, 1983), 97.

53. Beth A. Berkowitz, *Defining Jewish Difference: From Antiquity to the Present* (Cambridge, UK: Cambridge University Press, 2012), 41–59, doi:10.1017/CBO 9781139005159. The rabbis debated degrees of Hellenization; see Seth Schwartz, *Imperialism and Jewish Society* (Princeton, NJ: Princeton University Press, 2001), 103–75.

54. See *Special Laws* 1.33, 2.162–67, *On the Life of Moses* 1.148, *On the Posterity of Cain and His Exile* 91–93, *On Abraham* 98. Also Ellen Birnbaum, *The Place of Judaism in Philo's Thought: Israel, Jews, and Proselytes* (Atlanta: Society of Biblical Literature, 1996).

55. Kaufmann Kohler, *Jewish Theology, Systematically and Historically Considered* (New York: Macmillan, 1928), 323. Also Sforno (c. 1475–1550) on Exod. 19:5–6: God loves all the peoples of the world, especially the righteous; Israel is called to teach humanity so that all may serve God together.

56. Leo Baeck, *Das Wesen des Judentums*, as cited in Ze'ev Levy, "Judaism and Chosenness: On Some Controversial Aspects from Spinoza to Contemporary Jewish Thought," in *A People Apart: Chosenness and Ritual in Jewish Philosophical Thought*, ed. Daniel H. Frank (Albany, NY: SUNY Press, 1993), 101.

57. Cited in Renzo Fabris, "Modern Man and the Concept of the Chosen People," in *Seeds of Reconciliation: Essays on Jewish-Christian Understanding*, ed. Katharine T. Hargrove (North Richland Hills, TX: BIBAL Press, 1996), 100.

58. Irving Greenberg, *Living in the Image of God: Jewish Teaching to Perfect the World* (Northvale, NJ: Jason Aronson, 1998), 79. See David Novak, *The Election of Israel: The Idea of the Chosen People* (Cambridge, UK: Cambridge University Press, 1995); Soulen, *God of Israel and Christian Theology*; Michael Wyschogrod, *The Body of Faith* (Lanham, MD: Rowman and Littlefield, 2000); Kaminsky, *Yet I Loved Jacob*; Avi Beker, *The Chosen: The History of an Idea, and the Anatomy of an Obsession* (New York: Palgrave Macmillan, 2008); Reuven Firestone, *Who Are the Real Chosen People? The Meaning of Chosenness in Judaism, Christianity, and Islam* (Woodstock, VT: SkyLight Paths, 2008); Joel Lohr, *Chosen and Unchosen: Conceptions of Election in the Pentateuch and Jewish-Christian Interpretation* (Winona Lake, IN: Eisenbrauns, 2009).

59. The passage uses prooftexts from 1 Sam. 2:27, Isa. 43:14, and Deut. 30:3 to support the claim. Regarding the last of these, the Talmud notes that the verse states "God will return," not "God will cause to return."

60. Also Sifre Deut. 308: Even though you are full of blemishes, you are God's children. Rabbi Yehudah ostensibly maintained that Israel could lose its elect position for failing to behave as "children of the Lord," but it was a minority opinion that seemed to fade away (Sifre Deut. 96).

61. Regarding chosenness of the land of Israel, see David Novak, *Zionism and Judaism: A New Theory* (Cambridge, UK: Cambridge University Press, 2015); W. D. Davies, *The Territorial Dimension of Judaism* (Berkeley: University of California Press, 1982).

62. Soulen, *The God of Israel and Christian Theology*, 8, building on the reasoning of Michael Wyschogrod.

63. See David Stern, *Parables in Midrash: Narrative and Exegesis in Rabbinic Literature* (Cambridge, MA: Harvard University Press, 1994), 56–62 for an insightful reading of the passage.

64. The notion that any Jew could impact the cosmos through performance of mitzvot was transformative for the refugees expelled from Spain in 1492 (Rachel Elior, *Jewish Mysticism: The Infinite Expression of Freedom* [Oxford, UK: Littman Library, 2009], 1–32).

CHAPTER 9: ELECTION IN CHRISTIANITY

1. Mary is told that her son will sit on the throne of his father David (Luke 1:32). Echoing Abraham's trial, Jesus must go into the wilderness as soon as his election is announced (Mark 1:9–13). Jesus warns his listeners that they will be afflicted for their faith (Matt. 5, Mark 13). One who asks Jesus how to acquire eternal life is told to follow the commandments (Matt. 19, Mark 10).

2. Many ideas that became central in early Christianity were part of the Jewish conceptual universe at the time, and both religions were profoundly impacted by Hellenism. See E. P. Sanders, *Paul and Palestinian Judaism: A Comparison of Patterns of Religion* (Philadelphia: Fortress, 1977); Everett Ferguson, *Backgrounds of Early Christianity* (Grand Rapids, MI: Eerdmans, 2003); Hans-Josef Klauck, *The Religious Context of Early Christianity: A Guide to Greco-Roman Religions* (Minneapolis: Fortress, 2003); Daniel Boyarin, *The Jewish Gospels: The Story of the Jewish Christ* (New York: New Press, 2012).

3. See J. Christiaan Beker, *Paul the Apostle: The Essence of Paul's Thought* (Fortress, 1980), 59–93.

4. See, e.g., Shaye J. D. Cohen's introduction to Galatians in *The Jewish Annotated New Testament*, ed. Amy-Jill Levine and Mark Zvi Brettler (Oxford, UK: Oxford University Press, 2011), 373–74. Claims about the status of the Jewish covenant still ignites controversy; see Tom Heneghan, "Retired Pope Benedict Accused of Anti-Semitism after Article on Christians and Jews," *National Catholic Reporter*, August 6, 2018, https://www.ncronline.org/news/vatican/retired-pope-benedict-accused-anti-semitism-after-article-christians-and-jews.

5. Similarly, Malachi's call of "Have we not all one father?" (2:10) sounds universalist but is primarily making a case for Jewish unity. The Galatians passage follows Paul's dispute with Peter for sitting separately from Gentile followers (2:11–21).

6. Scholars debate catalysts and timing of the "parting of the ways," with growing conviction that separation from Judaism was a protracted process. See Annette H. Reed and Adam Becker, eds., *The Ways That Never Parted: Jews and Christians in Late Antiquity and the Early Middle Ages* (Minneapolis: Fortress, 2007). Abel Bibliowicz asserted that Christian anti-Judaism grew out of internal conflict in the Jesus movement in *Jews and Gentiles in the Early Jesus Movement: An Unintended Journey* (New York: Palgrave Macmillan, 2013).

7. Paul affirmed the law for Jewish believers in Jesus and access without it for Gentile believers. Recent scholarship emphasizes Paul's continuing identification as a Jew, e.g., John Gager, *Who Made Early Christianity? The Jewish Lives of the Apostle Paul* (New York: Columbia University Press, 2015).

8. "The law" is a poor rendering of Torah (literally "instruction"), playing into historical bias that Judaism is legalistic. The Koine Greek term *nomos* may capture a fuller semantic range, but it was flattened in patristic writings.

9. Origen wrote in *Homilies on Leviticus* 7.5.5, "For even in the Gospels, it is the letter that kills." Sanders, *Paul and Palestinian Judaism*, refuted Christian scholars who misrepresent late antique Judaism as concerned with "works" righteousness.

10. Cf. Exod. 19:6, Deut. 14:2, Hosea 2:2 to see how it incorporates language from Tanakh.

11. See Runesson, "Particularistic Judaism and Universalistic Christianity?" 58–60; Denise Kimber Buell, "Rethinking the Relevance of Race for Early Christian Self-Definition," *Harvard Theological Review* 94:4 (2001): 449–76, doi:10.1017/S0017816000 1038044.

12. See Paul Imhof and Hubert Biallowons, eds., *Karl Rahner in Dialogue: Conversations and Interviews, 1965–1982* (New York: Crossroad, 1986); Krister Stendahl, "From God's Perspective We Are All Minorities," *Journal of Religious Pluralism* 2 (1993): 4.

13. In *The Fate of the Unrepentant: A Study of Biblical Themes of Fire and Being Consumed* (Eugene, OR: Wipf and Stock, 2012), 52–55, Webb Mealy argued that eternal destruction means they cease to exist after death. Others maintain that the Greek term is best rendered by its English cognate (*aeon*), indicating a long period rather than eternity.

14. On conversion to Judaism in the late Second Temple period, see Shaye Cohen, *The Beginnings of Jewishness* (Berkeley: University of California Press, 1999), 129–62; Carleton Paget, "Jewish Proselytism at the Time of Christian Origins: Chimera or Reality?," *Journal for the Study of the New Testament* 18:62 (1996): 65–103, doi:10.1177/0142064X9601806204.

15. See Norman Beck, *Mature Christianity in the 21st Century: The Recognition and Repudiation of the Anti-Jewish Polemic of the New Testament* (New York: Crossroad, 1994); Paula Fredriksen and Adele Reinhartz, eds., *Jesus, Judaism and Christian Anti-Judaism: Reading the New Testament in a Post-Holocaust World* (Louisville, KY: Westminster John Knox, 2002).

16. Smith, *Relating Religion*, 245; see chap. 7 above.

17. Note Birger A. Pearson, "1 Thessalonians 2:13–16: A Deutero-Pauline Interpolation," *Harvard Theological Review* 64 (1971): 79–94, doi:10.1017/S0017816000018046.

18. Rosemary Radford Ruether, *Faith and Fratricide: The Theological Roots of Anti-Semitism* (New York: Seabury Press, 1974), 230.

19. See W. R. Herzog, *Parables as Subversive Speech: Jesus as Pedagogue of the Oppressed* (Louisville, KY: Westminster John Knox, 1994). Francisco Lozada and Greg Carey, eds., *Soundings in Cultural Criticism: Perspectives and Methods in Culture, Power, and Identity in the New Testament* (Minneapolis: Fortress Press, 2013).

20. Calvin J. Roetzl, "Election/Calling in Certain Pauline Letters: An Experimental Construction," in *Society for Biblical Literature 1990 Seminar Papers*, ed. David J. Lull (Atlanta: Scholars Press, 1990), 556.

21. See Michel Desjardins, *Peace, Violence and the New Testament* (London: T&T Clark, 1997).

22. Gregory of Nyssa, *De anima et resurrectione* 46, *Oratia catechetica* 26; Clement, *Stromata* 7.2, 16; Origen, *De principiis* 3.6.6 (elsewhere he asserted limits). See Acts 3:21; Brian Daley, *The Hope of the Early Church: A Handbook of Patristic Eschatology* (Cambridge, UK: Cambridge University Press, 1991); Ilaria L. E. Ramelli, *The Christian Doctrine of Apokatastasis: A Critical Assessment from the New Testament to Eriugena* (Leiden: Brill, 2013).

23. Such mystics include Isaac the Syrian (seventh century), Amalric of Bena (died c. 1207), Julian of Norwich (d. 1416). Rita Nakashima Brock and Rebecca Ann Parker reviewed Christian universalists dating from seventeenth-century England in *Saving Paradise: How Christianity Traded Love of This World for Crucifixion and Empire* (Boston: Beacon, 2008), 389–98. Numerous pluralist Christian theologies have emerged in recent decades.

24. *The Wisdom of St. Isaac the Syrian*, trans. Sebastian Brock (Oxford, UK: SLG Press, 1997), loc. 78–88, 307–320.

25. *On the Gospel of St. John* 86 (c. 419 CE). Cf. Thomas Aquinas's distinction between God's love, which causes good, versus our own which is incited by good that already exists (*Summa Theologica* I.23.4).

26. Justin Martyr, *Dialogue with Trypho* 11.

27. Paul identifies the seed of Abraham, written in the singular in Genesis 15:15, as Jesus (Gal. 3:16). See also Augustine, *On the Spirit and the Letter* 46; Irenaeus (130–202 CE), *Against Heresies* 4.21.

28. See Jon D. Levenson, *Death and Resurrection of the Beloved Son: The Transformation of Child Sacrifice in Judaism and Christianity* (New Haven, CT: Yale University Press, 1995), 198–219.

29. Irenaeus, *Against Heresies* 4.33. John of Damascus identified the tree in Eden as Jesus's cross: "For since death was by a tree, it is fitting that life and resurrection are bestowed by a tree" (*Exposition of the Orthodox Faith* 4.11).

30. The suffering servant motif is already absorbed in New Testament (Matt. 8:17, Acts 8:32–35).

31. Augustine, *Contra Faustum* 19:9–10.

32. Augustine, *On the Gospel of St. John* 11.8: "The former people is a figure for the present people. For in the Jewish people was figured the Christian people. There a figure, here the truth."

33. Tertullian, *Adversus Judaeos* 5.

34. Augustine, *Contra Faustum* 12:9–14. Cf. *On the Gospel of St. John* 9.11.1, 11.7.2, *The City of God* 15.26.

35. See 2 Corinthians 3:13–16; Daniel Boyarin, "Subversion of the Jews: Moses' Veil and the Hermeneutics of Supersession," *Diacritics* 23:2 (1993): 16–35. Alexandrian exegesis pursued typological readings more than the Antiochene school.

36. Soulen constructed a framework analyzing Christian ideas of supersession. Economic supersession maintains that carnal Israel was providentially ordered from the outset to become obsolete. Punitive supersession contends God punished Israel for its sinfulness, including refusal to embrace Christ. Structural supersession renders the "Old" Testament indecisive for Christian theology in imagining God's redemptive plan; the essential narratives become creation, the "fall," the incarnation of Jesus, and the final consummation, bypassing entirely God's involvement with the people of Israel (*The God of Israel and Christian Theology*, 28–33).

37. See Augustine, *Contra Faustum* and Paula Fredriksen, *Augustine and the Jews* (New Haven, CT: Yale University Press, 2010).

38. See, for instance, Justin Martyr's *Dialogue with Trypho*, Cyprian's *Three Books of Testimonies Against the Jews*, John Chrysostom's and Tertullian's *Adversus Judaeos*. For a compilation of polemical literature, see Heinz Schreckenberg, *Die christlichen Adversus-Judaeos Texte und ihr literarisches und historisches Umfeld* (Frankfurt: Peter Lang, 1988–1994). Christian tropes also adopted Hellenistic barbs, appropriating dominant modes of cultural power; see Andrew Jacobs, "The Lion and the Lamb: Reconsidering Jewish-Christian Relations in Antiquity," in *The Ways That Never Parted*, ed. Becker and Reed, 95–118.

39. David Nirenberg, "Slay Them Not: A Review of Paula Fredriksen's *Augustine and the Jews*," *New Republic* 240:4 (March 18, 2009): 42–47. See Fredriksen, *Augustine and the Jews*, 306–7; Jeremy Cohen, *Living Letters of the Law: Ideas of the Jew in Medieval Christianity* (Berkeley: University of California Press, 1999), 2–3; Miriam S. Taylor, *Anti-Judaism and Early Christian Identity: A Critique of the Scholarly Consensus* (Leiden: Brill, 1994).

40. See Amnon Linder, *The Jews in Roman Imperial Legislation* (Detroit: Wayne State University Press, 1988); Jacob Rader Marcus, *The Jew in the Medieval World: A Sourcebook, 315–1791* (Philadelphia: Jewish Publication Society, 1938), 3–7. Note also Norman Golb, "Jewish Proselytism—A Phenomenon in the Religious History of Early Medieval Europe," March 3, 1987, http://oi.uchicago.edu/pdf/jewish_proselytism.pdf.

41. "The Edict of Expulsion of the Jews," trans. Edward Peters, Foundation for the Advancement of Sephardic Studies and Culture, http://www.sephardicstudies.org/decree.html.

42. Jerusha Lamptey [Rhodes], *Never Wholly Other: A Muslima Theology of Religious Pluralism* (Oxford, UK: Oxford University Press, 2014), 2, doi:10.1093/acprof:oso/9780199362783.001.0001.

43. Ibn Ishaq (704–68) provided the earliest extant record; see Martin Lings, *Muhammad: His Life Based on the Earliest Sources* (Rochester, VT: Inner Traditions, 2006), 81–84.

44. See David Nirenberg, *Neighboring Faiths: Christianity, Islam, and Judaism in the Middle Ages and Today* (Chicago: University of Chicago Press, 2014), 16.

45. See David Thomas, ed. and trans., *Early Muslim Polemic against Christianity: Abu Isa al-Warraq's "Against the Incarnation"* (Cambridge, UK: Cambridge University Press, 2002), 14–15.

46. Risâlat al-Kindi, *Dialogue islamo-chrétien sous le Calife al-Ma'mûn (813–834): Les épitres d'Al-Hashimi et d'Al-Kindî*, trans. Georges Tatar (Paris: Nouvelles Éditions Latines, 1985).

47. John V. Tolan, *Saracens: Islam in the Medieval European Imagination* (New York: Columbia University Press, 2002), 23.

48. See Debra Higgs Strickland, *Saracens, Demons, and Jews: Making Monsters in Medieval Art* (Princeton, NJ: Princeton University Press, 2003).

49. Wolfgang Seiferth, *Synagogue and Church in the Middle Ages: Two Symbols in Art and Literature* (New York: Frederick Ungar Publishing, 1970), 5–7, 95–109, figs. 5, 31, 35–37.

50. Cited in Constant J. Mews, "Abelard and Heloise on Jews and *Hebraica Veritas*," in *Christian Attitudes toward Jews in the Middle Ages*, ed. Michael Frassetto (London: Routledge, 2007), 83. Cf. Marc Saperstein, "Christians and Jews: Some Positive Images," *Harvard Theological Review* 79:1/3 (1986): 237, doi:10.1017/S00178160000 20502.

51. Mews, "Abelard and Heloise," 96.

52. Tolan, *Saracens*, 175–78; Nirenberg, *Neighboring Faiths*, 26.

53. Rita George-Tvrtković, *A Christian Pilgrim in Medieval Iraq: Riccoldo Montecroce's Encounter with Islam* (Turnhout, Belgium: Brepols, 2012).

54. Martin Luther, "That Jesus Christ Was Born a Jew," https://www.uni-due.de /collcart/es/sem/s6/txt09_1.htm.

55. Martin Luther, *The Christian in Society IV*, vol. 47 of *Luther's Works* (Philadelphia: Fortress Press, 1971). See Adam S. Francisco, *Martin Luther and Islam: A Study in Sixteenth-Century Polemics and Apologetics* (Leiden: Brill, 2007), doi:10.1163/ej .9789004160439.i-260.

56. Catherine Keller, *God and Power: Counter-Apocalyptic Journeys* (Minneapolis: Fortress, 2005), 115.

57. Jeremy M. Schott, *Christianity, Empire and the Making of Religion in Late Antiquity* (Philadelphia: University of Pennsylvania Press, 2008), 3–4, 69–76.

58. See George Kalantzis, *Caesar and the Lamb* (Eugene, OR: Wipf and Stock, 2012), 97–147; Lisa Sowle Cahill, *Love Your Enemies: Discipleship, Pacifism, and Just War Theory* (Minneapolis: Augsburg Fortress, 1994), 41–54.

59. Christians served in the Roman army by the second century; Athanasius (296–373) and Basil of Caesarea (330–379) wrote in support of their participation. See Louis J. Swift, *The Early Fathers on War and Military Service* (Wilmington, DE: Michael Glazier, 1984), 93–95; James Turner Johnson, *The Quest for Peace* (Princeton, NJ: Princeton University Press, 1987); David Hunter, "A Decade of Research on Early Christians and Military Service," *Religious Studies Review* 18:2 (1992): 87–94, doi:10.1111/j.1748–0922.1992.tb00084.x.

60. Symmachus, *Relatio* 3.10, Themistius *Orations* 68d–69a. Augustine wrote, "Union with wisdom is not achieved by a single road," but he later retracted it citing, "I am the way" (*Retractiones* 1.4.3).

61. Alexei M. Sivertsev, *Judaism and Imperial Ideology in Late Antiquity* (Cambridge, UK: Cambridge University Press, 2011), 10. Cf. Henry Chadwick, "Christian and Roman Universalism in the Fourth Century," in *Christian Faith and Greek Philosophy*, ed. Lionel Wickham and Caroline Bammel (Leiden: Brill, 1993), 26–42.

62. See *The Theodosian Code*, book 16. Constantius II and Theodosius I were the first emperors to persecute pagans.

63. Michael Gaddis, *There Is No Crime for Those Who Have Christ* (Berkeley: University of California Press, 2005), 1, 191. Note Romans 8:33–34: "Who shall bring any charge against God's elect? It is God who justifies; who is to condemn?"

64. Severus of Minorca, *Letter on the Conversion of the Jews* 31.3–4, trans. Scott Bradbury (Oxford, UK: Oxford University Press, 1996), 125.

65. For an anthology on just war theory, see Arthur Holmes, ed., *War and Christian Ethics: Classic and Contemporary Readings on the Morality of War* (Grand Rapids, MI: Baker Academic, 2005).

66. See Swift, *The Early Fathers on War*, 149–54; Frances Young, "The Early Church: Military Service, War and Peace," *Theology* 92:750 (1989): 491–503.

67. Robert Chazan, *European Jewry and the First Crusade* (Berkeley: University of California Press, 1996), 85–98, 173–78; *The Jews of Medieval Western Christendom 1000–1500* (Cambridge, UK: Cambridge University Press, 2006). Rabbi Ephraim of Bonn corroborated his intervention. See James Brundage, *The Crusades: A Documentary History* (Milwaukee, WI: Marquette University Press, 1962), 115–121; Cohen, *Living Letters*, 73–94.

68. Robert the Monk, *Historia Hierosolymitana*, https://sourcebooks.fordham.edu/source/urban2-5vers.asp#robert. His record was composed approximately twenty-five years after the fact; no contemporaneous record of the speech survives.

69. Christophe T. Maier, *Preaching the Crusades: Mendicant Friars and the Cross in the Thirteenth Century* (Cambridge, UK: Cambridge University Press, 1998), 15.

70. *Nicholas of Cusa on Interreligious Harmony: Text, Concordance and Translation of De Pace Fidei*, ed. and trans. James Biechler and H. Lawrence Bond (Lewiston, NY: Edward Mellen, 1991), 1.2.

71. See Tatha Wiley, *Original Sin: Origins, Developments and Contemporary Meanings* (New York: Paulist Press, 2002), 40–42.

72. See Brinley Rees, *Pelagius: Life and Letters* (Woodbridge, UK: Boydell Press, 1998).

73. *Commentarius in Epistolam ad Romanos*, ed. Éloi Marie Buytaert, Corpus Christianorum, Continuatio Mediaevalis 11 (Turnhout, Belgium: Brepols, 1969), 114–17; Mews, "Abelard and Heloise," 92. See also Paula Fredriksen, *Sin: The Early History of an Idea* (Princeton, NJ: Princeton University Press, 2012).

74. Brock and Parker, *Saving Paradise*, 84–114. Noting that Church art before the ninth century emphasized images of idyllic gardens, not crucifixions, they claimed the myth of redemptive violence did not overtake Christianity until later.

75. Albrecht Ritschl, *The Christian Doctrine of Justification and Reconciliation: The Positive Development of the Doctrine*, 3rd ed., ed. and trans. H. R. Mackintosh and A. B. Macaulay (Clifton, NJ: Reference Book Publishers, 1966), 121, 295, 301.

76. Karl Barth, *Church Dogmatics III/2*, trans. Geoffrey Bromiley and Thomas Torrence (London: T&T Clark, 1957). See Soulen, *God of Israel and Christian Theology*; Douglas John Hall, *The Cross in Our Context: Jesus and the Suffering World* (Minneapolis: Augsburg Fortress, 2003); Sallie McFague, *Life Abundant: Rethinking Theology and Economy for a Planet in Peril* (Minneapolis: Augsburg Fortress, 2001).

77. Examples include John Hick, *God Has Many Names* (Philadelphia: Westminster Press, 1980); John Hick and Paul F. Knitter, eds., *The Myth of Christian Uniqueness: Toward a Pluralistic Theology of Religions* (Maryknoll, NY: Orbis Books, 1987); Monica A. Coleman, *Making a Way Out of No Way: A Womanist Theology* (Minneapolis: Fortress Press, 2008); Jacques Dupuis, *Toward a Christian Theology of Religious Pluralism* (Maryknoll, NY: Orbis, 2002); Perry Schmidt-Leukel, *Religious Pluralism and Interreligious Theology* (Maryknoll, NY: Orbis Books, 2017); John R. Franke, *Manifold Witness: The Plurality of Truth* (Nashville: Abingdon Press, 2009).

78. Candida Moss, *The Other Christs: Imitating Jesus in Ancient Christian Ideologies of Martyrdom* (Oxford, UK: Oxford University Press, 2012), 19–20, doi:10.1093/acprof :oso/9780199739875.001.0001.

79. Tripp York, *The Purple Crown: The Politics of Martyrdom* (Scottdale, PA: Herald Press, 2007).

80. Peter Brown, *The Cult of the Saints: Its Rise and Function in Latin Christianity* (Chicago: University of Chicago Press, 2009), 72.

81. *The Martyrdom of St. Polycarp*, http://www.ccel.org/ccel/richardson/fathers.vii .i.iii.html. Texts often exaggerated and invented stories of Christian martyrdom in stylized rewritings of "noble death" traditions; see Candida Moss, *The Myth of Persecution: How Early Christians Invented a Story of Martyrdom* (New York: HarperCollins, 2013).

82. Jürgen Moltmann, *The Crucified God: The Cross of Christ as the Foundation and Criticism of Christian Theology*, trans. R. A. Wilson and John Bowden (Philadelphia: Fortress Press, 1974), 1.

83. Patrick M. Erben, "Book of Suffering, Suffering Book: The Mennonite *Martyrs' Mirror* and the Translation of Martyrdom in Colonial America," in *Empires of God: Religious Encounters in the Early Modern Atlantic*, ed. Linda Gregerson and Susan Juster (Philadelphia: University of Pennsylvania Press, 2011), 195.

84. Dietrich Bonhoeffer, *The Cost of Discipleship*, trans. R. H. Fuller (New York: Simon and Schuster, 2012).

85. James H. Cone, *A Black Liberation Theology, 40th Anniversary Edition* (Maryknoll, NY: Orbis Books, 2010), 2, 67, 59.

86. Don A. Pittman, Ruben L. F. Habito, and Terry C. Muck, eds., *Ministry and Theology in Global Perspective: Contemporary Challenges for the Church* (Grand Rapids, MI: Eerdmans, 1996), 223. For postcolonial understandings of Christian mission, see David Bosch, *Transforming Mission: Paradigm Shifts in Theology of Mission* (Maryknoll, NY: Orbis, 2011); Brian McLaren, *Why Did Jesus, Moses, the Buddha, and Mohammed Cross the Road? Christian Identity in a Multi-Faith World* (New York: Jericho, 2012).

CHAPTER 10: DIVINE GUIDANCE IN ISLAM

1. A related concept is found in rabbinic thought: "Fulfilling one commandment (mitzvah) leads to [fulfillment of another] commandment" (m. Avot 4:2).

2. Mattson, *Story of the Qur'an*, 56–57.

3. See Winter, "Last Trump Card," 137–45. Cf. William Adler, "The Jews as Falsifiers: Charges of Tendentious Emendations in Anti-Jewish Christian Polemics," *Translation of Scripture–JQR Supplement* (1990): 1–27.

4. Shahrastani (d. 1153) and Nawawi (thirteenth century) were among commentators who saw previous revelations as invalid. See Camilla Adang, *Muslim Writers on Judaism and the Hebrew Bible: From Ibn Rabban to Ibn Hazm* (Leiden: Brill 1996); Winter, "Last Trump Card," 146. Joseph Lumbard cited 5:43, 47; 16:43; and 48:29, challenging such uses of *naskh* (*Study Qur'an*, 1767–68). See Fatoohi, *Abrogation in the Qur'an*, 68–69.

5. See commentary in Nasr, *Study Quran*, 276; Reuven Firestone, "Is There a Notion of 'Divine Election' in Qur'an," *New Perspectives on the Qur'an*, ed. Gabriel Said Reynolds (London: Routledge, 2011), 404–7.

6. See commentary in Nasr, *Study Quran*, pp. 153–54, and discussion of primordial religion below.

7. Firestone, "Is There a Notion of 'Divine Election,'" 406–7.

8. Maulana Muhammad Ali (1874–1951), *The Holy Qur'an with English Translation and Commentary* (Dublin, OH: Ahamadiyya Anjuman Ishaat Islam, 2002), 863.

9. Islamic tradition denies that Jesus was among the prophets who were killed, by the Jews or by the Roman authorities. Instead, he was lifted up to dwell with God (Qur'an 4:157–58).

10. Cf. 2:65–66, 7:166, 5:82–83. Exegetes debate whether to interpret the image metaphorically or literally, but both dehumanize Jews. See Esack, "The Portrayal of Jews," 207–33; Amir Hussein, "Muslims, Pluralism and Interfaith Dialogue," in *Progressive Muslims*, ed. Safi, 254.

11. Commentary generally interprets this to mean that shirk is not forgiven unless wrongdoers repent. See http://m.qtafsir.com/Surah-An-Nisa/Allah-Does-not-Forgive-Shirk.

12. See discussion of dhimmitude below.

13. E.g., Makki b. Abi Talib (eleventh century), Abu Bakr ibn al-Arabi (twelfth century). See Fatoohi, *Abrogation in the Qur'an*, 114–21.

14. For discussion of nonviolence in Islam, see Mohammed Abu-Nimer, *Nonviolence and Peace Building in Islam: Theory and Practice* (Gainesville: University Press of Florida, 2003). For all three traditions, see Thistlethwaite, *Interfaith Just Peacemaking*.

15. See Abdulaziz Sachedina, "The Qur'an and Other Religions," in *Cambridge Companion to the Qur'an*, ed. McAuliffe, 296–97. Traditional exegesis applied such statements only to converts to Islam, but some modern readers challenge this conclusion; see Mahmoud Ayoub, "Nearest in Amity: Christians in the Qur'an and Contemporary Exegetical Tradition," *Islam and Christian–Muslim Relations* 8:2 (1997): 145–64.

16. Sachedina, "Qur'an and Other Religions," 294. Cf. Mohammad Fadel, "'No Salvation Outside Islam': Muslim Modernists, Democratic Politics, and Islamic Theological Exclusivism," in *Between Heaven and Hell*, ed. Khalil, 35–61.

17. Similar notions of God settling religious disputes on the Day of Rising appear in 2:113, 22:17, and 10:93, but without asserting that religious difference is part of God's plan. A darker version of human difference proclaims that conflicts "will fill up Hell with the jinn and mankind all together" (11:118–19).

18. Jonathan P. Berkey, *The Formation of Islam: Religion and Society in the Near East, 600–1800* (Cambridge, UK: Cambridge University Press, 2003), 72–74.

Contemporaneous Syriac sources refer to Muhammad as king of the Arabs, not a religious prophet.

19. Wink, "The Myth of Redemptive Violence," 3:278; see discussion in chap. 1.

20. The Fatamids extended dhimmi status to a broader range of religious others.

21. See Caner Dagli, "Conquest and Conversion, War and Peace in the Qur'an," in *Study Qur'an*, ed. Nasr, 1806.

22. As paraphrased in Roxanne L. Euben and Muhammed Qasim Zaman, eds., *Princeton Readings in Islamist Thought: Texts and Contexts from al-Banna to bin Laden* (Princeton, NJ: Princeton University Press, 2009), 307.

23. It also forbids killing animals except for sustenance, cutting down fruit-bearing trees, and other restrictions. See Khaled Abou el Fadl, "Between Functionalism and Morality: The Juristic Debates on the Conduct of War," in *Islamic Ethics of Life: Abortion, War, and Euthanasia*, ed. Jonathan Brockopp (Columbia: University of South Carolina, 2003), 103–28.

24. John Kelsay, "Antisemitism in Classical Islamic Sources," in *Not Your Father's Antisemitism: Hatred of the Jews in the Twenty-First Century*, ed. Michael Berenbaum (St. Paul, MN: Paragon House, 2008), 107–12.

25. See Shah-Kazemi, *Spirit of Tolerance in Islam*, 39, 123; C. E. Bosworth, "The Concept of *Dhimma* in Early Islam," in *Christians and Jews in the Ottoman Empire: The Functioning of a Plural Society*, ed. Benjamin Braude and Bernard Lewis (New York: Holmes and Meier, 1982): 1:37–51.

26. Norman Stillman, *The Jews of Arab Lands* (Philadelphia: Jewish Publication Society, 1979), 157–58.

27. Stillman, *Jews of Arab Lands*, 251, 201, 255–58. See the chronicles of Dionysius of Tel Mahré and Michael the Syrian, and the Charter of Privileges reportedly assigned by Muhammad to the community at St. Catherine's monastery.

28. Braude and Lewis, eds., *Christians and Jews in the Ottoman Empire*.

29. Ronald Grigor Suny, *They Can Live in the Desert but Nowhere Else: A History of the Armenian Genocide* (Princeton, NJ: Princeton University Press, 2015), xi–xxi. Shah-Kazemi, *Spirit of Tolerance*, 66, cites a hadith in which Muhammad warns, "On the day of judgment I myself will act as accuser of any man who oppresses a person under the protection of Islam."

30. Joshua Finkel, "A *Risala* of al-Jahiz," *Journal of the American Oriental Society* 47 (1927): 316, 318–319, 328–33. Hava Lazarus-Yafeh argued that anti-Christian polemic multiplied after the Crusades: "Some Neglected Aspects of Medieval Muslim Polemic against Christianity," *Harvard Theological Review* 89:1 (1996): 70, doi:10.1017/S0017816000031813.

31. Lamptey [Rhodes], *Never Wholly Other*, 23. See Gabriel Said Reynolds, "On the Qu'ranic Accusation of Falsification (*Taḥrif*) and Christian Anti-Jewish Polemic," *Journal of the American Oriental Society* 130:2 (2010): 189–202.

32. Ibn Hazm, *Al-fisal fi al-milal* (*Treatise on Religions, Sects and Creeds*), I:35; cited in Moshe Gil, "The Creed of Abā ʿĀmir," *Israel Oriental Studies* 12, ed. Joel Kraemer (Leiden: Brill, 1992), 45. See Ghulam Haider Aasi, *Muslim Understanding of Other Religions: A Study of Ibn Ḥazm's Kitāb Al-faṣl Fī Al-milal Wa Al-aḥwā' Wa Al-niḥal* (New Delhi: Adam Publishers, 2007); Theodore Pulcini, *Exegesis as Polemical Discourse: Ibn Hazm on Jewish and Christian Scriptures* (Atlanta: Scholars Press, 1998), 1–128.

33. Pulcini, *Exegesis as Polemical Discourse*, 133. See also Camilla Adang "Medieval Muslim Polemics and the Jewish Scriptures," in *Muslim Perceptions of Other Religions: A Historical Survey*, ed. Jean Jacques Waardenburg (Oxford, UK: Oxford University Press, 1999), 151–52.

34. Bernard Lewis, *The Multiple Identities of the Middle East* (New York: Schocken Books, 1998), 127.

35. Compare María Rosa Menocal, *The Ornament of the World: How Muslims, Jews, and Christians Created a Culture of Tolerance in Medieval Spain* (New York: Back Bay Books, 2002); and Darío Fernández-Morera, *The Myth of the Andalusian Paradise: Muslims, Christians, and Jews Under Islamic Rule in Medieval Spain* (Wilmington, DE: Intercollegiate Studies Institute, 2016).

36. Translation from Bernard Lewis, *Islam in History: Ideas, People, and Events in the Middle East* (New York: Open Court, 2013), 159–61.

37. James T. Monroe, ed. and trans., *Hispano-Arabic Poetry* (Berkeley: University of California Press, 1974), 332–36.

38. Similarly al-Amiri (d. 992). See Winter, "The Last Trump Card," 135, 146; and "Realism and the Real," in *Between Heaven and Hell*, ed. Khalil, 127. In *Islam and the Fate of Others: The Salvation Question* (Oxford, UK: Oxford University Press, 2012), however, Khalil offers a different reading of al-Ghazali, naming his perspective "optimistic inclusivism."

39. Kevin Reinhart, "Failures of Practice or Failures of Faith: Are Non-Muslims Subject to the Sharia?," in *Between Heaven and Hell*, ed. Khalil, 13–14, 19. In the same volume, see Mohammad Fadel, "No Salvation Outside Islam," 40.

40. Cited in Winter, "Realism and the Real," 125.

41. Ibn Kathir, *Tafsir al-Quran al-azim* I.103; II:67. See Sachedina, "Qur'an and Other Religions," 308n10; Jane Dammen McAuliffe, *Qur'anic Christians: An Analysis of Classical and Modern Exegesis* (Cambridge, UK: Cambridge University Press, 2010), 93–128.

42. See Sachedina, "Qur'an and Other Religions," 302. Al-Tabari and Shi'a commentator al-Tabarsi rejected the idea that 2:62 is abrogated by 3:65; *naskh* applies only to commands and prohibitions, not reports and promises. See Shah-Kazemi, "Beyond Polemics and Pluralism," 94.

43. Reza Shah-Kazemi, *Justice and Remembrance: Introducing the Spirituality of Imam Ali* (London: I. B. Tauris, 2006), 73–132, 219–34.

44. Bernard Lewis, *Origins of Isma'ilism: A Study of the Historical Background of the Fatamid Caliphate* (Cambridge, UK: W. Heffer and Sons, 1940), 94, 96.

45. Shah-Kazemi, *The Spirit of Tolerance*, 58; Ibn al-Arabi, *The Ringstones of Wisdom* (Fusus al-hikam), trans. Caner Dagli (Chicago: University of Chicago, 2004), 105–17; William Chittick, *Imaginal Worlds: Ibn al-'Arabi and the Problem of Religious Diversity* (Albany: State University of New York Press, 1994), 123–24, citing Ibn Arabi's *al-Futuhat al-makkiyya* II.116.7.

46. Ibn al-'Arabī, *The Tarjuman al-Ashwaq*, trans. Reynold Nicholson (London: Royal Asiatic Society, 1911), XI.

47. Rumi, *The Essential Rumi*, trans. Coleman Barks (New York: HarperOne, 1995), 32.

48. Abu'l Fadl as cited in Shah-Kazemi, *Spirit of Tolerance*, 35–36.

49. Cited in Chittick, *Imaginal Worlds*, 125.

50. Sidney H. Griffith, "The Monk in the Emir's *Majlis*: Reflections on a Popular Genre of Christian Literary Apologetics in Arabic in the Early Islamic Period," in *The Majlis: Interreligious Encounters in Medieval Islam*, ed. Hava Lazarus-Yafeh (Wiesbaden: Harrassowitz, 1999), 42.

51. See Sarah Stroumsa, "Ibn al-Rawandi's *su adab al-mujadala*: The Role of Bad Manners in Medieval Disputations," in *The Majlis*, ed. Lazarus-Yafeh, 75.

52. Griffith, "The Monk," 62; based on an eleventh-century biographical dictionary *Jadhwat al-Muqtabis*.

53. *Kitab al-Milal wa 'l-Nihal*; my translation from French in Daniel Gimaret and Guy Monnot, trans., *Livre des Religions et des Sectes* (Leuven: Peeters/UNESCO, 1986), 114.

54. See Steven Wasserstrom, "Islamicate History of Religions?," *History of Religions* 27:4 (1988): 405–11; Gimaret and Monnot, *Livre des Religions*, 160, 165.

55. Ahmad S. Dallal, Yoginder Sikand, and Abdul Rashid Moten, "Ummah," in *The Oxford Encyclopedia of the Islamic World*, Oxford Islamic Studies Online, http:// www.oxfordislamicstudies.com/article/opr/t236/e0818.

56. Malcolm X with Alex Haley, *The Autobiography of Malcolm X* (New York: Grove Press, 1965), 344–45.

57. Seyyed Hossain Nasr, *Islam: Religion, History and Civilization* (New York: HarperOne, 2001), 5.

58. Jacques Waardenburg, "World Religions as Seen in the Light of Islam," in *Islam: Past Influence and Present Challenge*, ed. Alfred Welch and Pierre Cahia (Albany, NY: SUNY Press, 1979), 246–47. Tim Winter calls it "non-categoric supersession" ("The Last Trump Card," 138, 152).

59. Narrated by Ibn Abbas, a Companion of the Prophet, and collected by Ahmad b. Hanbal; "The Most Beloved Religion: Primordial and Generous Faith," December 31, 2015, http://islamicuniversality.com/tag/din-al-hanif. A parallel report is found in *Sahih al-Bukhari*, ed. and trans. Muhammad Muhsin Kahn (Chicago, 1976), I:34.

60. Shah-Kazemi, *Spirit of Tolerance*, 80. See discussion of humanity's noble stature in Qur'an 17:70, 95:4.

61. Fatoohi, *Abrogation in the Qur'an*, 32–33; Tariq Ramadan, "Salvation—The Known and the Unknown," in *Between Heaven and Hell*, ed. Khalil, x.

62. Asghar Ali Engineer, "Islam and Pluralism," in *The Myth of Religious Superiority*, ed. Knitter, 214–16.

63. Seyyed Hossein Nasr, "Religion and Religions," in *The Religious Other: Toward a Muslim Theology of Other Religions in a Post-Prophetic Age*, ed. Muhammad Suhail 'Umar (Lahore, Pakistan: Iqbal Academy Pakistan, 2008), 59–81.

64. Mahmut Aydin, "A Muslim Pluralist: Jalaluddin Rumi," in *The Myth of Religious Superiority*, ed. Knitter, 223–24, 232–36.

65. Shah-Kazemi, *Spirit of Tolerance*, 75–111. Also *The Other in the Light of the One: The Universality of Qur'an and Interfaith Dialogue* (Cambridge, UK: Islamic Texts Society, 2006).

66. See Pim Valkenberg's review of *The Religious Other*, ed. Umar, in *Modern Theology* 27:3 (2011): 549–51, doi:10.1111/j.1468–0025.2011.01702.x.

67. Mohammad Hashim Kamali, *Shari'ah Law: An Introduction* (London: Oneworld, 2008), 2–3.

68. Abdullahi Ahmed An-Na'im, "Shari'a and Islamic Family Law: Transition and Transformation," in *Islamic Family Law in a Changing World: A Global Resource Book* (London: Zed Books, 2002).

69. There is also a distinct realm for secular law (*siyasa*). See Asifa Quraishi, "Taking Shari'a Seriously," *Constitutional Commentary* 26:297 (2010): 299–305, https://scholarship.law.umn.edu/concomm/71.

70. Seyyed Hossein Nasr, *Ideals and Realities of Islam* (New York: Praeger, 1967), 96.

71. See Mahmoud Ayoub, *The Qur'an and Its Interpreters*, 2:294.

CHAPTER 11: ENDURING CHALLENGES

1. Abraham Isaac Kook, "The Moral Principles," in *The Essential Writings of Abraham Isaac Kook*, ed. and trans. Ben Zion Bokser (Teaneck, NJ: Ben Yehuda Press, 2006), 138.

2. Kook, "*Derech haTechiya*," available in English translation as "Rav Kook: The Road to Renewal," trans. Ben Zion Bokser, *Tradition: A Journal of Orthodox Thought* 13:3 (1973): 141.

3. See, e.g., Todd Gitlin and Leil Leibowitz, "The Centrality of Jewish Chosenness," *Tablet*, June 7, 2010, https://www.tabletmag.com/scroll/35579/the-centrality-of-jewish-chosenness.

4. See Shai Held, "A Bolt from the Blue," *Sh'ma: A Journal of Jewish Ideas*, February 10, 2015, http://shma.com/2015/02/a-bolt-from-the-blue; Kaminsky, *Yet I Loved Jacob*, 77.

5. See Abraham Joshua Heschel, "No Religion is an Island," *Union Seminary Quarterly Review* 21:2:1 (1966): 125–26; Nancy Fuchs-Kreimer, "In the Spittin' Image of God," *Huffington Post*, December 20, 2010, modified May 25, 2011, https://www.huffingtonpost.com/nancy-fuchs-kreimer/appearance-on-whyys-this-_b_796398.html; and articles by Dalit Kaplan ("Let Us Hear") and Rachel Kohl Finegold ("The Choosing People") in *Sh'ma: A Journal of Jewish Responsibility*, February 10, 2015.

6. Mordecai M. Kaplan, "The Condition of Jewish Belief: A Symposium," *Commentary Magazine* 42:2 (1966): 108–10. For a feminist critique of chosenness, see Judith Plaskow, *Standing Again at Sinai: Judaism from a Feminist Perspective* (New York: HarperCollins, 1991), 96–103.

7. The yeshivah directed by Rabbi Shapira, Od Yosef Chai, published the manuscript. It was initially endorsed by several leading rabbis, only some of whom withdrew their support after they actually read it. See Daniel Estrin, "The King's Torah: A Rabbinic Text or a Call to Terror?," *Haaretz*, January 22, 2010, https://www.haaretz.com/1.5088576.

8. See Gadi Gvaryahu, "Don't Despair of Religious Zionism," *New Israel Fund*, April 2, 2012, https://www.nif.org/blog/dont-despair-of-religious-zionism; "Charges Filed against Rabbi for Racist Incitement and Violence," *New Israel Fund*, December 8, 2016, https://www.nif.org/stories/human-rights-democracy/charges-filed-rabbi-racist-incitement-violence.

9. Nancy Fuchs-Kreimer, "Reconstructing Chosenness in Ecumenical Perspective," *Zeek*, January 31, 2012, http://zeek.forward.com/articles/117482.

10. See Paul Mendes-Flohr, "In Pursuit of Normalcy: Zionism's Ambivalence toward Israel's Election," in *Many Are Chosen: Divine Election and Western Nationalism*, ed. William Hutchison and Harmut Lehmann (Minneapolis: Fortress Press, 1994),

203–24. Cf. Eisen, *Peace and Violence*, 141–204; Ehud Luz, *Wrestling with an Angel: Power, Morality and Jewish Identity* (New Haven, CT: Yale University Press, 2003).

11. Also Rabbis Zvi Hirsch Kalischer (1795–1874), Judah Alkalai (1798–1878), Isaac Jacob Reines (1839–1915); see Aviezer Ravitzky, *Messianism, Zionism and Jewish Religious Radicalism* (Chicago: University of Chicago, 1996), 211–34.

12. *Sihot be'et milchamah* [Discussions in Time of War], ed. Y. Haikin, cited in Ravitzky, *Messianism*, 84.

13. Yeshayahu Leibowitz, *Judaism, Human Values, and the Jewish State* (Cambridge, MA: Harvard University Press, 1995).

14. Eisen, *The Peace and Violence of Judaism*, 189–90. Purity of arms (*taharat haneshek*) is invoked in training Israel Defense Force soldiers, including instructions to minimize force, prevent civilian casualties, resist dehumanizing the enemy, and challenge criminal orders. See Aryeh Klapper et al., "Halakhah and Morality in Modern Warfare," *Meorot* 6:1 (2006) for differing analyses of its practical application.

15. Gitlin and Leibovitz, "Centrality of Jewish Chosenness."

16. Also, the Nation of Islam's publication of *The Secret Relationship between Blacks and Jews* deliberately distorts Jewish participation in the slave trade, promoting African American antisemitism. See Eli Faber, *Jews, Slaves, and the Slave Trade: Setting the Record Straight* (New York: NYU Press, 1998).

17. As in the writings of Abu al-Ala Mawdudi and Sayyid Qutb; see William Shepard, "Sayyid Qutb's Doctrine of "Jāhiliyya," *International Journal of Middle East Studies* 35:4 (Nov. 2003): 521–45; Quintan Wiktorowicz, "A Genealogy of Radical Islam," in *Political Islam: A Critical Reader*, ed. Frederic Volpi (London: Routledge, 2011), 274–75.

18. Marcia Hermansen, "How to Put the Genie Back in the Bottle? 'Identity' Islam and Muslim Youth Cultures in America," in *Progressive Muslims*, ed. Safi, 309–10.

19. See the website, www.acommonword.com.

20. Jerusha Lamptey [Rhodes], "Embracing Relationality and Theological Tensions," in *Between Heaven and Hell*, ed. Khalil, 234–52. Mahmud Shaltut, "The Qur'an and Fighting" in *Jihad in Classical and Modern Islam*, ed. Rudolph Peters (Princeton, NJ: Markus Wiener, 2005), 59–102, similarly advocates seeking a Qur'anic worldview rather than isolated verses.

21. Sachedina, "The Qur'an and Other Religions," 297, 306.

22. Winter, "The Last Trump Card," 135. A surprising range of thinkers accept the potential acceptability of other paths for "Peoples of the Book" as indicated in Qur'an (e.g., 2:62), even though they continue to privilege the truth claims of Islam; these include the Iranian mullah Sayyid Mahmud Taleqani, the Pakistani modernist intellectual Fazlur Rahman, the Egyptian Salafi Islamist reformer Rashid Rida, and the American philosopher Muhammad Legenhausen.

23. Pew Research Center, "The World's Muslims: Religion, Politics and Society," Pew Forum, April 3, 2013. http://www.pewforum.org/wp-content/uploads/sites/7/2013/04/worlds-muslims-religion-politics-society-full-report.pdf, 140.

24. Asef Bayat, ed., *Post-Islamism: The Changing Faces of Political Islam* (Oxford, UK: Oxford University Press, 2013), 4.

25. Euben and Zaman, eds., *Princeton Readings*, 4. Some view the conceptual frame of Islamism as a Western Orientalist construct; see Hasan Hanafi, "Islamism: Whose

Debate Is It?," in *Islamism: Contested Perspectives on Political Islam*, eds. Richard Martin and Abbas Barzegar (Stanford, CA: Stanford University Press, 2010), 63–66.

26. Al-Banna, "Toward the Light," in *Princeton Readings*, ed. Euben and Zaman, 58–61. He cited the aya that describes Muhammad's followers as "the best community" (3:110), a common trope in Islamist discourse.

27. Qutb, "In the Shade of the Qur'an," in *Princeton Readings*, ed. Euben and Zaman, 147.

28. Faraj, "The Neglected Duty," in *Princeton Readings*, ed. Euben and Zaman, 323–24, 327–43. Faraj was executed in 1982 as a co-conspirator in the assassination of President Anwar Sadat in Egypt.

29. Euben and Zaman, eds., *Princeton Readings*, 226. Qaradawi was among the prominent Islamists who condemned the September 11 attacks on the United States.

30. Euben and Zaman, eds., *Princeton Readings*, 307.

31. Michel Jobert, "L'Islam et sa modernité," *Revue du Tiers-Monde* 92 (1982): 773–84, https://www.persee.fr/doc/tiers_0040–7356_1982_num_23_92_4171; cited in Nadia Yassine, *Full Sails Ahead*, trans. Farouk Bouasse (Iowa City: Justice and Spirituality Publishing, 2006), 168–69.

32. Khalil al-Anani, "The Myth of Excluding Moderate Islamists in the Arab World" (The Saban Center for Middle East Policy at the Brookings Institution, March 2010): 2. He offered the Muslim Brotherhood as a test case, radicalized in some countries, elsewhere participating peacefully in elections, and sometimes presenting a relatively progressive democratic platform.

33. Mohsen Kadivar, "From Traditional Islam to Islam as an End in Itself," *Die Welt des Islams* 51:3–4 (2011): 459–84, doi:10.1163/15700601X611632; Center for Human Rights in Iran, "15 Prominent Iranians Call for a Referendum on the Islamic Republic," February 14, 2018, https://www.iranhumanrights.org/2018/02/15-prominent -iranians-call-for-a-referendum-on-the-islamic-republic.

34. Robert Hefner, "Islam, Southeast Asian," in *The Encyclopedia of Politics and Religion*, ed. Robert Wuthnow (London: Routledge, 2013), 1:396. See also Rushd as-Safaa, "Islamic Reform Against Islamism," *Reformer* (May 16, 2018) https://medium .com/reformermag/islamic-reform-against-islamism-c7ba1f7da9be.

35. Bassam Tibi, *Islamism and Islam* (New Haven, CT: Yale University Press, 2012), 186, 12, 106. Tibi was born in Syria but moved to Germany at age eighteen.

36. See Zaher Kazmi, "Beyond Liberal Islam," *Aeon*, December 21, 2017, https:// aeon.co/essays/is-it-time-to-look-beyond-the-idea-of-liberal-islam; Wael B. Hallaq, *The Impossible State: Islam, Politics, and Modernity's Moral Predicament* (New York: Columbia University Press, 2012); Cemil Aydin, *The Idea of the Muslim World* (Cambridge, MA: Harvard University Press, 2017); Edward Said, *Covering Islam: How the Media and the Experts Determine How We See the Rest of the World* (New York: Vintage, 1997); Adis Duderija, "Critical-Progressive Muslim Thought: Reflections on its Political Ramifications," *Review of Faith and International Affairs* 11:3 (2013): 69–79, https:// ssrn.com/abstract=2328581.

37. Saba Mahmood, "Feminist Theory, Embodiment, and the Docile Agent: Some Reflections on the Egyptian Islamic Revival," *Cultural Anthropology* 16:2 (2001): 224–25; Todd H. Green, *Presumed Guilty: Why We Shouldn't Ask Muslims to Condemn Terrorism* (Minneapolis: Fortress Press, 2018).

38. Jonathan Lyons, *Islam through Western Eyes* (New York: Columbia University Press, 2014), 195. In the now-classic essay, "Can the Subaltern Speak?," Gayatri Chakravorty Spivak asserted: "White men are saving brown women from brown men" is the animating collective fantasy of Western imperialism (in Patrick Williams and Laura Chrisman, eds., *Colonial Discourse and Post-Colonial Theory* [New York: Columbia University Press, 1994], 92).

39. Todd H. Green, *The Fear of Islam: An Introduction to Islamophobia in the West* (Minneapolis: Fortress Press, 2019), 205–36.

40. "The Islamic Veil Across Europe," *BBC News*, May 31, 2018, https://www.bbc .com/news/world-europe-13038095.

41. Saba Mahmood, *The Politics of Piety: The Islamic Revival and the Feminist Subject* (Princeton, NJ: Princeton University Press, 2004). See also Juliane Hammer, "(Muslim) Women's Bodies, Islamophobia and American Politics," *Bulletin for the Study of Religion* 42:1 (2013): 29–36, doi:10.1558/bsor.v42i1.29; Lila Abu-Lughod, "Do Muslim Women Really Need Saving? Anthropological Reflections on Cultural Relativism and Its Others," *American Anthropologist* 104:3 (2002): 783–90.

42. See Matti Bunzl, *Anti-Semitism and Islamophobia: Hatreds Old and New in Europe* (Chicago: Prickly Paradigm Press, 2007); Deborah E. Lipstadt, *Antisemitism Here and Now* (New York: Schocken Books, 2019); Joshua Trachtenberg, *The Devil and the Jews: The Medieval Conception of the Jew and Its Relation to Modern Anti-Semitism* (Philadelphia: Jewish Publication Society, 2002); William Nicholls, *Christian Anti-Semitism: A History of Hate* (Northvale, NJ: Jason Aronson, 1995); Jonathan Riley-Smith, *The Crusades, Christianity and Islam* (New York: Colombia University Press, 2008); Carole Hillenbrand, *The Crusades: Islamic Perspectives* (Edinburgh: Edinburgh University Press, 1999); Thomas S. Kidd, *American Christians and Islam: Evangelical Culture and Muslims from the Colonial Period to the Age of Terrorism* (Princeton, NJ: Princeton University Press, 2009).

43. FBI Hate Crimes Statistics, 2018, https://ucr.fbi.gov/hate-crime/2018/topic /tables/table-1.xls.

44. Laurie Goodstein, "Christian Leaders Denounce Trump's Plan to Favor Christian Refugees," *New York Times*, January 29, 2017, https://www.nytimes.com/2017/01 /29/us/christian-leaders-denounce-trumps-plan-to-favor-christian-immigrants.html; Harry Bruinius, "Why Evangelicals are Trump's Strongest Travel-Ban Supporters," *Christian Science Monitor*, March 3, 2017, https://www.csmonitor.com/USA/Politics /2017/0303/Why-Evangelicals-are-Trump-s-strongest-travel-ban-supporters; Ruth Graham, "Christian Leaders Nearly Unanimous in Opposing Trump's Muslim Ban," *Slate*, January 29, 2017, http://www.slate.com/blogs/the_slatest/2017/01/29/christian _leaders_oppose_trump_s_muslim_ban.html.

45. See the remarks of Revs. Jimmy Swaggart and Pat Robertson: "Bush vs. the Televangelists," *BeliefNet*, http://www.beliefnet.com/News/2002/11/Bush-Vs-The -Televangelists.aspx; WND Staff, "Pat Robertson: No Muslim Judges," *WorldNetDaily*, May 3, 2005, http://www.wnd.com/2005/05/30130. Christians are not the only advocates of this perspective; see Matthew Duss, Yasmine Taeb, Ken Gude, and Ken Sofer, "Fear, Inc. 2.0: The Islamophobia Network's Efforts to Manufacture Hate in America," Center for American Progress, 2015, https://cdn.americanprogress.org/wp-content /uploads/2015/02/FearInc-report2.11.pdf.

46. Douglas Pratt, *Christian Engagement with Islam: Ecumenical Journeys since 1910* (Leiden: Brill, 2017).

47. See Alan Race, *Christians and Religious Pluralism: Patterns in the Christian Theology of Religions* (London: SCM, 1983), and Gavin D'Costa, *Theology and Religious Pluralism: The Challenge of Other Religions* (Malden, MA: Blackwell, 1986). For critiques and reframings, see Knitter, *Myth of Religious Superiority*, especially Perry Schmidt-Leukel, "Exclusivism, Inclusivism and Pluralism: The Tripolar Typology—Clarified and Reaffirmed," and Rita Gross, "Excuse Me, but What's the Question? Isn't Religious Diversity Normal?"

48. See Suchocki, *Divinity and Diversity*; Peter C. Hodgson, "The Spirit and Religious Pluralism," in Knitter, *Myth of Religious Superiority*, 135–50; S. Mark Heim, *Salvations: Truth and Difference in Religion* (Maryknoll, NY: Orbis Books, 1995); John Hick, *An Interpretation of Religion: Human Responses to the Transcendent* (New York: Macmillan, 1989); Coleman, *Making a Way*; Cynthia M. Campbell, *A Multitude of Blessings: A Christian Approach to Religious Diversity* (Louisville, KY: Westminster John Knox, 2006).

49. Diana L. Eck, "What Is Pluralism?," Pluralism Project, Harvard University, 2006, http://pluralism.org/what-is-pluralism.

50. Vatican II, *Nostra aetate*, 1965, https://www.vatican.va/archive/hist_councils / ii_vatican_council/documents/vat-ii_decl_19651028_nostra-aetate_en.html.

51. Caryn Riswold, "Teaching the College 'Nones': Christian Privilege and the Religion Professor," *Teaching Theology and Religion* 18:2 (2015): 133–48, doi:10.1111 /teth.12275; see also Kwok Pui-Lan, *Postcolonial Imagination and Feminist Thought* (Louisville, KY: Westminster John Knox, 2005), 186–208.

52. Mary C. Boys, *Has God Only One Blessing? Judaism as a Source of Christian Self-Understanding* (New York: Paulist Press, 2000), 8. See also Amy-Jill Levine, "Bearing False Witness: Common Errors Made about Early Judaism," in Levine and Brettler, *Jewish Annotated New Testament*, 501–4.

53. Letty R. Russell, *Just Hospitality: God's Welcome in a World of Difference* (Louisville, KY: Westminster John Knox, 2009), 38.

54. Andrew Walls, *The Cross-Cultural Process in Christian History: Studies in the Transmission and Appropriation of Faith* (Maryknoll, NY: Orbis Books, 2002), 49. See also Norman Etherington, ed., *Missions and Empire* (Oxford, UK: Oxford University Press, 2005).

55. Roger Williams (1603–83) recognized the perils in championing a Christian nation chosen by God to rule the earth; he stood up for the rights of indigenous populations and was banished as a heretic (Rosemary Radford Ruether, *America, Amerikkka: Elect Nation and Imperial Violence* [London: Equinox, 2007], 251).

56. Josiah Strong, *Our Country: Its Possible Future and Its Present Crisis* (New York: Baker and Taylor, 1885), 219.

57. Andrew Porter, *Religion Versus Empire? British Protestant Missionaries and Overseas Expansion, 1700–1914* (Manchester, UK: Manchester University Press, 2004); Ambrose Mong, *Guns and Gospel: Imperialism and Evangelism in China* (Cambridge, UK: James Clarke and Co., 2017); Ruether, *America, Amerikkka*. Missions later played a role in dismantling colonial empires; see Brian Stanley, ed., *Missions, Nationalism, and the End of Empire* (Grand Rapids, MI: Eerdmans, 2004).

58. Michelle Goldberg, *Kingdom Coming: The Rise of Christian Nationalism* (New York: W. W. Norton, 2006).

59. Albert J. Beveridge, *Congressional Record* 56:1 (1900): 704–12, https://www.mtholyoke.edu/acad/intrel/ajb72.htm.

60. Woodrow Wilson, "A Campaign Address in Jersey City, New Jersey," May 25, 1912, in vol. 24, *The Papers of Woodrow Wilson*, ed. Arthur S. Link (Princeton, NJ: Princeton University Press, 1978), 443. See also Conrad Cherry, *God's New Israel: Religious Interpretations of American Destiny* (Chapel Hill: University of North Carolina Press, 1998); Todd Gitlin and Liel Leibovitz, *The Chosen Peoples: America, Israel, and the Ordeals of Divine Election* (New York: Simon and Schuster, 2010), 65–145.

61. Cited in W. R. Ward, "Response," in *Many Are Chosen: Divine Election and Western Nationalism*, ed. William Hutchison and Hartmut Lehmann (Minneapolis: Fortress Press, 1994), 51.

62. Anthony D. Smith, *Chosen Peoples: Sacred Sources of National Identity* (Oxford, UK: Oxford University Press, 2004), 7, 17, 255, 257–58.

63. Conor Cruise O'Brien, *God Land: Reflections on Religion and Nationalism* (Bloomington, IN: iUniverse, 1999), 41–42.

64. Abraham Lincoln, "Address to the New Jersey Senate," *Abraham Lincoln Online*, February 21, 1861, http://www.abrahamlincolnonline.org/lincoln/speeches/trenton1.htm.

65. Michael Fullilove, *Rendezvous with Destiny: How Franklin D. Roosevelt and Five Extraordinary Men Took America into the War and into the World* (London: Penguin, 2013), 130.

66. Langston Hughes, "Let America Be America Again," https://www.poets.org/viewmedia.php/prmMID/15609.

67. Gitlin and Leibovitz, *The Chosen Peoples*, xvi.

CHAPTER 12: RELIGION IN THE PUBLIC SQUARE?

1. John Rawls, *Political Liberalism* (New York: Columbia University Press, 1993). In the 2005 expanded edition, he made additional room for religious speech (l–liv). Note similarity to rules of the majlis discussed in chap. 10.

2. Barack Obama, "Call to Renewal," keynote address, June 28, 2006, available at https://www.nytimes.com/2006/06/28/us/politics/2006obamaspeech.html.

3. See Alexis de Tocqueville, *Democracy in America*, ed. J. P. Mayer, trans. George Lawrence (New York: Harper and Row, 1988), 295.

4. Stephen L. Carter, *The Culture of Disbelief: How American Law and Politics Trivialize Religious Devotion* (New York: Anchor Books, 1994), 230.

5. Wilfred M. McClay, "Two Concepts of Secularism," in *Religion Returns to the Public Square: Faith and Policy in America*, ed. Hugh Heclo and Wilfred McClay (Baltimore: Johns Hopkins University Press, 2003), 33.

6. Hervieu-Léger, "What Scripture Tells Me," 27.

7. David Hollinger, "Religious Ideas: Should They Be Critically Engaged or Given a Pass?," *Representations* 101 (2008): 147, doi:10.1525/rep.2008.101.1.144.

8. Rawls, *Political Liberalism*, xviii.

9. See the Supreme Court opinions in *Masterpiece Cakeshop, Ltd. v. Colorado Civil Rights Commission*; the First Amendment Defense Act introduced in the 115th Congress (S.2525, 2017–2018); and the recently established Health and Human Services

Department's Conscience and Religious Freedom Division, "Ensuring Compliance with Certain Statutory Provisions in Health Care; Delegations of Authority" (January 18, 2018). See also Rachel Mikva, "For Trump Administration, What Does Religious Freedom Really Mean?," *CNN Opinion*, August 12, 2018, https://www.cnn.com/2018 /08/08/opinions/trump-religious-liberty-opinion-mikva.

10. Robert Audi and Nicholas Wolterstorff, *Religion in the Public Square: The Place of Religious Convictions in Political Debate* (Lanham, MD: Rowman and Littlefield, 1997), 37.

11. See David Garland, *Punishment and Modern Society* (Oxford, UK: Oxford University Press, 1990), 252.

12. See, e.g., Dan Gilgoff, "6 Other Calamities Blamed on Divine Retribution," *CNN Belief Blog*, March 16, 2011, http://religion.blogs.cnn.com/2011/03/16/6-other -calamities-blamed-on-divine-retribution.

13. See the nuanced treatment of prosperity gospel in Kate Bowler, *Blessed: A History of the American Prosperity Gospel* (Oxford, UK: Oxford University Press, 2018).

14. Russell H. Conwell, *Acres of Diamonds* (New York: Harper and Brothers, 1915), 21.

15. John Locke, *Some Thoughts Concerning Education* (London: J. and R. Tonson, 1779), 55. Maimonides said an untutored soul observes mitzvot to avoid punishment, but we learn to serve God out of love (*Mishnah Torah Hil. Tesh.* 10.1–2).

16. Phillip Smith, *Punishment and Culture* (Chicago: University of Chicago Press, 2008), 5; Garland, *Punishment and Modern Society*, 186.

17. Statistics vary, but recent studies reveal a recidivism rate over 60%, more than 2.2 million people incarcerated, and 1 in 37 Americans caught "in the system" ("Trends in U.S. Corrections," Sentencing Project, June 2019, https://sentencingproject.org /wp-content/uploads/2016/01/Trends in US-Corrections.pdf; "Criminal Justice Fact Sheet," NAACP, https://www.naacp.org/criminal-justice-fact-sheet, accessed December 19, 2019; Mariel Alper, Matthew R. Durose, and Joshua Markman, "2018 Update on Prisoner Recidivism: A 9-Year Follow-up Period (2005–2014)," Bureau of Justice Statistics, May 2018, https://www.bjs.gov/content/pub/pdf/18upr9yfup0514.pdf.

18. Michelle Alexander, *The New Jim Crow: Mass Incarceration in the Age of Colorblindness* (New York: New Press, 2010), 4.

19. Michel Foucault, *Discipline and Punish: The Birth of the Prison* (New York: Pantheon, 1977).

20. See, e.g., T. Richard Snyder, *The Protestant Ethic and the Spirit of Punishment* (Grand Rapids, MI: Eerdmans, 2000); Herman Bianchi, *Justice as Sanctuary: Toward a New System of Crime Control* (Bloomington: Indiana University Press, 1994); James Logan, *Good Punishment? Christian Moral Practice and U.S. Imprisonment* (Grand Rapids, MI: Eerdmans, 2008).

21. Conrad G. Brunk, "Restorative Justice and the Philosophical Theories of Criminal Punishment," in *The Spiritual Roots of Restorative Justice*, ed. Michael L. Hadley (Albany: State University of New York Press, 2001), 31–56.

22. "Justice," *Merriam-Webster*, https://www.merriam-webster.com/dictionary /justice.

23. Cf. Jacob Rosenberg and Avi Weiss, "Land Concentration, Efficiency, Slavery and the Jubilee," in *The Oxford Handbook of Judaism and Economics*, ed. Aaron Levine (Oxford, UK: Oxford University Press, 2010), 74–88, doi:10.1093/oxfordhb/9780195398625 .013.0003.

24. Jonathan Sacks, *To Heal a Fractured World: The Ethics of Responsibility* (New York: Schocken Books, 2005), 33; Elliot Dorff, *To Do the Right and the Good: A Jewish Approach to Modern Social Ethics* (Philadelphia: Jewish Publication Society, 2002), 114–25.

25. Moshe Weinfeld, *Social Justice in Ancient Israel and in the Ancient Near East* (Jerusalem: Magnes Press, 2000), 25.

26. See Eliezer Segal, "Jewish Perspectives on Restorative Justice," in Hadley, *The Spiritual Roots of Restorative Justice*, 184.

27. See Maimonides, *Mishneh Torah Hilchot De'ot* 6.6–7, Nachmanides in his Torah commentary, op. cit.

28. Daniel Elazar, *Covenant and Polity in Biblical Israel: Biblical Foundations and Jewish Expressions* (New Brunswick, NJ: Transaction Publishers, 1998).

29. See m. Yoma 8 and y. Yoma 8:9 (45c), for discussion of atonement, the methods and importance of restoring right relationship. In b. Ber. 10a, Beruria chastised her husband, Rabbi Meir, for praying for the death of bandits rather than their repentance. See Aryeh Cohen, *Justice in the City* (Boston: Academic Studies Press, 2012).

30. This argument is not considered conclusive proof that *eye for an eye* means monetary compensation, but its obsessive focus on equal punishment highlights the difficulty of measuring retribution. David Daube argued that Tanakh intends compensation (*Studies in Biblical Law* [1946; repr., Clark NJ: Lawbook Exchange, 2004]), 102–53. Cf. Matt. 5.

31. A striking, rather strange example is the list of sins and their consequent afflictions in b. Shabb. 32b–33a.

32. US Conference of Catholic Bishops, "Responsibility, Rehabilitation, and Restoration: A Catholic Perspective on Crime and Criminal Justice," November 15, 2000, http://www.usccb.org/issues-and-action/human-life-and-dignity/criminal-justice -restorative-justice/crime-and-criminal-justice.cfm.

33. Christopher Marshall, *Compassionate Justice* (Eugene, OR: Wipf and Stock, 2012), loc. 943–949.

34. See Levine and Brettler, *Jewish Annotated New Testament*, 123.

35. See, e.g. Ezra 4, Neh. 4; Josephus, *Antiquities* 13.74–79, 18.19–20; *Jewish War* 2.232–37.

36. "Letters of St. Augustine" 133, composed in 412 CE, http://www.newadvent .org/fathers/1102133.htm.

37. Thomas Hughson, "Social Justice in Lactantius' *Divine Institutes*: An Exploration," in *Reading Patristic Texts on Social Ethics*, ed. Johan Leemans, Brian Matz, and Johan Verstraeten (Washington, DC: Catholic University of America Press, 2011), 193. See Oliver O'Donovan and Joan Lockwood O'Donovan, eds., *From Irenaeus to Grotius: A Sourcebook in Christian Political Thought 100–1626* (Grand Rapids, MI: Eerdmans, 1999), 46–47.

38. See Gary Anderson, *Charity: The Place of the Poor in Biblical Tradition* (New Haven, CT: Yale University Press, 2014).

39. Timothy Patitsas, "St. Basil's Philanthropic Program and Modern Microlending Strategies for Economic Self-Actualization," in *Wealth and Poverty in the Early Church and Society*, ed. Susan Holman (Grand Rapids, MI: Baker Academic, 2008), 270.

40. See Mohammed Hashim Kamali, *Freedom, Equality and Justice in Islam* (Cambridge, UK: Islamic Texts Society, 2002), 133–42. (Note: It somewhat misrepresents Jewish and Christian teachings, but frames Muslim teachings of distributive justice.)

41. Brown, *Misquoting Muhammad*, 180. Hanafi jurist al-Kasani (twelfth century) and many others published lists of multiple circumstances that seed doubt and avert severe retribution.

42. Mutaz M. Qafisheh, "Restorative Justice in the Islamic Penal Law: A Contribution to the Global System," *International Journal of Criminal Justice Sciences* 7:1 (2012): 496–97, https://www.sascv.org/ijcjs/pdfs/mutazaicjs2012istissue.pdf.

43. Susan C. Hascall, "Restorative Justice in Islam: Should *Qisas* Be Considered a Form of Restorative Justice?," *Berkeley Journal of Middle Eastern and Islamic Law* 35 (2011): 36.

44. Qafisheh, "Restorative Justice," 488.

45. Yildirim, "Peace and Conflict Resolution in the Medina Charter," *Peace Review: A Journal of Social Justice* 18 (2006): 109–17.

46. See Abdul Aziz Said, Nathan C. Funk, and Ayse S. Kadayifci, eds., *Peace and Conflict Resolution in Islam: Precept and Practice* (Lanham, MD: University Press of America, 2001).

47. Maimonides, *Mishneh Torah Sanhedrin* 11:4. See Dorff, *To Do the Right and the Good*, 120.

48. Conciliation processes were also prevalent in pre-Islamic Arabia; see Doron Pely, *Muslim/Arab Mediation and Conflict Resolution: Understanding Sulha* (London: Routledge, 2016), 16.

49. Qafisheh, "Restorative Justice," 491.

50. Heather Thomson, "Justice and Gender: On Feminist Theology and Restorative Justice," in *The Bible, Justice, and Public Theology*, ed. David J. Neville (Eugene, OR: Wipf and Stock, 2014), 143.

51. Rudolph Peters, *Crime and Punishment in Islamic Law: Theory and Practice from the Sixteenth to the Twenty-First Centuries* (Cambridge, UK: Cambridge University Press, 2005), 187.

52. See Thomas Noakes-Duncan, "The Emergence of Restorative Justice in Ecclesial Practice," in *Journal of Moral Theology* 5:2 (2016).

53. Marshall, *Compassionate Justice*, loc. 218.

54. Howard Zehr, *Changing Lenses: Restorative Justice for Our Times* (1990; repr., Harrisonburg, VA: Herald Press, 2015), 83.

55. Bryan Stevenson, *Just Mercy: A Story of Justice and Redemption* (New York: Spiegel and Grau, 2015), 309.

CHAPTER 13: THE SPACE-IN-BETWEEN

1. Dawkins, 1996 address accepting the American Humanist Association's 1996 Humanist of the Year award, *The Humanist* (1997).

2. Hollinger, "Religious Ideas," 145.

3. Originally, it restricted only congressional (i.e., national) action; states were allowed to have official religions and only gradually disestablished them. Since the Supreme Court adopted the doctrine of selective incorporation (early twentieth century), constitutional protections apply to the states as well. One consequence is that atheists may hold public office even in the seven states that still have laws on their books prohibiting them from doing so.

4. Cathleen Kaveny, *Prophecy Without Contempt: Religious Discourse in the Public Square* (Cambridge, MA: Harvard University Press, 2016), ix–x.

5. Diana L. Eck, "Prospects for Pluralism: Voice and Vision in the Study of Religion," *Journal of the American Academy of Religion* 75:4 (2007): 771, doi:10.1093/jaarel/lfmo61.

6. Peter Ochs, ed. *The Return to Scripture in Judaism and Christianity: Essays in Postcritical Scriptural Interpretation* (Eugene, OR: Wipf and Stock, 1993), 3.

7. Hans-Georg Gadamer, *Truth and Method* (orig., 1975; repr., London: Bloomsbury Academic, 2013), 308.

8. Paul Ricoeur, *Interpretation Theory: Discourse and the Surplus of Meaning* (Fort Worth: Texas Christian University Press, 1976).

INDEX